Vestiges of a Proud Nation

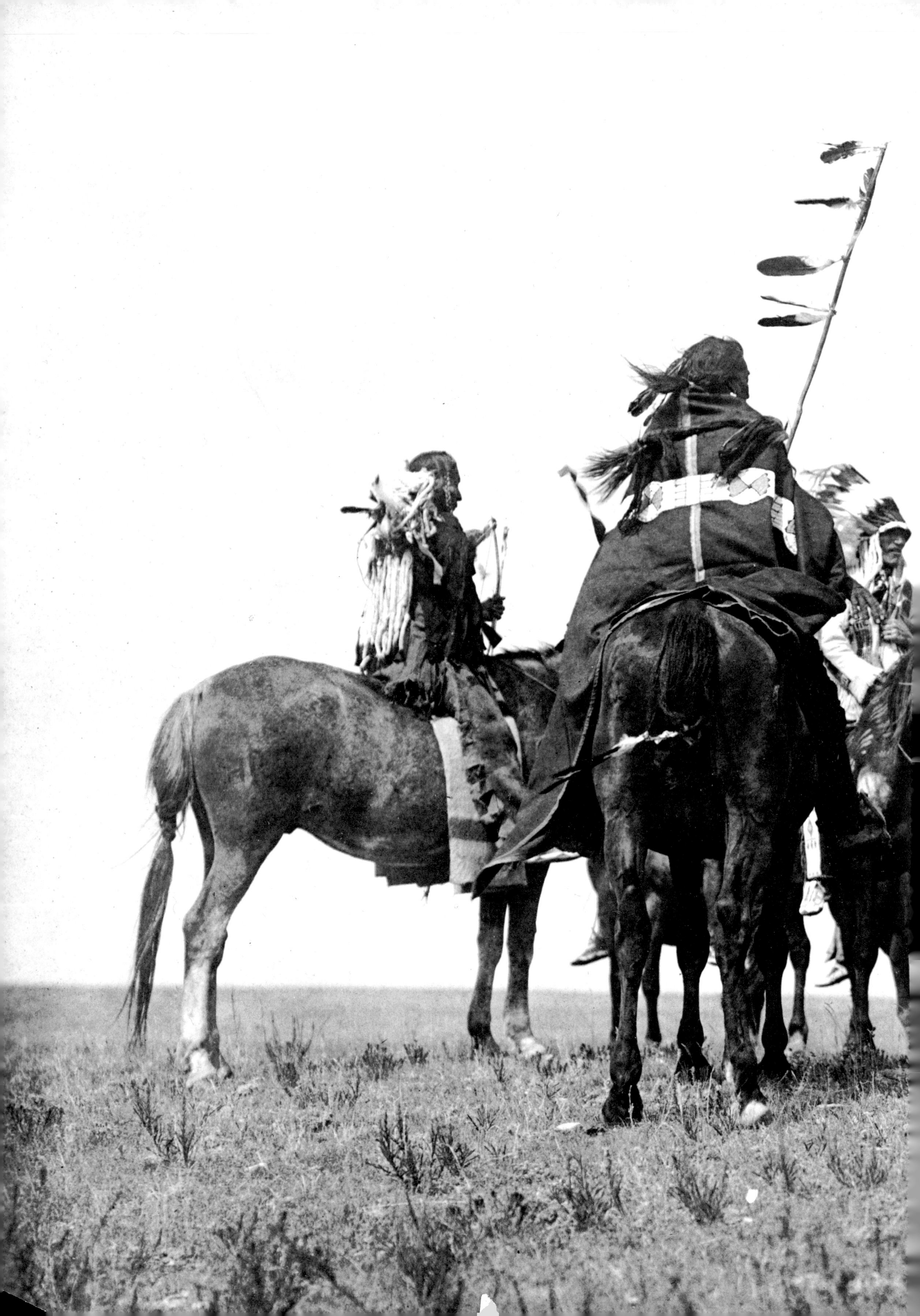

Vestiges of a Proud Nation

The Ogden B. Read Northern Plains Indian Collection

Edited by Glenn E. Markoe

Raymond J. DeMallie
Royal B. Hassrick

Robert Hull Fleming Museum • Burlington, Vermont • 1986

The publication of this catalogue was supported by a generous grant from the National Endowment for the Humanities.

Copyright © Robert Hull Fleming Museum
University of Vermont, 1986
All rights reserved
Library of Congress Catalog Card Number 86-061726
ISBN 0-934658-01-3

Photographer: Wes Disney
Designer: Leslie Fry
Copy editor: Jill Mason

Typography by Quad Left Graphics
Color separations by Champlain Color Corporation
Printed by Meriden-Stinehour Press

Historic photographs: State Historical Societies of Nebraska, Montana and North Dakota; Bureau of Indian Affairs. Fort Peck, Montana; National Anthropological Archives, Smithsonian Institution; The Library of Congress.

Cover: Sioux Hand Drum (Cat. no. 27)
Title page: War Party of Atsinas. Photo by Edward Curtis. Courtesy Library of Congress.
Page 70: Brulé Sioux with travois. Rosebud Agency. Ca. 1900. Photo by John Anderson. Courtesy Nebraska State Historical Society.
Pages 78, 79: Brulé Sioux woman preparing painted rawhide for parfleches. Rosebud Agency. Ca. 1900. Photo by John Anderson. Courtesy Nebraska State Historical Society.

Robert Hull Fleming Museum
The University of Vermont
Burlington, Vermont 05405
Tel: 802-656-0750

Distributed by the University of Nebraska Press

Contents

Director's Foreword   7
Ildiko Heffernan

Preface: Sioux Indian Art   9
George P. Horse Capture

Introduction   13
Glenn E. Markoe

The Sioux in Dakota and Montana Territories:
Cultural and Historical Background of the Ogden B. Read Collection   19
Raymond J. DeMallie

The Culture of the Sioux   71
Royal B. Hassrick

The Read Collection   79
Catalogue by Royal B. Hassrick and Glenn E. Markoe

    Men's Costume and Accessories   80
    Women's Costume and Accessories   96
    Ornaments and Jewelry   107
    Ritual and Ceremonial Objects   109
    Weapons and War Paraphernalia   126
    Horse Gear and Riding Accessories   137
    Pipes and Smoking Equipment   143
    Bags and Containers   151
    Utensils, Implements, and Vessels   163

The Ogden B. Read Inventory   169

Appendix: Other Documented Nineteenth-Century Plains Indian Collections

Director's Foreword

The publication of a catalogue of the Ogden B. Read Northern Plains Indian Collection is an event of special significance for the Robert Hull Fleming Museum of the University of Vermont. This catalogue is the first major scholarly publication devoted to an aspect of the Museum's permanent collections. It is particularly fitting that the Read Collection be so honored, for it is the oldest collection in the Museum's holdings and was the first important gift to the Museum under its first director, George Henry Perkins.

Beyond its importance to the Museum and the University, the collection is significant as a historical document of Sioux Indian art and culture. Its unique historical value stems from the fact that its collector, Ogden Benedict Read, had an intrinsic interest in documenting the material culture of the Sioux. The artifacts he collected were items of traditional workmanship fashioned by Native Americans who still pursued the way of life of their ancestors. Ironically, this traditional lifestyle was soon to disappear through a policy of forced settlement which Read, as a United States military officer, was entrusted with carrying out. By the end of Read's military career in the West in 1887, nomadic Sioux culture, along with the buffalo, its chief resource, had been eliminated from the Plains. This collection, remarkable not only for the variety of its contents but also for its extraordinary historical context, allows a unique glimpse at the traditional work of a Native American people.

As in any undertaking of this size, there are a great many individuals who have contributed to its success. An especial debt of gratitude is due to the publication's two primary co-authors, Raymond J. DeMallie and Royal B. Hassrick. The Museum owes them both a great deal of appreciation for the time they devoted to this project — Dr. DeMallie for his long hours of preparatory research at the National Archives of the Smithsonian Institution; and Mr. Hassrick for his extended correspondence and repeated visits in order to catalogue the collection. Special thanks are also due to George P. Horse Capture, Curator of the Plains Indian Museum, Buffalo Bill Historical Center, for his thoughtful essay on Sioux art.

I would like to thank the Museum's Curator of Collections, Glenn E. Markoe, for his patient and energetic work as editor of this volume. It was Dr. Markoe who conceived the idea for this publication and saw it through from start to conclusion. My sincere appreciation also goes to Fleming Museum Registrar Leigh Rickes for his careful work in surveying and inventorying the collection.

Several other individuals deserve special mention for their generous assistance, most particularly Roy A. Whitmore, Dean of the School of Natural Resources at the University of Vermont, for his help in identifying the wood used in the manufacture of objects in the collection; and William Merrill and Joseph Brown of the Department of Anthropology at the National Museum of Natural History, the Smithsonian Institution, for their assistance in making the Smithsonian's extensive files and collections available for comparative study. Especial thanks go to Dennis and Jane Piechota for their expert conservation work on a number of items from the collection. This conservation work was made possible through support from the Fleming Museum's Earl Fund. The State Historical Societies of Montana and North Dakota, the Bureau of Indian Affairs at Fort Peck, Montana, and the National Anthropological Archives of the Smithsonian Institution are to be acknowledged for their cooperation in providing photographs for this publication.

Aside from its contribution to scholarship and research, the importance of a collection catalogue may be measured in its visual impact and pictorial value. A number of individuals have contributed to this end. My sincere appreciation goes to photographer Wes Disney for his subtle handling of difficult material and his patient efforts throughout the project. I would like to thank Leslie Fry for her thoughtful and effective design of a challenging publication project. Special thanks are also due to Merlin Acomb and Melinda Sargent for the production of the two maps. Lastly, the Museum's appreciation extends to Jill Mason for her editorial work on the catalogue.

Most important, we are indebted to the National Endowment for the Humanities for its generous funding of this publication. Without its support, the project could not have taken place.

I wish to extend my appreciation to Tony Perry for his financial support of the project.

Ildiko Heffernan
Director
Robert Hull Fleming Museum

Preface: Sioux Indian Art

The image of the Plains Indian which persists in the general public's mind is that of a feather-bedecked, painted, whooping warrior, mounted on his spotted pony, thundering across the prairie to the attack. It matters little that the so-called Indian Wars ended almost a century ago. The spectacle, maintained and exaggerated by commercial films and artists, has become a stereotype of most Indian people, and of the Sioux Indian people in particular.

To recognize and admire a group solely for its ability to wage war is confining and unfair to everyone concerned. One way of broadening this limited perspective is through a study of the traditional art of the Plains Indian people. Refreshingly unlike European styles, this art intimately reflects the diverse lifeways of the First People of this hemisphere.

The story begins, naturally, with the First People themselves, who arrived in this hemisphere tens of thousands of years ago, who learned to live with nature and the earth, and who developed lifestyles compatible with their own specific environment and philosophy. The native people of the Northwest Coast, for example, centered their lives around the bounty of the sea and the forests, fashioning shelters, clothing, and many other items from wood and other natural materials. The people from the Southwest dry-farmed their arid region for food, wove much of their clothing, and created pottery for their sedentary world. Blessed by a favorable climate, the first Californians lived in relative ease, having little need for clothing and living in an abundance of small game, berries, and acorns. Farther inland, in the semi-arid regions known as the Great Plains, the tribes extending from central Canada to Texas and from the Rocky Mountains to beyond the Mississippi River shared a common environment and developed similar cultures.

After an extended period, the people of the Great Plains developed a buffalo-oriented economy, initially procuring the magnificent animals by ambush in pounds or "corrals," or by chasing them off cliffs. Dependent upon the buffalo for food and most other supplies (such as utensils from bones and horns, clothing and robes from hides, rope from hair, and hundreds of additional items), the inhabitants of the Plains centered their cycle of life around the animal and around the spiritual forces that ruled the earth and sky. Like the buffalo herds they followed, the tribes traveled in small groups in the harsh winter and gathered together in the summer for feasts and other activities.

The horse, or "Big Dog," delivered to the continent by the Spanish in the Southwest, created a revolution among the people by allowing them to obtain buffalo almost at will and with relative ease, and to travel farther and carry more material. No longer required to devote enormous amounts of time and energy to subsistence activities, they could now afford to refine other essential aspects of their culture, such as religion and art.

Despite a rigorous lifestyle, an innate love of color and beauty compelled the Plains inhabitants to create a style of art that satisfied their cultural requirements. In prehistoric times the surfaces of cave walls and cliffs or large rocks were adorned with images and symbols, perhaps for hunting or other spiritual power, but in the historic period the migratory life of the tribes fashioned their culture. Everything used had to be sturdy, lightweight, and easily transportable — there were few luxuries. The people decorated the items they used on a daily basis: vessels, weapons, garments, and horsegear, to name a few. The object had to serve two purposes: its practical function and a decorative one. Shirts, dresses, footwear, and many other items of clothing and gear were intricately ornamented in materials and fashions that are still admired today. Other utilitarian items were decorated more simply: examples in the Read Collection include a horn drinking cup with simple incisions, and a wooden bowl, carved from the burl of a tree, its surface highly polished to highlight the fine twisted grain of the wood.

Originally, decorative materials were obtained directly from nature and included bone "beads," shells, animal teeth and hooves, and berries; porcupine quillwork embroidery, painting, and featherwork were among the more spectacular forms of decorative media. A little before 1800, foreign trade goods became available in the Northern Plains. The native artists quickly adapted many of them for their own use, often abandoning natural materials. Foreign trade items were often used intact and became a part of the tribal repertory. An excellent example of this practice of wholesale borrowing is the pipe tomahawk (cat. no. 53).

The styles of Plains Indian art were usually determined by the artist's gender. Men often executed realistic forms on their clothing, shields, tipis, robes, and military equipment. Artistic forms and concepts frequently came to the artist in visions or dreams, or memories of actual military exploits. Tribal historians painted a well-known symbol for each year on calendar robes called "winter counts." Women excelled in abstract design. Although they, too, applied paints to robes and parfleches, their primary decorative materials were porcupine quills and, later, glass beads. Many of the items they produced, such as the quill-decorated moccasins and the beaded bonnet case (cat. nos. 4 and 85) in the Read Collection, are exquisite works of art in their own right.

One of the most enduring and attractive of the decorative trade items associated with Plains Indian art is the glass bead. Manufactured primarily in Italy, the first examples to reach the Plains were fairly large (roughly ⅛ inch in diameter) and were known as "pony beads," so called, it is said, because they arrived on the backs of ponies. First imported around 1790, these glass beads became so popular that, by 1840, they had virtually replaced the use of traditional porcupine quillwork; black, white, and blue beads were preferred. The smaller seed beads supplanted pony beads by the mid-nineteenth century. The popularity of glass beads over porcupine quills can be attributed to at least three reasons: first, they offered a wider choice of colors; second, they were more easily obtained; and third, they fit within the linear orientation of the traditional patterns.

The female artists developed two basic methods of applying the beads to the material. In the first, known as the "appliqué," or "overlay," stitch, a beaded strand is fastened down to the material after every two or three beads, resulting in a firm, flat appearance. The other technique is called the "lazy" stitch. After the thread is fastened to the material, a number of beads are threaded and stitched down at a distance that is shorter than if they were laid flat — the result is a string of beads that arcs slightly at the center. The next row is applied parallel to and almost touching the first row in the same manner. The parallel lines eventually create a "ribbed," or "washboard," appearance that allows more surface flexibility.

Besides the glass beads, a whole host of European trade goods infiltrated the native repertory of materials. Trade thread eventually replaced animal sinew; aniline dyes were preferred over natural tints for their brighter colors; metal bells sounded clearer than dewclaws. Numerous other substitutions took place as well, but the traditional forms and sense of aesthetics remained.

The hides of animals provided the background for the ornamentation. Depending upon the use, various types of hides were preferred. For the lighter requirements of clothing, deerskin, elkskin, and the hides of the smaller buffalo prevailed. The larger buffalo hides, either tanned or as rawhide, functioned as horse equipment, robes, parfleches, bags, and other items until shortly after 1880, when the herds were largely eliminated. Later, canvas, muslin, wool, and cowhide partially filled the requirements for support materials.

As a way of expressing their religious beliefs and philosophies and of commemorating personal exploits, as well as for purely aesthetic reasons, the beadwork artists incorporated specific colors and designs into their art. Red could represent power, or life's blood and energy. Spring and new life could be expressed in green. A cross might be a star; a circle, the sun or stars; and a crescent, the moon, all of these motifs acknowledging the celestial element. For many, the stepped pyramid abstractly symbolized tipis, mountains, or Mother Earth.

Other symbols, patterns, and colors probably held a particular meaning for individual artists, as anthropologists have recorded. As these same elements were incorporated into the work of others, their meanings were undoubtedly interpreted differently. As a result, personal interpretations became associated with symbols or colors that may have been completely different from that originally intended, but still representing something special to each artist and group. Most of the recorded meanings of these figures and colors are, therefore, suspect because of interpretive subjectivity. It may also be the case that many of the images and colors were chosen solely for their aesthetic value.

Indian artists, particularly the Sioux, were amazingly inventive. Although somewhat limited by traditional techniques and by the structure of the object itself, the modes of bead decoration and color combinations they created were often spectacular.

Despite a common environment and shared cultural traits, no single artistic standard ever emerged among the Plains tribes. Before 1840, their art was generally expressed in geometric designs, although such designs were not identifiable as unique to one tribe. Only after the mid-1800s did distinct tribal styles develop, and even then many of them were not limited to one tribe but were shared, to varying degrees, within a region. Over a period of time a tribe's preference would change slightly, and new or altered designs would be favored. Floral patterns from the East entered the Plains in great number during this period (cat. no. 107). Compounding the difficulties of attributing art pieces to a specific tribe were the traditions of trading, gift-giving, intertribal marriages, close alliances, warfare, and other practices which encouraged the interchange of art styles among diverse groups.

Within the Northern Plains area three major centers of tribal art influence have been identified: the Blackfeet, the Crow, and the Sioux; each of these centers is named after a large tribe whose distinctive art styles have influenced many of the smaller, adjacent tribes. Nevertheless, specific tribal preferences complicate any systematic explanation of stylistic diffusion. Consider the question of beadwork application: the Assiniboine of Montana, who are close relatives of the Sioux (who use the lazy stitch) and long-term allies of the Cree in Canada (who use the appliqué stitch) have practiced both the lazy stitch and appliqué techniques. The Arapaho of Wyoming and the Cheyenne of Montana, long-time friends of the Sioux, also favor the lazy stitch, while the Gros Ventre of Montana, even though closely related to the Arapaho, generally prefer the appliqué technique.

The period between 1885 and 1895 appears to have been the most productive for the traditional Indian artists in spite of the outside forces which engulfed them. Overrun by the ever-encroaching whites, the tribes lost most of their land base, their native religion, and their military might. Enclosed on remote and barren reservations and subject to the whims of a far-off government and often corrupt Indian agents, the tribes somehow survived — and with them their art.

Today we are in the midst of an Indian renaissance. Religious practices long dormant are being revived across Indian country. Each year the Sun Dance lodges fill and the buttes see a growing number of vision questers, all fasting and praying for the required four days and nights. Quillwork, too, is reappearing, revived primarily by the Sioux people.

The overt manifestation of contemporary tribal art takes place at the celebrations or powwows that occur every summer in most Indian communities across the plains. Brightly colored feathers and rayon shawls take their place alongside the traditional eagle feathers and deerskin dresses as the people dance and sing to celebrate life.

The objects in the Ogden B. Read Collection testify to the quality of the art produced by the Sioux people. The majority of articles in the collection can, in fact, be identified as the creations of the Sioux and their relatives, as Read's own notes confirm. Problems of authorship nevertheless remain, even with a collection as well documented as the Read. The fact that objects were acquired from Yanktonai or Hunkpapa Sioux Indians does not mean that their "owners" were necessarily their makers. Due to the dynamics of interchange among Plains people, many factors often came into play. As the Sioux expanded westward, they came into conflict with various tribes. Booty and treasures were carried from the battlefield or were received as gifts or trade items. The elkskin dress (cat. no. 13; Read no. 28) was probably made by a Plateau Indian tribe, perhaps the Nez Percé, as Read records. Very possibly, it made its way eastward by a combination of gift-giving and transfer of war spoils. The Crow Indian buffalo robes (cat. nos. 15 and 16; Read nos. 18 and 20) offer another example of this category.

Sioux art is comprised of many elements that unite to form unique styles. These styles, such as the geometric and the floral, are shared to a lesser degree with allied or related tribes, including the Cheyenne, the Arapaho, and the Fort Peck Assiniboine. The Sioux favored use of the lazy stitch to attach the white or blue beads that usually formed the background of their decorated work. Before 1870, the beaded geometric symbols and designs on the background were bold and strong, and were usually worked in red, white, blue, green, yellow, and a few other colors. Vast empty spaces separated the simple but forceful rectangles, triangles, and circles of the central forms, conveying a sense of pride, strength, and confidence.

After 1870, as the disruption of their traditional life accelerated, the simple artistic forms became more complex. Smaller triangles, linear projections, and terraced zigzag extensions filled the empty spaces. Designs became spidery and attenuated. In the 1880s, stylized forms emerged, featuring standing or mounted men in warbonnets, women, animals, and other motifs. American flags were incorporated into the designs and appeared in great profusion. The turbulence of the period caused great unrest among the tribes, and they experimented in many areas, seeking to make a transition from the traditional motifs to new ones. Hats, shirts, trousers, vests, and other articles of clothing were often completely covered with beadwork in a manner which, although to some degree attractive, could be considered excessive.

The Ogden B. Read Collection of Plains Indian materials faithfully represents the art and ethnology of the Sioux and other Plains Indian tribes. The publication of this collection adds an important chapter to the continuing story of the First People.

George P. Horse Capture
Curator, Plains Indian Museum
Buffalo Bill Historical Center
Cody, Wyoming, 1986

Introduction

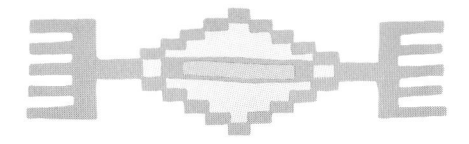

Vestiges of a Proud Nation documents a unique collection of Plains Indian artifacts. The proud nation referred to is that of the Sioux people, from whom the collection was acquired. The term "vestiges" may be aptly applied to the material remains of a people, such as the Sioux, whose traditional way of life was disappearing at the very moment of the Read Collection's formation. Implicit is the realization that any collection of historical artifacts, no matter how comprehensive, is but the material remnant of a vibrant culture whose past traditions — religious, political, and social — cannot be measured in physical or tangible terms.

The collector, Ogden Benedict Read, served as an army officer in the Northern Plains during the last quarter of the nineteenth century. In and of itself, this circumstance is not a unique one; quite a number of Plains Indian collections survive whose contents were assembled by military officers posted in the area during the last century. What makes the Read Collection unique is the documentation that accompanies it. Every object is recorded in an annotated list provided by Read to the University of Vermont along with the collection. This list furnishes precise information about the objects' original owners as well as the dates, locations, and (in some instances) circumstances of their acquisition by Read. Such scholarly attention to detail is rare indeed in an era when Indian relics were normally collected as curios or mementos.

The collection is also remarkable for its variety of materials. Although relatively small, numbering slightly more than a hundred objects, it encompasses a wide range of items — from eating utensils and implements to elaborate articles of ceremonial dress. To be sure, it contains a number of war trophies and curios, such as tomahawks and scalps, but these represent a relatively small proportion of the collection as a whole. Unlike that of most nineteenth-century private collectors, Read's primary purpose was not to amass a group of impressive show pieces but, rather, to document the material culture of a people. His interest in collecting was that of an antiquarian. (Read had a large personal library of volumes on historical and natural historical subjects and was himself a member of the Smithsonian Institution, the American Ethnology Society, and the American Antiquarian Society.) In fact, his ultimate intention was to build a study collection for his alma mater, the University of Vermont. With this purpose in mind, Read selected a wide range of objects that provided valuable information about the society and the technology that produced them.

The collection, as Read's inventory informs, was assembled through a variety of means. A great many of the items were purchased by Read himself; others were presented as gifts to him or members of his family by Indian friends or visiting dignitaries. Yet others were acquired from local traders and scouts with whom Read came into contact. The most notable of the latter was Joseph Culbertson, a white scout and interpreter in Read's employ. Not everything in the collection was peaceably obtained; a large group of objects was appropriated during a single military operation — an attack upon a neighboring Hunkpapa camp on January 2, 1881 — in which Read was directly involved. With this one exception, however, it appears that few objects, save for some firearms and ammunition (nos. 15, 16, 104), were taken forcibly from their Indian owners.[1] Unlike many of his military colleagues, Read seems to have been sensitive enough to the situation and mindful enough of military propriety not to have abused his authority in appropriating Indian goods and possessions.

The great majority of pieces in the Read Collection were acquired over the years 1879–1882, during an era traditionally defined as the "early reservation" period in the Northern Plains. Read himself was instrumental in transferring large numbers of Sioux to the government agencies recently established in the area. The bulk of the collection was acquired either from such agency Sioux or from those Indians (referred to by the military as "hostiles") who so far had managed to resist the army's efforts at reservation settlement. Within Read's jurisdiction, these "hostiles" belonged to Sitting Bull's Hunkpapa tribe, a division of the Teton Dakota who had settled in western Dakota Territory. Unlike the settled Indian populations of the later reservation period (from circa 1890 onward), who, in response to economic pressures, produced their wares largely for a western market, both the Yanktonai at the agencies and the Hunkpapa still at large continued to pursue the nomadic lifestyle of their ancestors. As a result, most of the items in the collection are utilitarian in function and were made and ornamented in the traditional manner.

As far as date is concerned, the earliest recorded piece in the collection (tobacco pouch no. 63) was acquired in 1876 at Standing Rock Agency, Dakota Territory, Read's first military assignment in the Northern Plains. The latest recorded date of acquisition is 1882. Given the perishable nature of the materials used in construction and the fact that a wood or hide object in constant use would have had a relatively short lifespan, we may assume that most, if not all, of the objects in the collection were made during the decade 1870–1880. Read's own records indicate that certain items were presented as gifts to him and to his family and were probably new or relatively unused at the time of their presentation. Other items, such as the parfleches (no. 23) and painted rawhide container (no. 24), are in such pristine condition that it is clear that they received little if any use, whether intended as gifts or not. Certainly, for all of these objects, we may assume a date of manufacture within a year or two of their date of acquisition.

A small number of items that appear to be of considerably earlier date have been included in the catalogue: a hair-fringed shirt (cat. no. 7), a pair of leggings (cat. no. 8), a quiver (cat. no. 44), a knife case (cat. no. 107), and a pad saddle (cat. no. 65). Stylistically, all of them belong to the period of the mid-nineteenth century and are distinguished from the remainder of the collection by their use of pony beads and native-dyed porcupine-quill decoration. Significantly, none of these objects is included in Read's original inventory. The hair-fringed shirt, in fact, may be identified with a "fine scalp jacket" mentioned as already part of the Museum's collection in a letter written by Director Perkins to Read in January of 1882. The quill-decorated leggings are very similar in style and probably entered the Museum's collections at the same time. Since none of these items can be identified as later acquisitions, all can be safely assumed to have been part of the Museum's holdings before the acquisition of Read's collection.

In addition to furnishing dates, the Read Collection provides valuable information about tribal origins and sources of manufacture. As previously stated, the majority of the objects were obtained from either Hunkpapa or Yanktonai Dakota Indians who were living in proximity to Read's Poplar River post in the late 1870s and early 1880s. In his inventory, Read normally designates the article's owner, frequently by name. Generalized sources of tribal manufacture are given for certain items (e.g., rawhide bag no. 24 ["Yanktonai manufacture"] and saddlebag no. 27 ["Uncapapa manufacture"]). More frequently, however, such ethnic information is appended to specific individuals when they are identified as makers (e.g., "made by wife of Two Bears, Yanktonais" [nos. 57, 58, 60, 75, and 116]). These comments regarding maker are carefully differentiated from the bulk of the entries which objectively list the source of the gift or purchase ("purchased from," "presented by," "captured from") without venturing any inference as to source of manufacture. Thus, it appears that Read designates the artisan only when he has been given direct or specific information about tribal or personal origin.

While the majority of items in the collection are Sioux, articles from other Northern Plains tribes are included and identified. Crow material (nos. 8, 18, 20, 46, 84, 85, 97, 102), including two decorated buffalo robes, forms the largest outside group; most of the pieces were obtained at Terry's Landing, Montana Territory, from female relatives of what appear to have been Crow scouts. Long-standing enemies of the Sioux, the Crow were employed by the army for their intimate knowledge of the terrain.[2] A number of objects bear vivid testimony to the fierce and continuous rivalry between the Sioux and other tribes, including the Crow. One example is the war club recorded in entry number 12; as its Yanktonai owner proudly pointed out, the red paint on the club head marked the point to which it had been driven through the skull of a Crow Indian. A scalp and pipe (nos. 48 and 69) were taken from a Blackfoot Indian killed by a Yanktonai near Camp Poplar River in 1881.

The importance of both Native American and European trade items to the Sioux is underlined by the collection. The necklace and earrings recorded in entry no. 95 attest to long-distance Native American trade. Purchased from a Yanktonai woman at Camp Poplar River, they are made of abalone and dentalia shells imported from the Pacific Coast. The value of elks' teeth as items of Indian trade is discussed under entry no. 81.

American- and European-manufactured trade goods are equally present. Weapons and hunting implements stand at the top of the list (cf. the commercial steel-bladed knives [no. 16] and the pipe tomahawk [no. 8]). Native-manufactured items such as the beaded guncase (no. 137) and the cartridge pouch (no. 79) attest to the use of western firearms.

European trade goods, such as brass beads and upholstery tacks, nails and tin cone ornaments, glass beads, textiles (stroud, calico, ribbon, and English chintz [no. 59]), and commercial leather, were incorporated in the design and decoration of Native American goods. In addition to the imported items obtained up the Missouri from the southeast, many of the trade goods represented in the Read Collection are likely to have come from the north by way of French-Canadian traders from the neighboring trade post at Wood Mountain, North West Territory. At least one trade item, a pair of snow shoes (no. 38), is recorded as having come from this post — a present to Read from a French-Canadian trader named Cadd.

Valuable as an anthropological resource, the Read Collection is of even greater interest as a historical document. The first half of this publication is therefore devoted to a historical examination of the Sioux in the Northern Plains. Ogden B. Read's military career encompassed a crucial period at the end of the Indian Wars. He was transferred to the northern territories within a few months of the Custer defeat at Little Big Horn (in June of 1876),[3] and, with the Eleventh Infantry, was soon actively involved in field operations against the northern tribes in Montana Territory. For the next decade, Read was to occupy a series of military-post positions in the North, among them the command, in 1880, of newly created Camp Poplar River in eastern Montana Territory. It was here that he became directly involved in the army's efforts to settle the remainder of Sitting Bull's Hunkpapa tribe on the government reservations.

The most significant of the military engagements in which Read was involved during his residence at Camp Poplar River was that of January 2, 1881, a date which occurs repeatedly throughout his inventory list. With Captain Read's assistance, Major Guido Ilges, who had been brought in to assume temporary command of the post shortly after Read's arrival, waged an apparently unprovoked assault on a camp of "hostile" Hunkpapas established above the post. Following the surrender of its inhabitants, the camp and its lodges were burned to the ground. Some sixteen items in the collection are recorded as having been taken from the Hunkpapa camp during or after the burning of the lodges. Shortly after the assault, Read, with a detachment of the Eleventh Infantry, conducted the remaining Hunkpapa captives (numbering over three hundred people and two hundred horses) under Chief Crow King to Fort Buford for temporary internment, an event referred to in the entry for war club no. 10. Over the next six months, Read was involved in negotiating the surrender of the remaining bands of hostile Hunkpapas, many of whom (like Iron Dog and his followers [entry no. 81]), forced by military pressures and starvation, offered themselves up to the authorities. As entry no. 77 indicates, this process of negotiation continued well into the summer of 1881.

Read was directly involved in reconnaissance operations against Sitting Bull during the chief's final years in Canada, and his collection inventory contains the names of many of Sitting Bull's Hunkpapa subordinates: Chiefs Crow (no. 111), Crow King (no. 26), and Black Eagle (nos. 10, 78); his messengers, "Umpato Wakan" (no. 15) and Little Shield (no. 36); his stepson, Man Who Hides Under the Snow (no. 40); and his chief advisor, Little Assiniboine (no. 90). The military's ultimate objective was to secure Sitting Bull's surrender, as Read acknowledges in his annual report to the Assistant Adjutant General's Office on September 19, 1881. After tabulating the number of hostile Indians secured and transferred to Fort Buford over the past year, he adds: "The most important result of all was [the] weakening of Sitting Bull's force to such an extent as to compel his final surrender with all but a small remaint [sic] of the hostile Sioux." The momentous event to which he refers had taken place at Fort Buford on July 19, precisely two months before.

The Museum's acquisition of the Read Collection has an interesting history. The collection was presented by Read to the University as a long-term loan.[4] According to the correspondence between Read and the Museum's director, George Henry Perkins (transcripts of which are preserved in the Museum's archives), the collection was shipped from Camp Poplar River to the University in two installments, the first (nos. 1–112) in the fall of 1881 and the second (nos. 113–138) sometime in the following year. The first shipment arrived from Bismarck, North Dakota, by express rather than by freight, as had been anticipated. It appears that the University was in financial straits at the time and its president, Horace Buckham, was unwilling to assume the steep transportation costs (over $29) despite Director Perkins' urgings. Read later sent a check to the University to cover the amount.

Perkins' delight upon receiving the Read Collection was evident. In a letter to Read, dated October 25, 1881, he writes: "Your collection has arrived safely and I have today opened the large box and taken out most of the articles. I am astonished at the variety and value of the collection. It is simply invaluable, and to everyone, but especially to ethnologists, will be of very great value and will attract a great deal of attention." Perkins had every reason to be delighted. Prior to its receipt, the Museum's holdings had consisted of little more than a small study collection of birds, mammals, shells, and geologic specimens. Read's gift was the first major ethnographic collection acquired by the University.

Despite the University's financial troubles, Perkins did manage to secure $50 for the construction of new cases especially designed for the collection. In a letter from Perkins to Read (then stationed at Fort Yates, Montana Territory) in 1887, we learn that the collection had been recently installed in a special room in the University's Old Mill, where the Museum's collections had been housed since Read's student days in 1861. The collection was displayed in its entirety in thirteen newly constructed cases with glazed fronts; "articles of similar use" were grouped together and accompanied by specially printed labels. Shortly after the installation, Read and his family moved back east to Plattsburgh, New York, directly across from Burlington, Vermont, on Lake Champlain. In May of 1888, not long after his return, Read delivered a lecture at the Museum, entitled "The Indians of the Northwest," at the close of which he exhibited a variety of objects from his collection.[5] How often Read visited the Museum at this time is not known. Tragically, his stay at Plattsburgh proved a short one. In 1889, just over two years after his return, Read took his own life. He was only forty-six years old.

The Read Collection remained in Torrey Hall through the end of the nineteenth and early decades of the twentieth century. The University's burgeoning collections, however, soon outgrew the old museum's limited facilities and a new building was constructed in 1931. Installation shots taken at the time of the Fleming Museum's opening show that highlights of the Read Collection were incorporated within a large ethnographic gallery that housed a selection of artifacts from Asia, Africa, Oceania and the Americas. Over the ensuing decades, with the growth of the ethnographic holdings and a change in collection priority from ethnographic works to works of fine art, an increasingly smaller share of the collection was exhibited. Since the Fleming's renovation during 1980–83, the Read Collection, along with the rest of the ethnographic holdings, has been removed from permanent display and resituated in a newly equipped storage facility, where it has been surveyed and studied by a number of specialists. A generous grant from the National Endowment for the Humanities awarded to the Fleming in 1984 enabled the Museum to undertake the research and publication of the collection. In preparation for this publication, the entire collection was assessed as to its conservation needs, and a select number of objects were chosen for treatment; this work was successfully completed in 1985. A special exhibition of the entire Read Collection is being planned for the year 1989.

The publication necessitated a full re-inventory of the Read Collection. Sometime after their arrival at the Museum, the items in the collection had been tagged by Director Perkins according to the numbered list provided by Read, but, unfortunately, they were not permanently numbered. By the early 1930s, when the objects were assigned permanent numbers, most of Perkins' original tags had either fallen off or been removed. Many other Plains Indian pieces had entered the Museum's holdings in the intervening years, adding to the confusion. As a result, a number of objects, both pre- and postdating the collection, were mistakenly assigned to it, while other pieces original to the collection were misidentified and unwittingly divorced from it. By a careful process of elimination and a thorough re-evaluation of all items identifiable as potential entries, it has been possible to reconstruct the list with a fair amount of certainty. For every object that can be clearly assigned to an original Read entry (from Perkins' surviving identification tags or through incontrovertible correspondence in description), the original Read number has been listed in the catalogue entry. To those pieces for which a one-to-one correspondence between object and inventory entry cannot be established, a late-accession number (annotated LA) beginning with number 139 (Read's list ends with number 138) has been assigned and the possible numbered entries in Read's inventory recorded. (In the case of three unidentified tobacco bags, "no. 62, 63, or 66" is appended to each, indicating that each of the bags in question could correspond to any of the three entries.) In some instances, items have been included in the catalogue which cannot be located on the original list; these are noted accordingly.

At the end of the catalogue section, Read's original inventory has been reproduced in its entirety, with editorial comments and annotations. This list has been preserved in the form of a typed transcription made from what must be assumed to have been Read's handwritten original (now lost, unfortunately). With the exception of some minor corrections and punctuation added for clarity and grammatical consistency, the inventory reproduced in this publication conforms faithfully to the transcription, preserving the spellings and abbreviations as they were presumably copied from the original. Each entry is preceded by an annotation that indicates the current status of the object(s) correlated with it. In those instances where Museum records indicate that a particular object recorded on the list had been sold or discarded, this information is noted. For the majority of items unaccounted for, however, no information exists in the Museum's records. The natural historical items (hides, skins, and zoological specimens) were very likely transferred out of the collection or discarded owing to their deteriorating condition. (Perkins expressed his concern to Read about moth-related damage to hides and furs when the collection first arrived.) A number of items on the original inventory have never been listed in the Museum's records, suggesting that these objects were never accessioned; some may have been returned to Mrs. Read during the negotiations over the purchase of the collection after her husband's death.

In the catalogue entries, tribal identifications are based primarily upon the information (concerning an object's owner or maker) furnished by Read himself. Where a specific tribal identification is not possible, the generic term "Sioux" or "Northern Plains" is used. For each catalogue entry, Read's information regarding origin, date of acquisition, and find circumstance is provided. The physical descriptions of the objects adhere to the standardized format and terminology established by Barbara Hail in her publication *Hau, Kóla!* These descriptive entries were written by the editor of this publication; the commentaries that follow the descriptions are those of Royal Hassrick. In certain instances, comparisons are cited with documented objects of comparable date and origin in other museum collections. The most noteworthy of these collections (presently known to the editor) are listed in an appendix at the end of the book.

Glenn E. Markoe
Curator of Collections
Robert Hull Fleming Museum

1. Medicine shield cover no. 72 is recorded as having been taken from a Sioux grave near Camp Poplar River in 1881, but it is unclear who was directly responsible for the action.

2. Dress no. 28, for instance, was captured by Crow scouts under General Miles during a military engagement with the Nez Percé under Chief Joseph at Bear Paw Mountains, M.T., in 1877.

3. In fact, the collection contained a number of souvenirs and mementos of the battle either given to Read or picked up by him on the battlefield (nos. 6, 107, 108, 109, 111).

4. The collection was later purchased from Read's widow sometime around 1893.

5. Burlington *Daily Free Press*, May 16, 1888, p. 8.

Sitting Bull. Hunkpapa. Photo by O. S. Goff. Read Collection 1881.3.136.1.

The Sioux in Dakota and Montana Territories: Cultural and Historical Background of the Ogden B. Read Collection

When Lieutenant Ogden B. Read was assigned to Dakota Territory in 1876, the Sioux Indians it was his duty to fight and to administer were facing a critical period in their history, the events of which would determine whether they would survive as a people. The crisis with which the Sioux found themselves confronted was threefold: political, economic, and religious.

The political crisis stemmed from the legal system of the United States government, which, since 1871, no longer considered American Indian peoples to be the sovereign "domestic dependent nations" of earlier U.S. policy, articulated in 1831 by Supreme Court Chief Justice John Marshall. Indian rights — both in theory and in practice — were subordinated to the needs of the United States at large. Tribes were to be localized on reservations where they would pass away, either by physical death or by assimilating to the Christian civilization of the United States. For the Sioux, this amounted to a choice between freedom and submission. The cost of the former was unrelenting war with the U.S. Army, while the cost of the latter was restriction to a reservation and subjugation to the rules and regulations of a government Indian agency.

The economic crisis was just as dire. Game animals were disappearing at a rate that defied comprehension; tribes were being drawn into ever-diminishing hunting areas and forced to compete with one another over the remaining buffalo herds. The choice was to be hemmed in by enemy tribes and fight or starve on the plains, or to go to the agencies and hope that the government would provide the necessities that hunting no longer could.

Fusing these crises into one pattern of cultural choice was the religious crisis: the old prayers and rituals no longer fulfilled the people's needs. Game didn't always come; victory didn't always follow; death and suffering from war and disease and hunger were eroding even the fundamental religious values of their traditional way of life. If their old gods had deserted them, if old values no longer applied, the only alternative was the new way offered by the white men. This period in Sioux history presented the people the choice between holding on to the old life on the plains and dying off like the buffalo, or accepting — no matter how tentatively — the new life on the reservations and surviving in the white man's world. Faced with this choice, the Sioux thought of their children and the future and took the harder road: they chose life on the reservations.[1]

The historical forces that brought the Sioux to this critical turning point gathered in the space of a single generation. As Colonel Richard I. Dodge remarked in *The Plains of the Great West* (1877), what had only a half-century earlier been the unexplored Great American Desert had become fully known and was rapidly filling up with white frontier settlers bringing with them all the technological innovations of American civilization. The great emigrant trails to California and Oregon provided the opening wedge into Sioux country, followed by the florescence of steamboat traffic on the Missouri River. The discovery of gold in Montana in

1863 and in the Black Hills of Dakota in 1874 sparked the blazing of new trails and lured hordes of fortune seekers to the region that would serve as the final stage for the contest between the Sioux and the white invaders. The Sioux were not oblivious to the impending danger. Speaking to a group of U.S. treaty commissioners in 1865, Lone Horn, leading chief of the Minneconjous, spoke his mind: "Our buffalo are all being scared away because the whites are traveling through our country. You have sent for us to come in and talk with you. The reason we could not all come is because we have to go away so far on the buffalo hunt, and it is the fault of the whites who drove them away that we have to follow the game so far. The game we must have to live, and have to go after it." But the conflict between the whites and the Sioux was not to be resolved through diplomacy.[2]

The story of the struggle between the Sioux and the white Americans has been told time and again; it is a chronicle of bloodshed and betrayal that has crystalized in American legend around the personalities of remembered leaders: General George A. Custer, Sitting Bull, Crazy Horse, Gall. The final act, the 1890 massacre at Wounded Knee, the last bloodshed of the Sioux wars, occurred in the year declared by historian Frederick Jackson Turner to mark the end of the American frontier and has come to symbolize the defeat of the American Indian.[3] But the history of those times and the challenges faced by the Sioux people are not adequately summarized in the accounts of marches and battles, nor can they be responsibly relegated to the frontier that is past and gone. The legacy is with us yet; the battles are remembered — the victories together with the defeats — but the real dynamic that has brought the Sioux people from the close of the frontier into the atomic age results from a social process, the adaptation of the Indian peoples to the new world of the reservations during the last decades of the nineteenth century and their integration as distinctive peoples into the social fabric of twentieth-century America.

In the nineteenth century the name "Sioux" designated not a single tribe or national entity, but a complex web of bands and tribes spread from the forested regions of the upper Mississippi, across the prairies of Minnesota and Dakota Territory, and beyond the Missouri on the high plains of Nebraska, Dakota, Wyoming, and Montana. The word "Sioux" (in the early nineteenth century pronounced with a French accent: *see-ou*, not *sou*) is a shortened form of a French borrowing of a Chippewa word. *Nadowe-is-iw* ("little adders"), signifying enemies, was the name the Chippewas used to designate the Sioux, with whom they contested the forests of Minnesota. What gave unity to the Sioux as a people was the commonality of language. In Sioux ideology, all who spoke any other language were enemies unless a formal peace had been entered into. The Sioux called themselves *Dak'óta* (or *Lak'óta*, in the western dialect), meaning "allies," and other tribal groups with whom peace had been made — notably the Cheyennes and Arapahoes during the nineteenth century — were incorporated into this alliance and designated "allies." The result of such identity was to impart a fluidity to Sioux society. Depending on the situation, the term *Dak'óta* might be used exclusively, to designate only certain bands or tribes, or it might be used inclusively to designate all the Sioux and their allies (or even, as it is frequently used today, to designate "Indians" as opposed to non-Indians). Who was or who wasn't *Dak'óta* or *Lak'óta* was therefore a matter to be negotiated in each specific context.[4]

While the Sioux people did not represent a kind of political union that acted in concert to control tribal territories or enforce tribal laws, they nonetheless articulated an ideology that symbolized their unity. This was the idea of the Seven Fireplaces, representing seven council fires, each fire symbolic of the autonomy of a political group. First mentioned by European writers in the nineteenth century (150 years after the Sioux had come to be known by Europeans), the Seven Fireplaces were identified as the seven tribes of the Sioux: *Mdéwak'ant'unwan*, "Spirit lake village"; *Wahpék'ute*, "Leaf shooters"; *Sisít'unwan*, meaning unknown; *Wahpét'unwan*, "Leaf village"; *Ihánkt'unwan*, "End village"; *Ihánkt'unwanna*, "Little end village"; and *T'íntat'unwan*, "Prairie village." Conventionally, the first four groups — Mdewakantons, Wahpekutes, Sissetons, and Wahpetons (using English forms) — are classed as Santee Sioux (from the name *Isán'at'i*, "Knife dwellers," referring to the name of a lake, the term by which the Tetons designated the eastern Sioux). These four groups call themselves *Dak'óta*. The next two groups — Yanktons and Yanktonais — are classed together as Yankton or "middle" Sioux, reflecting their geographical position between the Santees and the Tetons. They called themselves *Dak'óta*, also, but in other phonological contexts the prominent *d* of the Santee dialect became *n*. The last group, the Tetons, or western Sioux, called themselves *Lak'óta*, substituting the *l* for *d* or *n*.[5]

In actuality, the intermarriage of these groups and the extent to which some of them habitually camped with others during the nineteenth century blurred the precision of group identity. Rather than a static structure, the differentiation of social groups was a continuing process. Given the Sioux lack of concern over tribal boundaries and precise identities, such a continually developing structure posed no difficulties. The myth of the Seven Council Fires, representing an ancient political alliance of all the Sioux, and centered at Spirit Lake, served in the nineteenth century to symbolize unity by reference to past events. (In fact, however, lack of any corroborating evidence in the European written sources for the previous century and a half strongly suggests that the Seven Council Fires as an ideological concept expressing unity represents a non-historical myth rather than a dimly remembered legend.)

The symbol of the Seven Fireplaces was used in other ways as well, reflecting the flexibility of the term *Dak'óta*. Sometimes in listing the seven groups other tribes were included, most frequently the Cheyennes. Among the Tetons, in the late nineteenth century, the Seven Fireplaces referred primarily to the seven Teton tribes. From the single tribe referred to in the story of the Seven Fireplaces, the Tetons themselves developed a social order that replicated the whole. By the time of Lewis and Clark, there were four named Teton tribes, and by the 1860s the seven tribal names familiar to the history of the Indian wars had evolved: *Oglála*, "Scatters their own"; *Sic'áŋǧu*, "Burned thighs" (known by the French name Brulé); *Mnik'ówoju*, "Planters by water" (Minneconjou); *O'óhenuŋpa*, "Two kettles" (literally, "two boilings"); *Itázipco*, "Without bows" (known by the French name Sans Arcs); *Sihásapa*, "Black feet" (sometimes confused with the Algonquian-speaking Blackfeet Indians of Montana and Alberta); and *Húŋkpap'a*, "Campers at the opening of the circle."[6] All these peoples called themselves (and, situationally, the other Sioux and the Cheyennes and Arapahoes as well) *Lak'óta*.

Nor were the Tetons the only group to develop a more complex structure. The Yanktonais seem to have been well on the way to replicating the pattern of seven divisions as well. They divided into Lower and Upper Yanktonais, and one group of the latter — the Cutheads, under the leadership of Wa'ánatan ("Charger"), representing an amalgamation of Yanktonai and Sisseton families — seems by mid-nineteenth century to have become a separate group.

At the core, the flexibility of the Sioux social system reflected its smallest unit, the extended family, a group of relatives who lived together. Before the advent of the horse to the plains, extended families lived in single dwellings; later, with increased mobility and transportation capabilities, each nuclear family (or unit of mother and children) had a lodge of its own. For the vast majority of the Sioux people (excluding some of the eastern Sioux who lived in Woodlands-style bark lodges or European-style log houses, and some Yanktonais who lived in Missouri River-style earth lodges), home was a circular tipi, each in cultural symbolism a microcosm of the universe. With doorway facing east, the place of honor at the inside west, the fire in the center symbolizing autonomy, the lodge itself was simultaneously social nucleus and cultural symbol.

The band, *t'iyóšpaye* ("lodge group"), was a named social unit, a collection of lodges of related people, whose daily interaction was in terms of kinship roles, and whose daily salutations were kinship terms. On special occasions the *t'iyóšpaye* camped in circular form, facing east, the headman's lodge in the place of honor at the west, the ceremonial center being the middle of the camp circle, where within the council lodge a fireplace glowed, symbolizing the autonomy of the band. Basically a kinship unit, headed by a recognized elder chief (*itáŋc'aŋ*, "leader") and guided by a council of respected adult men, the *t'iyóšpaye* was the basic unit of society. Many *t'iyóšpaye* were linked with one or two others in larger, named units; some bore the names of leaders, but most were called by enigmatic nicknames whose referents and even meanings quickly became the subjects of legend. Groups composed of several of these *t'iyóšpaye* recognized common identity in named tribal units called *oyáte* (a term meaning tribe or people that could be applied at any level of social order). These *oyáte* correspond to the "fireplaces" of the Seven Fireplaces.

When large gatherings occurred, the people might camp in one circle, replicating that of the formal *t'iyóšpaye* camp, the chiefs exercising influence according to the ranking among them (based on kinship or respect), the councils of each band merging to meet as a single council. On these occasions special leaders might be appointed for the management of such a large encampment. The model of the *t'iyóšpaye* could be generalized upwards to any size; it provided the mechanism for maintaining social order in the large encampments that came together during the time of the Sun Dance and summer buffalo hunts, and — as Lieutenant Colonel George A. Custer learned the hard way — also gathered for defense against the U.S. Army.[7]

The *t'iyóšpaye* as a culturally prescribed model for organizing society provided the structure for the Sioux political system. The council of adult men represented the will of the people and met to deliberate on all matters that pertained to group welfare. The chief, representing the council, was an elder relative — a symbolic father — to the *t'iyóšpaye*, and was expected to voice the council's wishes. His only authority was to be accorded precedence in speaking at meetings of the council, and his effectiveness depended entirely upon his persuasiveness and his oratorical abilities. All council decisions were by consensus; no formal voting took place, which would result in dissenters publicly losing face. Under ordinary circumstances, any man who disagreed with council decisions was free to take his family and move away, but in times of war or during a communal hunt, dissenters were required to obey the council's decisions. The results of the council's deliberations were announced by a crier, usually an old man with a loud voice, whose duty it was to circle the camp and cry out the news to the people. Council decisions were enforced by the *akíc'ita*, frequently called the "soldier lodge" in English, which was an incipient police force appointed by the council to see that all the people cooperated for the common good. The badges of office were special black stripes painted on the face and sometimes special costumes or clubs of ash wood — hard, but bending, symbolizing the camp soldiers' duty to carry out the council's orders strictly but fairly. Individuals who violated the council's edicts, usually by leaving camp or attempting to hunt alone at a time that might endanger the success of a communal hunt, were punished: their tipis might be slashed to pieces and the poles broken, their dogs or horses killed, their weapons broken or confiscated, or their persons whipped. Resistance made the punishment stronger, and the camp soldiers were empowered to kill an offender if necessary. The camp soldiers were answerable to the council; if their punishments were judged to be unjust, the guilty soldiers would receive comparable punishment in return.[8]

This political structure — council, chief, soldier lodge — was replicated in every camp, small or large, and served to create and maintain social order. The council members were men whose brave deeds and skills made them respected by the people; they were formally invited to sit in the council meetings and apparently continued to do so for life. The band chief had the support and respect of his kinsmen; the office frequently passed from father to son, but did not necessarily do so. In some cases, a band might die with its chief, the members joining other bands. Thus, the political autonomy of a band was dependent on the success of its leader to maintain confidence in its viability. Any man could try to establish an independent band of his own, a mechanism allowing for the proliferation of social groups as populations became too large to remain together as single bands. In contrast to the fixedness of the council and chiefs, the camp soldiers were appointed anew each time a formal encampment was established. This provided the potential, at least, for the police function to rotate among all qualified men.

From a Sioux point of view, the whole of their society was an extension of the individual's web of kinship interconnections; the image of the web applies equally well to the family, band, tribal, or ethnic level of social order. Sioux emphasis was on pattern rather than group and was reflected in the lack of positive rules for recruitment to social groups (for example, an individual could freely choose the band of which he considered himself a member) and in the lack of a common, consensual understanding of the constituent groups and boundaries of society. The models of the *t'iyóšpaye* and *oyáte* served to provide the necessary pattern. Only in times of crisis, such as in dealings with the U.S. government, did issues of social boundaries arise.

The Sioux social system, so different from the bounded systems of European society, was a confusing one for the frontier Americans who dealt with the Sioux people in peace and war throughout the nineteenth century. Whites strove to impose a structured order on the Sioux in order to understand them and deal effectively with them. Methodically, the federal government made treaties with the various bands and tribes, naming them as political entities and appointing chiefs whom they recognized afterwards as the legitimate spokesmen for their people. One by one, the treaties relieved the Sioux groups of title to their lands and settled them on reservations where the traditionally fluid social boundaries became fixed.

When the United States took possession of the lands occupied by the Sioux, through the Louisiana Purchase and the War of 1812, the Indian peoples of the region had already experienced the effects of encroaching European civilization for more than a century. Through the mechanism of the fur trade with British and French traders from Canada, French and Spanish traders from Louisiana, and American traders from the United States, the Sioux had been drawn into commercial networks of international scope. Manufactured trade goods, including metal items of every kind — knives, awls, needles, kettles, traps, guns, and ammunition — gunpowder, cloth, foods, rum, brandy, and whiskey, became not mere luxuries but actual necessities of Indian life. Depending on a foreign market beyond their comprehension, the Indian peoples trapped beavers for their pelts until European technology found a cheaper substitute for beaver fur in felt making; then the Sioux turned to the trade in buffalo hides and dried meat to supply the nearer American markets. Trading, and the rituals of trade, had become integral to Indian life, a part of the yearly economic cycle. At the same time, horses, traded from the south and west, pervaded Plains Indian culture and remodeled the old pedestrian and canoe-based nomadic patterns into an equestrian one. Plains cultures flourished, both materially and spiritually. But the forces that nurtured this cultural florescence also carried the seeds of its destruction.[9]

The first written treaty signed by the Sioux with the United States was negotiated by Lieutenant Zebulon M. Pike on the upper Mississippi River in 1805. By its terms, the Sioux ceded to the United States two small areas of land for the purpose of establishing military posts. At the time, such military presence was required to keep British interests in the area in check; later, in 1819, the army built Fort Snelling, the first military post in Sioux country, on one of these sites. The treaty recognized "the Sioux Nation of Indians" as party to the treaty, creating thus a political entity in the eyes of U.S. law that had no real counterpart in Sioux cultural understanding. A series of treaties with various groups of Sioux followed, establishing on paper a relationship of dependence between the Indians and the United States and gradually eroding Sioux lands.[10]

During the first half of the nineteenth century, as white settlers filtered into Minnesota and Iowa, most of the Sioux were attracted westward, taking advantage of the mobility provided by the horse to follow the buffalo herds, already retreating before European advancement. Epidemic diseases at the end of the eighteenth and in the early decades of the nineteenth century decimated all the peoples of the plains, but especially the sedentary earth-lodge-dwelling tribes of the Missouri River valley. This opened the route for the Teton Sioux to cross the river and move into the rich buffalo plains. Even as the Sioux pressed their advantage to the west, white emigration followed. The California gold rush of 1848 drew thousands of emigrants across the new Sioux lands following the Oregon and California Trail along the south bank of the Platte River, soon paralleled on the opposite bank by the Mormon Trail. In 1849 the United States purchased Fort John, a small fur-trading post in what is now eastern Wyoming, and garrisoned it as Fort Laramie, the first military establishment among the western Sioux.[11]

While the Teton Sioux were pushing their territory westward, fighting the other tribes who blocked their way — Omahas, Pawnees, Shoshones, Kiowas, and Crows — the eastern Sioux were experiencing a new phase of interaction with the white men. In 1819 the federal government established the St. Peter's Agency to coordinate relations with the Minnesota Sioux. Government programs aimed at permanent settlement of the eastern Sioux, development of horticulture, and the introduction and promotion of white American values and patterns of life. Beginning in 1834, Christian missionaries settled among the eastern Sioux, providing some minimal education for a few of the children as well as preaching the gospel and teaching the arts of civilization by example. The missionaries devised a system for writing the Sioux language and by mid-century had completed a grammar, a dictionary, and extensive translations of the Bible, as well as hymns and other religious materials.[12]

The year 1851 proved to be a turning point. The four tribes of eastern Sioux signed treaties by which they surrendered title to all their lands in Minnesota and Iowa and agreed to settle on two small reservations along the Minnesota River. The same summer, representatives of many western tribes met near Fort Laramie to sign a treaty of peace and friendship with the United States and with one another as a preliminary step toward stabilizing the northwestern frontier. Included in this treaty, in theory at least, were all the other bands of Sioux not party to the Minnesota treaties. While not a treaty of land cession, the 1851 Fort Laramie treaty nonetheless had far-reaching consequences, for it defined the territorial boundaries of the western tribes, providing the basis from which the United States would later seek to extinguish Indian land titles to the entire region. It also granted permission to the United States to establish roads and military posts in the Indian country. In 1858 the Yanktons, who had been included in the Fort Laramie treaty but whose territory actually lay east of the Missouri River, ceded to the United States all of their lands in eastern Dakota Territory and Minnesota, reserving only a small reservation along the east bank of the Missouri. In that same year, the eastern Sioux signed new treaties calling for the allotment of lands to individual heads of families. In exchange for the lands surrendered, the eastern Sioux were to receive money, goods, and services — including education — with the understanding that the reservations would serve as homelands where the Indians would be transformed into civilized farmers and would ultimately become citizens of the United States.[13]

In surveying this history of events, the period can be interpreted as one characterized by good intentions on both sides. The Sioux would blame the greed and corruption of their Indian agents for the failure of the reservation experiment in Minnesota. The white settlers of Minnesota would blame the implacable "savagery" of the Sioux themselves, not yet sufficiently "advanced" to accept a civilized way of life. But a realistic appraisal from a modern perspective reveals tremendous tensions on both sides even as the original treaties were being negotiated. The Sioux realized full well that they were being pressured out of their lands; they did not want to give in, but found no way to resist. The eastern groups of Sioux clearly recognized the power of the United States to compel their unwilling capitulation to federal demands. Among themselves, dissension occurred over the right of any one group to sell lands. Sioux concepts of land ownership were distinct from those of the whites; like social boundaries, geographical boundaries were not clearly demarcated. To leave them flexible avoided strife. The trader Edwin Denig commented that Plains tribes did not recognize tribal boundaries: "The Indian, therefore, occupies any section of prairie where game is plentiful and he can protect himself from enemies." Thus, though the more westerly Sioux left behind the lands in eastern Dakota and western Minnesota where they had been born, there is nothing to indicate that they intended to abandon them. Speaking to a treaty commission in 1865, Two Lances, a chief of the Two Kettle Tetons, commented that he had given the Yanktons over four hundred horses "to take care of my land...and here, directly, the Yankton starts out and sells part of the land." Two Lances moralized: "A great liar lives and gets rich." Similar complaints were made against the Santees moving west onto the prairies and plains. Running Antelope, a Hunkpapa chief, asserted of the Santees: "They are coming here to push us off from our land, and I do not like to see them." The greatest affront, however, was not from other Indians but from the whites themselves. Speaking as head chief of the Minneconjous to the 1865 treaty commissioners, Lone Horn articulated what may be considered as the Sioux point of view on the entire proceedings: "You ask to go through my country, and you are trying to scare me out of it. I do not like it." To this remark the assembled Indians rumbled their assent, *"Hau!"* ("Yes!").[14]

The Sioux people, both in the east and in the west, were not uncomprehending victims of the advance of civilization. They were well aware of the political dynamics. Speaking to the 1851 treaty council at Fort Laramie, Black Hawk, an Oglala, protested the drawing of tribal boundaries:

> You have split the country and I don't like it. What we live upon we hunt for, and we hunt from the Platte to the Arkansas, and from here up to the Red But[t]e and the Sweet Water.... These lands once belonged to the Kiowas and Crows, but we [the Oglalas, Cheyennes, and Arapahoes] whipped these nations out of them, and in this we do what the white men do when they want the lands of the Indian.[15]

The Sioux felt swindled by their treaties, but they also found themselves in an impossible situation, unable to refuse to sign. Lone Horn expressed his people's frustration when speaking to the 1865 treaty commission: "As for this signing a treaty, I do not understand anything about it. Therefore, I do not like to sign it. It is well enough to ask us to make peace. We are all willing to do so." With these words, the chief seemed to have divorced his willingness to sign the treaty from the actual contents of the document, agreeing only to make peace. And when he finally came forward and touched his hand to the pen as the recorder made a mark opposite his name, he said: "You can write and read; we can talk." The Sioux leaders signing the treaty affirmed all that was said and recorded at the councils; the white commissioners signing the treaty affirmed only the specific contents of the document. Thus was the 1865 treaty, like all other treaties, "negotiated" and "signed" without any significant communication across the gap that separated Indian from white.[16]

Given the climate of misunderstanding and barely suppressed tension — the chiefs never claimed to be able to control the actions of the young men — it is not surprising that the tenuous peace established by the 1851 treaties was destroyed before it even had a fair trial. A number of bloody events stand out in those years following the treaties, landmarks of the increasing domination of the Indians by the whites.

In 1854, a lame cow belonging to a Mormon emigrant was killed by Sioux waiting near Fort Laramie for the arrival of the Indian agent and the annual distribution of treaty annuity goods. The chief of the camp, Brave Bear — the man recognized at the 1851 treaty council to be the head chief of the Sioux, through whom all dealings with the whites would take place — was unable to compel the offender to surrender. Placing his field gun in position, Lieutenant John L. Grattan prepared to take the man by force. In the ensuing melee, Brave Bear, Lieutenant Grattan, and all twenty-nine men of his detachment were killed by the angry Sioux. The resulting tumult escalated into the Sioux War of 1855, in which General William S. Harney, mad as a hornet (Hornet was a name by which the Sioux would later call him), fell upon the first camp of Sioux he met, a Brulé band under Little Thunder, camped at Ash Hollow on the Oregon Trail. Although they had been completely uninvolved in the Grattan affair, Harney attacked the camp, killing eighty-six Indians and marching seventy captive women and children to the new military post he had established at Fort Pierre, on the Missouri River. The business was resolved in the spring of 1856 at a treaty council held at Fort Pierre, when Lone Horn, the Minneconjou chief, turned over to General Harney The Man Who Killed the Cow (as the offender had come to be known). Fully prepared to see the man executed, the Sioux could only have been puzzled when the general allowed him to go free. Meanwhile, Spotted Tail, incarcerated for his part in holding up a mail coach, was sent to Fort Leavenworth, where he spent the winter of 1855–56 learning enough about the white men's ways of life to put aside any further notions of resisting their advance.[17]

The next incident occurred in 1857 in the area of Lake Okoboji and Spirit Lake, on the Iowa-Minnesota border, when a small group of Wahpekute Sioux under the leadership of Inkpaduta attacked local settlers, killing forty or more and taking four women prisoners. A military expedition to punish the murderers was countermanded by the Commissioner of Indian Affairs, and in the end it was Little Crow, a chief of the Mdewakantons, who led a war party against Inkpaduta, killing some of the Wahpekutes and driving the others out of the country. A special agent sent from Washington to investigate the incident concluded that the government's failure to fulfill treaty stipulations was the major cause of dissatisfaction leading to the outbreak. The Sioux told him that war against the United States, though futile, might at least lead to more favorable treatment afterward.[18]

Bad feelings escalated between Indians and whites in Minnesota, and in 1862 the Sioux revolted against domineering agents and conniving traders in what has become known as the Great Sioux Uprising. Not all the eastern Sioux participated in the fighting; many spent their time trying to avoid combatants on both sides. Military reprisals developed into full-scale war during 1863 and 1864, United States soldiers tracking the fleeing Sioux out onto the prairies of eastern Dakota. There the fighting spread to the Tetons at the Battle of Killdeer Mountain on July 28, 1864, remembered for involving the western Sioux in the Santees' war. In the end, over five hundred whites were killed, mostly settlers, and the eastern Sioux were driven away from their homes and scattered, prohibited by law from returning to Minnesota. Some fled to Canada or moved west to Montana;

the Bureau of Indian Affairs relocated many of them on the Missouri River, first at Crow Creek, then at Santee, Nebraska; others were later established at Sisseton and Devils Lake Reservations in Dakota; and remnant groups returned quietly to Minnesota, where, during the 1880s, they finally gained government recognition and were given tiny reservations.[19]

The military expedition of 1864 against the Sioux in Dakota, commanded by General Alfred Sully and General Henry H. Sibley, cannot be divorced from the wider panorama of Plains Indian history. In that year, hostilities developed between the southern Cheyennes and the military, culminating in the Sand Creek Massacre on November 29, 1864, when Colonel John M. Chivington of the Colorado volunteer militia led his troops against Black Kettle's Cheyennes, camped at Sand Creek under a flag of truce. The wanton slaying of 137 men, women, and children, compounded by the well-publicized atrocities committed by the soldiers on the Indians' bodies, turned public opinion in the eastern United States against a military solution to the western Indian question.[20]

At the close of the Civil War, the army prepared for the inevitable transcontinental railroads that would be built across Indian lands, and on the northern plains sought to protect the fortune hunters headed for the gold fields of Montana. Military opinion opted for a sound whipping of the Plains Indians, who, misled by the withdrawal of federal troops from their lands during the Civil War years, had grown to doubt the army's ability to punish them. But when President Andrew Johnson sent a commission to investigate the Sand Creek affair, its report led to a strategy of seeking peace with the Plains tribes and trying the more humane — and cheaper — alternative of settling the Indians on reservations. Thus, the control of Indian affairs was taken out of reach of the army, and treaty commissions, composed of both civilian and military members, traveled throughout the plains in 1865, 1866, 1867, and again in 1868, each year signing treaties with the Indian tribes and laying the basis for a system of reservations that would isolate Indians from the main routes of transcontinental travel.[21]

Even as the peace commissions were performing their work, the army was called on to protect the lives and property of citizens traveling through Indian territory. The Bozeman Trail, a cutoff from Fort Laramie (on the Oregon Trail) to Montana, passed through the middle of the Teton Sioux hunting grounds. To protect the route, the army constructed Fort Conner in 1865 (renamed Reno the following year), Forts Philip Kearny and C. F. Smith in 1866, and Fort Fetterman in 1867. The Sioux harassed Colonel Henry B. Carrington and his command even as they were building Fort Philip Kearny, keeping it under a continual state of seige. Then, on December 21, 1866, the Indians lured Lieutenant Colonel William J. Fetterman and a detachment of eighty men out of the post, led them into ambush, and killed them all.[22]

News of Fetterman's demise electrified the nation and prompted yet another investigatory commission. Rather than mount the all-out military campaign that would be necessary to chastise the Sioux, the government decided to continue negotiations for peace. By the treaty of 1868, the United States agreed to abandon Forts C. F. Smith, Philip Kearny, and Reno, and to close the Bozeman Trail to further travel. The decision was a pragmatic and economic one in part; having agreed to underwrite the expense of building the Northern Pacific Railroad, the government realized that speed in seeing it to completion was essential. All military support was to be given to the railroad project. In the meantime, by appearing to capitulate to Sioux demands to close the Bozeman Trail, the government hoped to propitiate the Sioux and convince them to withdraw opposition to railroad construction. Both the government's promise to abandon the Bozeman Trail and the Indians' guarantee not to oppose the railroad were written into the treaty.[23]

The 1868 Peace Commission, balanced between civilian and military members, reflected the confusion that reigned in U.S. Indian policy. Each side blamed failure of the system on the other, claiming that complete control of Indian affairs by the Interior Department (or, alternatively, by the War Department) would prove beneficial in the long run. There seems to have been little agreement between the two factions, and, although they wrote a joint report in which the military point of view took precedence — reflecting the strong hand of Lieutenant General William T. Sherman — it is clear that little consensus was achieved. Most significantly, the commission argued that the formality of making treaties with Indian tribes as though they were sovereign nations had become pretense and that Indians should be treated as groups of individuals, not tribes. This recommendation led to the 1871 act of Congress abandoning the treaty-making system with the Indians. Although Congress continued to make formal agreements with Indian tribes, these agreements were no longer given the solemn attention shown to treaties with foreign nations.[24]

For the western Sioux, the 1868 treaty was a crucially important document that would guide all future relations with the federal government. It set aside a reservation comprising all of present South Dakota west of the Missouri, and recognized the area in Nebraska north of the North Platte and the region of Wyoming and Montana west of the reservation to the summit of the Big Horn Mountains as "unceded Indian territory." The terms of the treaty specify that the Sioux relinquish "all right to occupy permanently the territory outside their reservation," but "reserve the right to hunt on any lands north of North Platte, and on

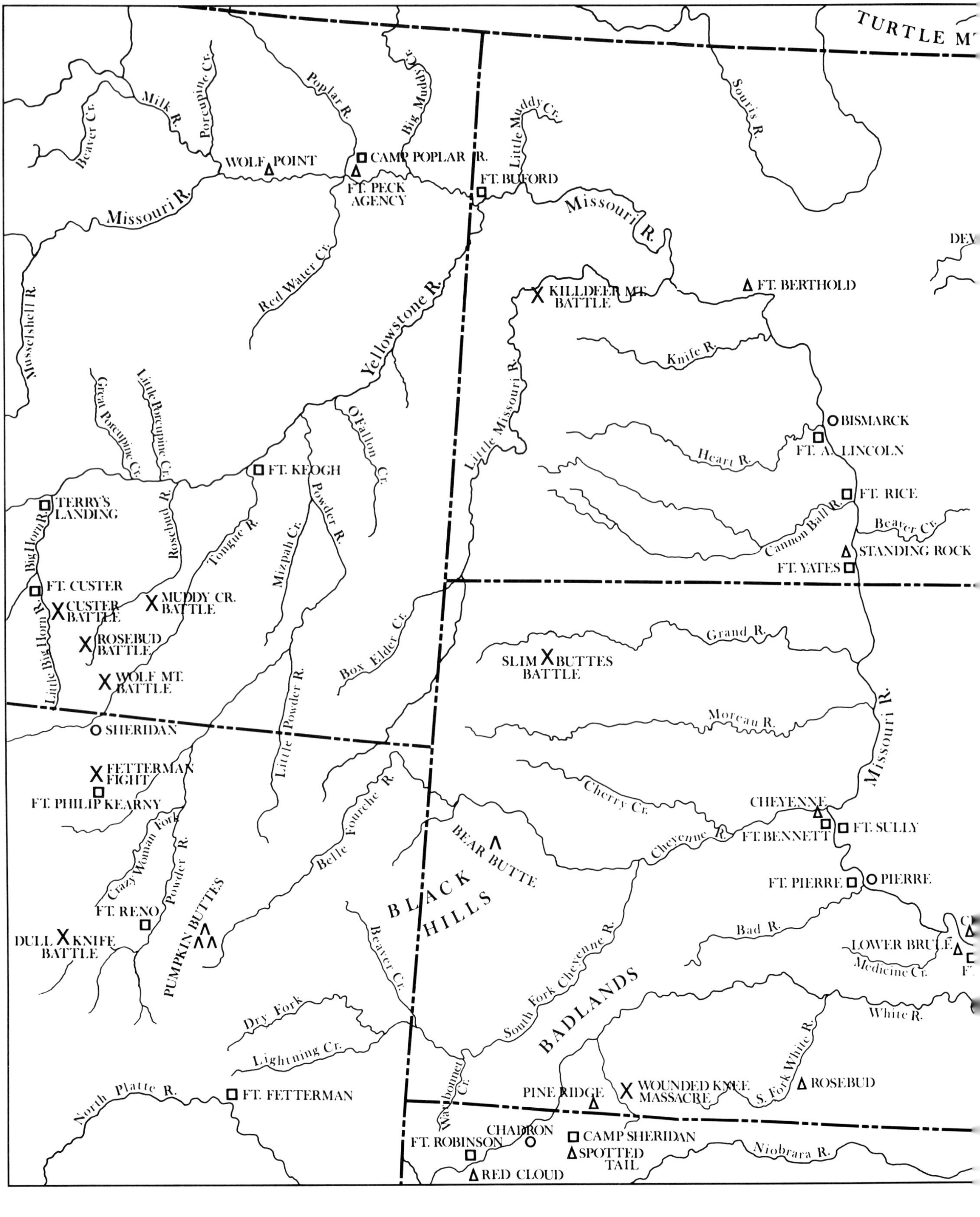

TURTLE M
Milk R.
Porcupine Cr.
Beaver Cr.
Poplar R.
Big Muddy Cr.
Little Muddy Cr.
Souris R.
WOLF POINT
CAMP POPLAR R.
FT. PECK AGENCY
FT. BUFORD
Missouri R.
Missouri R.
DEV
Musselshell R.
Red Water Cr.
Yellowstone R.
KILLDEER MT. BATTLE
FT. BERTHOLD
Knife R.
Little Missouri R.
Great Porcupine Cr.
Little Porcupine Cr.
O'Fallon Cr.
BISMARCK
FT. A. LINCOLN
Heart R.
FT. KEOGH
TERRY'S LANDING
Big Horn R.
Rosebud R.
Tongue R.
Mizpah Cr.
Powder R.
FT. RICE
Beaver Cr.
Cannon Ball R.
STANDING ROCK
FT. YATES
FT. CUSTER
CUSTER BATTLE
MUDDY CR. BATTLE
ROSEBUD BATTLE
Little Big Horn R.
WOLF MT. BATTLE
Box Elder Cr.
Little Powder R.
Grand R.
SLIM BUTTES BATTLE
Moreau R.
Missouri R.
SHERIDAN
FETTERMAN FIGHT
FT. PHILIP KEARNY
Crazy Woman Fork
Powder R.
Belle Fourche R.
Cherry Cr.
CHEYENNE
FT. BENNETT
FT. SULLY
Cheyenne R.
BEAR BUTTE
BLACK HILLS
FT. PIERRE
PIERRE
FT. RENO
PUMPKIN BUTTES
DULL KNIFE BATTLE
Beaver Cr.
South Fork Cheyenne R.
Bad R.
LOWER BRULE
Medicine Cr.
BADLANDS
White R.
Dry Fork
Lightning Cr.
S. Fork White R.
North Platte R.
FT. FETTERMAN
Warbonnet Cr.
PINE RIDGE
WOUNDED KNEE MASSACRE
ROSEBUD
CHADRON
CAMP SHERIDAN
FT. ROBINSON
SPOTTED TAIL
Niobrara R.
RED CLOUD

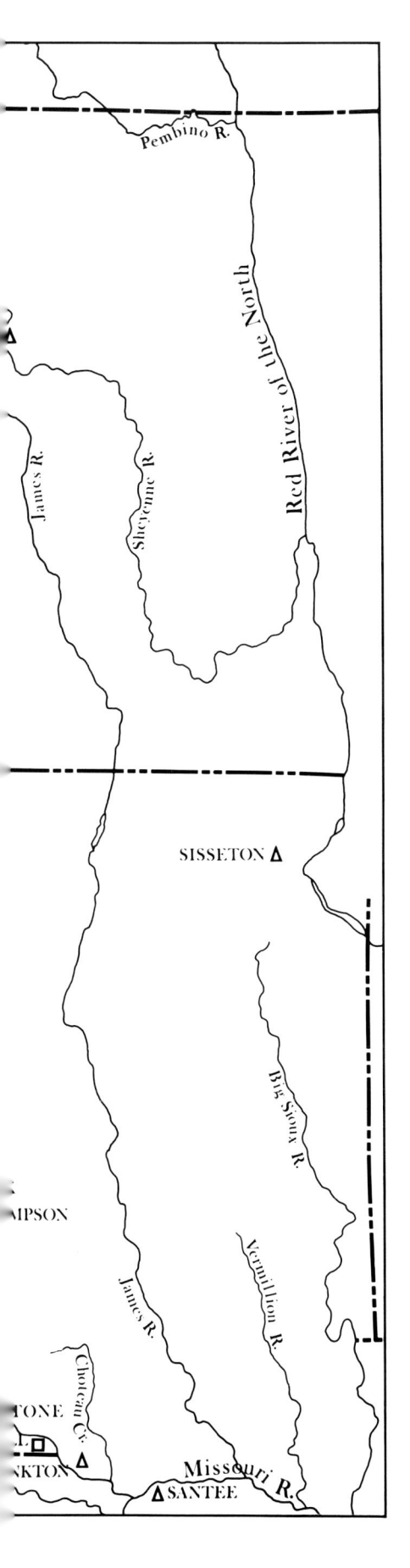

KEY
▲ INDIAN AGENCY
☐ MILITARY POST
○ TRADING POST, TOWN

Map 1. Western Sioux Homeland. Based on map ONC-17, "United States, Canada," Defense Mapping Agency Aerospace Center, St. Louis, Mo., ed. 5 (1979), and "Map of the Department of Dakota..." (1886), NARS, RG 77, map no. PRS 1886 #1.

the Republican Fork of the Smoky Hill River, so long as the buffalo may range thereon in such numbers as to justify the chase." The Sioux may have interpreted this as allowing them hunting rights outside the reservation forever, but government officials operated on the assumption that with the imminent extinction of the buffalo, these reserved hunting areas soon would be opened for white settlement.[25]

The 1868 treaty was ratified by the Senate and formally proclaimed by President Johnson in February of 1869. It called for the construction of an agency on what would become known as the Great Sioux Reservation and specified various annuities to be distributed for thirty years. It also provided for education and laid the basis for the ultimate allotment of lands in severalty. In appropriating the necessary funds, Congress stipulated that fiscal responsibility for carrying out the terms of the treaty would rest with the War Department. General Sherman appointed the retired General Harney, who had been one of the treaty commissioners, to head a new military district embracing the Sioux lands.[26]

The Peace Commission had selected Fort Randall, on the Missouri River at the southern boundary of the reservation, to serve as agency headquarters, and there in the autumn of 1868 Harney began his duties. The rationale for the location of the agency was the availability of cheap steamboat transportation to supply the Indians, but Fort Randall was too far from actual Sioux camping areas and too remote from the buffalo herds to attract any Indians but the most devoted supporters of the whites. It was clear, too, that given the large population of the Sioux, more than one agency would be required to administer them. Accordingly, the Bureau of Indian Affairs created four Sioux agencies on the west bank of the Missouri River: Whetstone, about 30 miles upstream from Fort Randall, established for the Brulés and Oglalas; Lower Brulé, 15 miles below Crow Creek Reservation (the latter home for the Lower Yanktonais, located on the east side of the river) and administered by the Crow Creek agent; Cheyenne (River), near Fort Sully, established for the Minneconjous, Sans Arcs, and Two Kettles; and Grand River, near Fort Rice, established for the Hunkpapas, Blackfeet Sioux, and Yanktonais. Delegations from the Great Sioux Reservation visited Washington, D.C., in 1870 to meet the president and other officials; as a result of their requests, Red Cloud and Spotted Tail were allowed to locate the Oglala and Brulé agencies, respectively, on the North Platte and White River, south and east of the Black Hills. The former site was actually found to be in Wyoming and the latter in Nebraska, both locations outside the boundaries of the Great Sioux Reservation. It was not until 1878 that, after a complicated series of moves, the Oglala agency, renamed Pine Ridge, and the Brulé agency, renamed Rosebud, were permanently situated in the White River country on the reservation.[27]

27

When the new agencies were created, they were placed in the charge of military officers, who served as agents. However, the inauguration of Ulysses S. Grant as President in March of 1869 brought about sweeping changes in Indian policy. Under the Grant Peace Policy, Christian churches were given the prerogative of choosing candidates for Indian agents, each agency being assigned, in theory, to the church that had already expended the greatest amount of missionary effort at that location. The distribution of agencies to the churches roughly followed the percentages of the population of the United States at large that belonged to each religious denomination. Under this policy, the Sioux agencies were quickly removed from military jurisdiction and the Peace Commission's plan for controlling the situation on the Great Sioux Reservation was foiled.[28]

While the new Sioux agencies were being built on the Missouri, a large proportion of the Indians represented by the 1868 treaty were residing outside the limits of the reservation in the unceded Indian country of Dakota and Montana territories. In November of 1868, reports received at Fort Buford (located on the Missouri at the confluence of the Yellowstone) indicated that large camps of Teton Sioux were moving down the Yellowstone River, fresh from fights with the Crows. The Upper Yanktonais, who were camped at the mouth of the Yellowstone opposite the fort, were reported to have been fighting the Red River Métis from Canada, the itinerant traders of the northern plains. Hunting in the Yellowstone country as well were groups of eastern Sioux from Canada — refugees from Minnesota who had fled across the line to escape the army after the 1862 uprising — and Yankton Sioux from east of the Missouri River in the southern part of Dakota Territory, who had sold most of their lands to the United States and were searching for new hunting grounds. Large numbers of Indians were camped around Fort Buford — Lower Assiniboines near the post, and further down the Missouri, Hidatsas and Mandans from Fort Berthold Agency. Other camps of Lower Assiniboines were a hundred miles up the Missouri, at the mouth of the Milk, while the Upper Assiniboines were camped up the Milk River. Beyond them were the River Crows, Gros Ventres, and Blackfeet.[29]

Here in this unceded Indian country — embracing the rich valleys of the upper Missouri, the Yellowstone, the Milk, and the Musselshell — the stage was being set for the final confrontation over the last great herds of buffalo in America, a conflict that would involve the warring tribes of the northwestern plains, Métis from Canada, and hunters from the Montana settlements. Within fifteen years, the buffalo would be gone from the plains, the traditional Indian way of life would pass with them, and the tribes would have no recourse but to turn to the government agencies for support.

When Montana Territory was organized in 1864, the Assiniboines, Gros Ventres, and River Crows were the principal tribes living along the Missouri and Milk rivers in the northeastern portion of the territory. No Sioux were reported to be living in this region. In 1868 an Indian agency was established at Fort Browning, a trading post of Durfee, Peck & Company on the Milk River, for the Gros Ventres and River Crows. The following year, Major General Alfred Sully, newly appointed Superintendent of Indians in Montana Territory, dispatched Special Agent A. S. Read (who was no relation to O. B. Read) to the new agency. There Agent Read found the two tribes gathered, awaiting their treaty annuities. The agent's instructions were to persuade the River Crows to move southwest to the Yellowstone and join the Mountain Crows at their new agency near Fort Ellis. At the same time, he was to persuade the Gros Ventres to share their agency with the Assiniboines. The Gros Ventres replied that they would be happy to accept the Upper Assiniboines, and, in fact, Agent Read discovered that there were already a considerable number of Upper Assiniboines camped at Milk River Agency. But the Gros Ventres objected to any relationship with the Lower Assiniboines; the latter were allies of the Sioux, with whom the Gros Ventres were at war. The River Crows objected to the proposal that they be removed to the Yellowstone. They were enjoying fine buffalo hunting on the Milk, as well as the proximity of the Blackfeet, with whom they warred for horses and scalps. The Bureau of Indian Affairs, however, was not inclined to listen to the Indians' objections, and the River Crows were assigned to the Mountain Crow Agency, while all the Assiniboines were assigned to Milk River Agency.[30]

Early in September of 1869, Lieutenant Colonel Henry A. Morrow reported from Fort Buford that one thousand Yanktonais had arrived at his post, asking to enter into a treaty of peace with the United States. These Indians told the commander that they were not bound by previous treaty obligations to the government, but that they were at peace with the whites and wanted to receive annuities like other tribes. Morrow prepared a formal petition for them in which the Indians pledged peace and friendship and asked to be granted a reservation of their own. This was signed by representatives of the Cuthead band of Upper Yanktonais (Medicine Bear, Thunder Bull, and His Road to Travel), the C'an'óna band of Upper Yanktonais (Shoots the Tiger, Afraid of Bear, Catches the Enemy, and Heart), and a band of Sissetons (Brave Bear and Your Relation to the Earth). A week later the *Takíni* band of Upper Yanktonais arrived at Fort Buford, and their leaders (Calumet Man, Afraid of Bull, Long Fox, Eagle Dog, and Standing Bellow) signed a similar petition asking to be included in the new reservation. Lieutenant Colonel Morrow encouraged the Indians to winter in the vicinity of Fort Buford and assured them that the army would supply them with food until the government could prepare a treaty for them.[31]

These bands of Upper Yanktonais and the consolidated band of Sissetons had long been associated with one another. As early as the 1830s they were reported to have been very much intermixed, living at that time on the prairies of western Minnesota and eastern Dakota Territory. Although both Medicine Bear and Thunder Bull had signed the 1868 treaty, they obviously did not feel bound by it. That treaty had been concerned with those Sioux living on the west (south) side of the Missouri River, whereas they identified themselves as Sioux of the east (north) side. They claimed the prairies of eastern Dakota Territory as far as the Chippewa country in Minnesota. But buffalo were becoming scarce in that country, and the Upper Yanktonais found it necessary to move farther west in order to find game on which to live. Moreover, there was the press of white settlement in Minnesota and eastern Dakota; in the aftermath of the 1862 uprising, the settlers had little sympathy for Indians, no matter how peaceably disposed, and the soldiers showed no inclination to differentiate between the guilty Santees and the innocent Yanktonais. Together, these two factors led the Upper Yanktonais and their Sisseton allies westward, along the north bank of the Missouri.[33]

This movement on the part of the Upper Yanktonais was a purposeful migration. Just as the Santees, driven out of Minnesota, had migrated — some to Canada, others to a reservation west of the Missouri — so the Upper Yanktonais were leaving their old territory for new. Thunder Bull had told the 1868 peace commissioners: "Our country, that you speak about, is ruined. But it is ourselves who ruin the country; not the whites. I know the reason why our game is giving out; it is the big guns that drive our game away."[35] The fault may have been the Indians' own, but the instruments of their misfortune were the guns provided by white traders. The disappearance of the buffalo was therefore directly linked to a kind of moral failing on the part of the Sioux, an abandonment of their old ways in favor of those of the white men.

These Upper Yanktonais had long been associated in friendly relationship with the Lower Assiniboines. According to Sioux tradition, the Assiniboine people had originally broken away from the C'an'óna band (also known as Wazík'ute) — a tradition that reflects more of long-standing relationship between the two groups than of actual historical origins. In 1866 the peace commissioners had met Medicine Bear's Upper Yanktonais, together with Red Stone's Lower Assiniboines, on the Missouri River near the mouth of White Earth River. On that occasion the Yanktonais numbered three hundred lodges and the Lower Assiniboines, two hundred lodges. The two groups frequently camped and hunted together, and one Yanktonai band of thirty lodges, led by Little Thigh, was intermarried with the Lower Assiniboines and lived with them permanently, although members of the band still identified themselves as Sioux. Red Stone informed the commissioners that there were more Yanktonais who also wished to join the Assiniboines.[34]

During the winter of 1869–70, two hundred lodges of Red Stone's Assiniboines and a large number of the Upper Yanktonais chose again to camp near Fort Buford, despite the scarcity of game in the vicinity of the post. In October, Lieutenant Colonel Morrow warned his superiors at Department of Dakota headquarters that unless he was permitted to issue food to the Indians camped around the fort, they would starve. In November he received authorization to do so until the Bureau of Indian Affairs could come to some decision concerning them. That same winter, a large group of Teton Sioux, principally Hunkpapas, wintered on the Missouri River above the Yellowstone, hunting and warring on the Crows.[35]

From Morrow's perspective at Fort Buford, the Sioux were clearly pushing their way westward in their quest for game, displacing other tribes. In June of 1870, he noted that the north bank of the Missouri from Buford to the mouth of the Milk was the territory of the Lower Assiniboines, but that some 2,500 Upper Yanktonais had moved into the area with them, and he suspected that they intended to drive the Assiniboines — in this case, probably the Upper Assiniboines — out of their way. Evidence of Sioux hostilities was not long in coming. Agent Read, at Milk River, reported that during the summer of 1870 his agency was attacked five times by parties of Sioux whom he identified as "Yancton Sioux, Yanctonais, Cutheads, and Santees." The Indians at the agency were recovering from a serious smallpox epidemic during the previous winter, and were in a weakened condition. The primary objective of these attacks on the agency was to steal horses from the Gros Ventres. The agent accused the Lower Assiniboines of participating in the attacks, but Red Stone, their chief, denied the charge.[36]

Confusion over the identity of various groups of Sioux was an ever-present reality. In August of 1870, Lieutenant Colonel C. C. Gilbert, the new commander at Fort Buford, received a letter from Black Eye, a Lower Yanktonai chief (written for him by a trader). The chief, with his band of 375 lodges, was camped near the mouth of Poplar River, upstream from Fort Buford. Black Eye wished to inform the soldiers that he was for peace, not war, and that he should not be blamed for the hostile acts of the Santees and Hunkpapas.[37]

Late in 1870, F. D. Pease, the Crow agent, prepared an informative survey of Indian tribes in eastern Montana. In all, the Assiniboines numbered about 430 lodges; their hunting grounds lay between the Missouri River and the British line. The Upper and Lower Assiniboines (so designated from their relative positions on the Missouri River) each constituted about half of the total. To the east of the Assiniboines, Pease reported some 460 lodges of "I-Santees, Cut-head and Yanktonees and other Sioux." South of the Assiniboines, various bands of Teton Sioux were occupying the area that the Assiniboines had ceded to the United States by the treaty of 1866. Pease wrote that the Tetons "have taken possession of the lower Yellowstone country, and between it and the mouth of Milk River, on the south side of the Missouri river." He reported that there had been some trouble between these Tetons and those living at Grand River Agency, and they had therefore received no annuities since 1864. They refused to return to Grand River because of the scarcity of game there, but requested to be settled on a reservation north of the Missouri, in buffalo country.[38]

To administer this large number of Indians living without attachment to any agency, J. A. Viall — who had replaced Major General Sully as Superintendent of Indians for Montana Territory — recommended in December of 1870 that a new reservation "for the Assinaboines, Mixed Santee, Cut Head and Yanktonees and the Teton tribes of the Sioux Indians be set apart for these Indians extending from the Missouri River to the British Boundary Line, and from the 109th to the 106th degree of Longitude." He further recommended that the new agency be established "at or near Muscleshell which is but a short distance above Wolf Point."[39]

During the fall and winter of 1870–71, the Upper Yanktonais again camped immediately west of Fort Buford, depending on the post for supplies. The Hidatsas, Mandans, and Arikaras from Fort Berthold Agency wintered in the same area. Repeated acts of violence in the vicinity of the post were blamed on these friendly groups, rightly or wrongly, and the commanding officer at Buford complained to his superiors that the Indians should not be allowed to roam about so freely. An Arikara scout reported that the Hunkpapas and other Sioux were wintering on the Yellowstone in twenty separate camps beyond the head of the Rosebud, near the foot of the "White Snow" (Big Horn) Mountains. Although there was no evidence to support the judgment, the army considered these Sioux to be "hostiles," a word used for any Indians not living at an Indian agency or absent from their agency without authorization. Reports indicated that the Sioux on the Yellowstone were trading with the Red River Métis for gunpowder and whiskey. The Upper Assiniboines evidently wintered near Milk River Agency, while the Lower Assiniboines spent the winter hunting along the Missouri from Fort Buford to the Milk River.[40]

When spring came, the Sioux made a further push westward. Special Agent A. J. Simmons, now in charge of Milk River Agency, reported that 260 lodges of "Santee and Yancton Sioux including Sissetons, Wahpetons, Cutheads, Blackfeet Sioux, and Tetons" had camped some 20 miles below the agency on April 30, 1871. Simmons wrote:

> They have steadily been moving west for years past, following up the game and great herds of buffalo which now appear to be almost surrounded and cornered in the northern part of this [Montana] Territory. Heretofore they have only sent war parties to this vicinity; now they have come in force with their whole encampment asserting *they have come to stay!*[41]

When the agent invited the Sioux chiefs to visit him for a talk, they refused and insisted that he come to their camp instead. The Lower Assiniboines were at this time camped within a half mile of the agency, and since they were on friendly terms with the Sioux, served as intermediaries. On May 4, Simmons went out to the Sioux camp, accompanied by Red Stone and Little Bull, two Lower Assiniboine chiefs, and a wagonload of provisions to feast the entire camp. At the council, held in the soldier lodge of the Santees, Standing Buffalo, the leading chief, proclaimed their peaceful intentions. According to Simmons' official report, the chief told him that:

> Their country below was burnt and dead, the game was all gone, they couldn't live in it; they had now come here, they liked this country, here they could make plenty of robes and make plenty of meat. Their country was wherever the buffalo ranged, here was plenty of buffalo, it was their country and they had come to live in it.

Simmons explained to them that this was the country of the Gros Ventres and Assiniboines and that the Great Father (the president) had not sent any goods for the Sioux to this place; he invited them to return his visit at the agency and have a further talk.

The next day, Standing Buffalo, with fifty of his warriors, came to the agency. After more talk and professions of mutual friendship, Simmons conceded to their demands for flour, sugar, coffee, tobacco, and other supplies, made them a present of a few blankets, and then said that he would request that provisions for them be sent to Milk River Agency before winter. Standing Buffalo was satisfied and demonstrated his good faith by spending the night at the agency. The next day, Struck By the Ree's son, one of the Yankton leaders, came to the agency with some of his warriors, and the feasting, speech making, and distribution of presents were repeated. Simmons reported that these Yanktons "are but the vanguard of a large body of Yanctons numbering I am informed over two hundred lodges who are also moving up Milk River to this point." Simmons was convinced of the good intentions of the Santees, who composed most of the camp then present, because he was confident of Standing Buffalo's ability to lead his people. The Yankton camp, on the other hand, the agent characterized as composed of "renegades from various bands," and reported that they had no chief among them who could exercise much influence or control. Simmons advised the Sioux to accompany the Assiniboines on a buffalo hunt, and shortly afterwards the combined camps moved toward the Little Rocky Mountains.

Simmons judged that to maintain friendship with the Sioux, "it is absolutely necessary to feed and clothe them," and recommended that supplies for that purpose be sent to his agency at once. Given the high priority placed on maintaining peaceful relations with the Sioux and the apparent impossibility of removing them to the Great Sioux Reservation without military force — at least as long as there were buffalo left in Montana to hunt — Superintendent Viall supported the agent's recommendation that the Sioux be attached to the Milk River Agency. On May 20, 1871, the Commissioner of Indian Affairs authorized Viall by telegram to feed the Sioux "to a limited extent," and in July the superintendent reported that nearly $16,000 worth of supplies had been sent to Milk River Agency for the Sioux, with instructions that Simmons issue them "in the most limited and economical manner possible."[42]

Agent Simmons reported in August of 1871 that 4,850 Assiniboines and 6,800 Sioux were within his jurisdiction. The Assiniboine figure apparently represents both the Upper and Lower Assiniboines and probably some of the North (Canadian) Assiniboines as well. The Sioux figure includes 2,500 Santees under Standing Buffalo's brother (Standing Buffalo himself having been killed in a fight with the Gros Ventres), as well as 4,300 "Yanctons, Yanctonais, Cut-heads and others," whose principal chief was Medicine Bear. The agent warned his superiors that supplies on hand were insufficient to support this large number of Indians through the winter. Game was being rapidly depleted; Simmons estimated that 50,000 buffalo had been killed that summer in Montana and predicted that without government support the Indians would be reduced first to eating their dogs and horses, then to actual starvation.[43]

Government officials were more concerned about the Tetons, reportedly under the leadership of the Hunkpapa chief Sitting Bull, than about the other Sioux in Montana. Military surveys to determine a route for the Northern Pacific Railroad had begun in the summer of 1871 and were met with hostility from the Sioux. In September, Agent Simmons was directed to make contact with these Tetons, determine their disposition toward peace, and induce them to send a delegation to Washington to sign a treaty. Simmons again relied on the Lower Assiniboine chiefs as intermediaries and arranged to hold a council with the Tetons at Fort Peck, a trading post established five years earlier on the Missouri near the mouth of the Milk. The traders at Peck had been in friendly relations with the Tetons and other Sioux, Sitting Bull himself having visited the fort to trade. On November 14, a group of Hunkpapa chiefs — Black Moon, Iron Dog, Long Dog, Little Wound, Sitting Eagle, and Bear's Rib — accompanied by two hundred lodges of their people, arrived at Fort Peck. They spent the next ten days counciling with Agent Simmons. From these long sessions, Simmons was able to come to a clear understanding of the Teton Sioux position. They had been hostile to whites for many years, refusing to have anything to do with them, obtaining their ammunition and necessary trade goods mostly from the Métis traders. The agent wrote: "From their standpoint all whites found in or traveling through their country are regarded as enemies, intruding upon their hunting grounds, and interfering with their game."[44]

Simmons was disappointed that Sitting Bull himself had not come to meet with him, but was satisfied with the explanation, which he heard repeated over and over, that the soldier lodge of Sitting Bull's camp had refused to allow the chief to leave. A war party in Sitting Bull's camp had announced its intention to leave the village on an expedition against both Indians and whites up the Missouri River. Sitting Bull and the camp council had ordered the soldier lodge to prevent any war parties from leaving the camp, and accordingly the soldier lodge punished the members of this party by killing some of their horses and slashing their lodge covers — the usual punishment for disregarding the pronouncements of the council. Some of the war party refused to obey the soldier lodge and resisted them; a general fight broke out in which eight men were killed. Out of fear of further bloodshed within the camp, the soldier lodge had refused to allow Sitting Bull to leave.

During the councils, Agent Simmons presented the Indians with the message from the Bureau of Indian Affairs requesting peace and asking that a delegation of leading men be sent to Washington, D.C., to sign a treaty. Black Moon declared that both he and Sitting Bull were for peace. However, if the whites wished peace, he said, they must stop the construction of the railroad which would pass through their country and destroy the game; all whites, including the soldiers, must be kept out of their country; Fort Buford and the Musselshell trading post must be abandoned. If these things were done, there would be peace. Other chiefs spoke to the same effect. The railroad would destroy the game, without which they could not live. They preferred to die fighting like brave men than to stand by and watch the buffalo destroyed by the white men.

Simmons replied by saying that there could be no stopping the railroad, but that when it was completed it would bring them presents and provisions from the Great Father. He would help them to live if they would cease their warfare. The whites were so numerous, Simmons cautioned, that they could exterminate the Indians if they wished, but instead their Great Father wanted to take pity on them, "because they were weak and inferior." He advised them that instead of throwing their lives away in battle, they should think about their women and children.

Confronted with conflicting statements, Simmons was unable to arrive at a close estimate of the number of lodges of Tetons in the vicinity of Fort Peck, but he estimated them to be about 1,400 — approximately 11,200 people. During his stay at Fort Peck, Simmons met parties of Sioux from both Grand River and Devils Lake agencies, whom he scolded for associating with the "hostiles" and sent back to their homes.

Black Moon and the other chiefs doubtless discussed Red Cloud's success in 1868 in having the Bozeman Trail closed and its three military posts abandoned. Perhaps they believed they could accomplish the same in Montana. The military was in no mood to conciliate the Indians; however, the Secretary of War advised the Interior Department to feed the Sioux in Montana again during the winter of 1871–72, since it was impracticable to fight them at the moment. For the time being, General Sherman commented, all measures in regard to the hostile Sioux would be "defensive." In the spring, the garrison at Fort Buford would be strengthened, and the military proposed building two new forts in the Yellowstone country. While the Bureau of Indian Affairs talked peace, the army prepared for war.[45]

In the summer of 1872 the president appointed a commission to visit the Teton Sioux in Montana. More than 450 lodges of Sioux gathered in August at Fort Peck to meet the representatives of the Great Father. Nearly three thousand Indians were in the camp, mostly Yanktonais, with a small number of Hunkpapas. Some five hundred lodges of Tetons, mostly Hunkpapas, under the leadership of No Neck, Black Moon, and Sitting Bull were reported to be in the Powder River country, together with some three thousand Oglalas from Red Cloud Agency, as well as others from other agencies. None of these "hostiles," who opposed the building of the railroad through Montana, would come to meet the commissioners.[46]

The council met in formal session at Fort Peck on August 21, with some two hundred chiefs and warriors in attendance. When the commissioners returned to Washington, they took with them a number of Yanktonai chiefs and warriors including Medicine Bear, Afraid of Bear, Black Eye, Black Catfish, Skin of the Heart, Eagle Packer, Red Thunder, Long Fox, and Gray Crane Walking, as well as the Hunkpapas Bloody Mouth, Bulrushes, Lost Medicine, and Black Horn. Apparently the Santee chiefs from Milk River Agency did not attend the council; in any case, they were not included in the delegation. Groups of chiefs from each of the other Sioux agencies made the trip east as well, the Grand River delegation including three Upper Yanktonai chiefs — Big Head, Black Eye (another chief of that

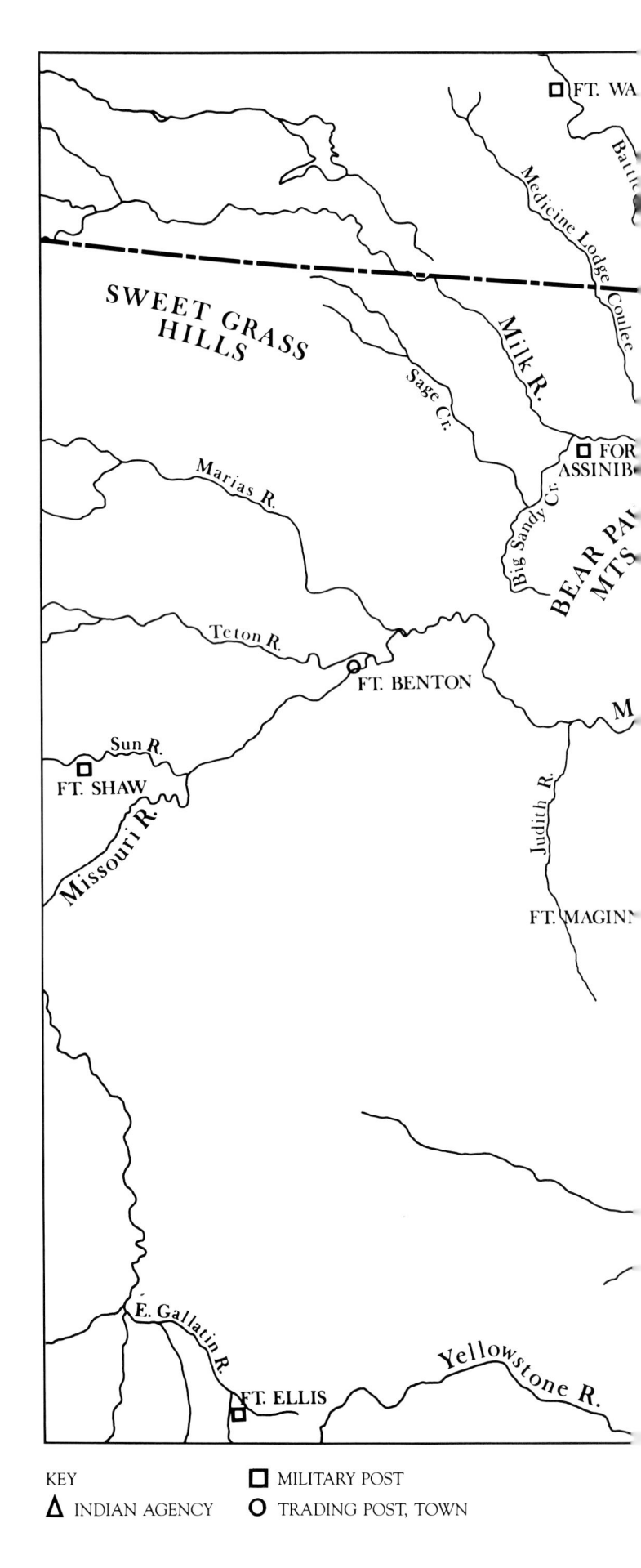

KEY
△ INDIAN AGENCY
☐ MILITARY POST
○ TRADING POST, TOWN

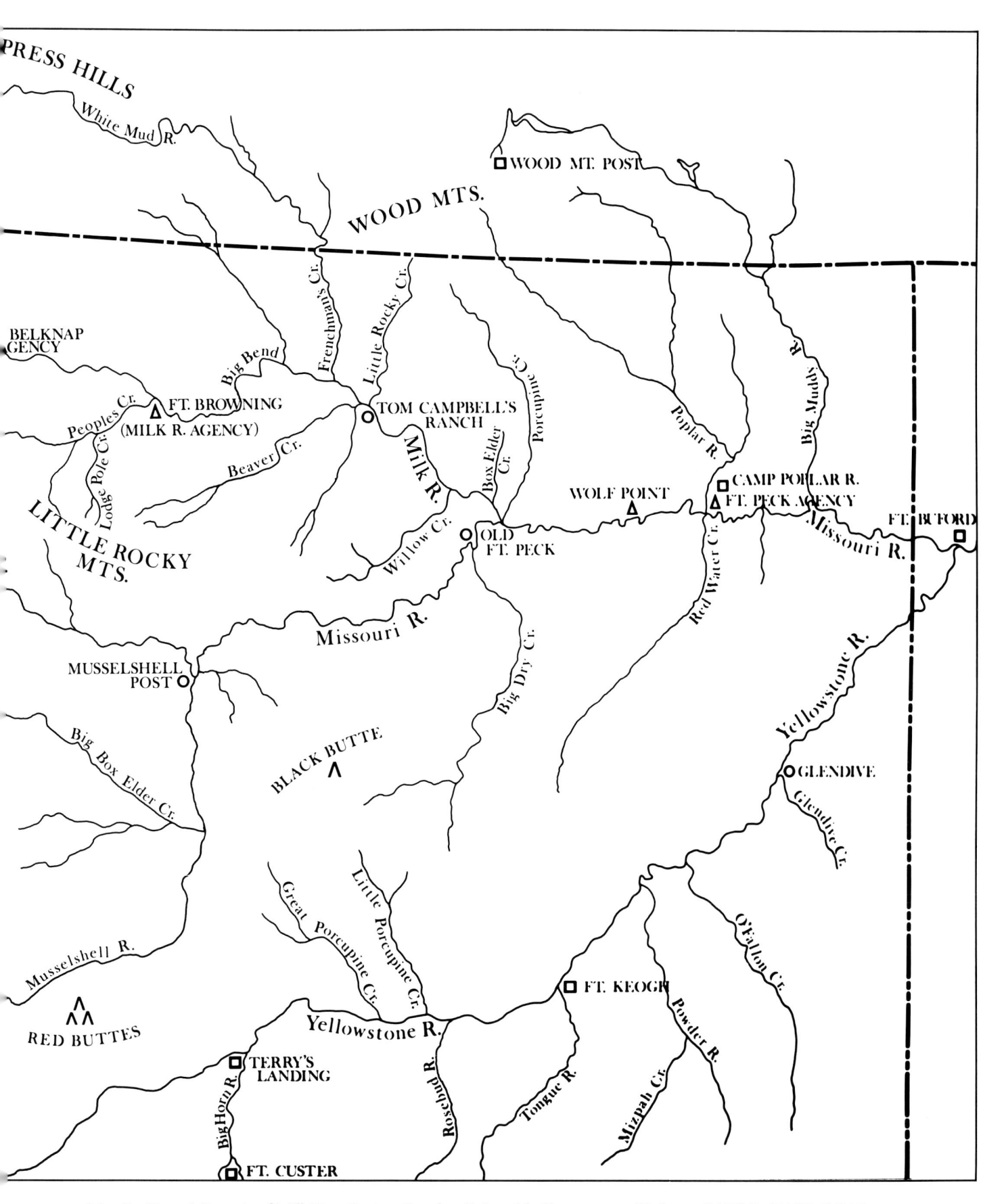

Map 2. Upper Missouri and Milk River Region. Based on "Map of the Department of Dakota..." (1886), NARS, RG 77, map no. PRS 1886 #1, and "War Department Map of the Yellowstone and Missouri Rivers..." (1976), NARS, RG 75, map no. 485.

name), and Big Razee — as well as three Lower Yanktonai chiefs — Two Bears, Red Bear, and Bull's Ghost. Some Hunkpapa chiefs from Grand River, including Bear's Rib, Running Antelope, and Thunder Hawk, also accompanied this delegation. However, since these delegations did not include any of the chiefs of the Montana Sioux who posed the immediate threat to peace and to the security of the railroad survey parties, the commissioners had clearly failed to accomplish their original goals.[47]

For the Sioux of Milk River Agency, the commission of 1872 and the subsequent delegation to Washington had important consequences. The commissioners recognized the right of the Sioux to remain in Montana and recommended that an agency be built for them at Fort Peck and that the Santees and Assiniboines from Milk River Agency be transferred to the new agency, thus separating them from the Gros Ventres. The basis for this decision seems to have been the idea that since the Sioux and Assiniboines spoke dialects of the same language, they should share the same agency. The proposed solution ignored the hostility of the Upper Assiniboines toward the Sioux, as well as the extent to which the Upper Assiniboines were intermarried with the Gros Ventres. It was a classic case of eastern politicians attempting to cut the Gordian knot of western Indian problems on the basis of too little knowledge.

The summer of 1872, despite all the movements toward peace, saw bloodshed in Montana. The military escort for the Northern Pacific Railroad survey crew was a formidable expedition of some six hundred men, under command of Colonel David S. Stanley, which headed west from Fort Rice, Dakota Territory. At the same time, a parallel expedition of about four hundred men, under Major Eugene M. Baker, headed east from Fort Ellis, Montana Territory. Although they planned to meet at the mouth of the Powder River, both columns engaged in battles with the Indians and returned to their respective posts. The Sioux under Sitting Bull, and their Cheyenne and Arapahoe allies, repeatedly attacked the survey parties. While the delegations were on their way to Washington to talk peace, the angry Teton Sioux in Montana were waging war. On August 14, they fought a major battle with Baker's command; Black Moon later told Agent Simmons that 1,400 warriors took part in the fight. The chief said that the Indians had been camped at the big bend of Powder River — more than two thousand lodges of Oglalas, Brulés, Minneconjous, Hunkpapas, and others — preparing to send a large war party against the Crow agency. On the way to attack they discovered Baker's troops and returned to their village, abandoning the raid on the Crows. Black Moon reported that the Brulés had launched the attack on Baker, and that they had all joined in.[48]

Agent Simmons and the Montana Sioux delegation arrived back at Fort Peck from Washington on November 20, the entire delegation returning "in excellent health with good hearts and without accident." They had won the right to an agency outside the Great Sioux Reservation, much to the annoyance of military authorities. Such a move undermined the entire strategy that lay behind the 1868 treaty. Simmons had prolonged the Indians' return trip, taking them by way of the Montana settlements to give them a good idea of the strength of the whites in the territory. They were treated kindly everywhere they went. "It was a big card," Simmons wrote, "in bringing them home that way to show them the settlements west of their country and to let them see that the people there were their friends." The delegation had enjoyed the benefits of railroad travel — speed and comfort — and could perhaps better appreciate the white men's insistence on building more of them. The members of the delegation became, in Simmons' words, "heartily tired" of the long stage ride through Montana: "Good Hawk expressed the sentiments of the party on the subject, in language more forceable perhaps than elegant he remarked, 'Railroad nena dosia [nína dúza, very fast], washta [wašté, it's good], wagon Son a b--ch you bet!'"[49]

When the delegation reached Fort Peck, they found "nearly the whole tribe" camped on the north side of the river, waiting for the party to return and for the promised issue of blankets, clothing, and other supplies. Two days later, on November 22, more than two hundred lodges of Hunkpapas under Black Moon arrived, having waited until the delegation returned to move to Fort Peck. They camped separately on the south side of the river. Simmons reported that only Sitting Bull, with fourteen lodges, still held back and refused to come in. Black Moon had an altercation with Simmons when he came to the fort with seventy warriors and demanded to be issued gunpowder. Simmons refused, the members of the delegation offering to stand by him in case of trouble. The agent declared that the Hunkpapas would have to cross the river and join the main camp before any annuities would be issued to them. Black Moon and his chiefs refused, but their people, unwilling to be left out of the distribution of presents, broke camp and crossed the Missouri. They erected their lodges around that of Bloody Mouth, one of the Hunkpapa delegates to Washington, thereby selecting him as the leader they would — for the moment — follow. They declared that they would never return to the other side of the river. Afterwards, the agent issued them their goods, and they seemed well satisfied. According to Simmons, this diplomatic move was engineered by the delegates themselves, who feasted the people and persuaded them to follow Bloody Mouth. Black Moon was left on the south bank of the river with only twenty lodges. As the agent phrased it, "after wrangling among themselves for some time at last *they* threw up the sponge, moved across the river, joined the main camp and took their annuities." It was a good lesson in Sioux political dynamics.[50]

The Bureau of Indian Affairs authorized the establishment of the new Fort Peck Agency in December. Simmons was directed to remove the Milk River Agency as soon as possible, consolidating it with Fort Peck. He reported that before he left Fort Peck for Helena on December 29, in order to make arrangements for removal of the old agency, 844 lodges of Tetons and Yanktonais had established their winter quarters around the new agency site. Chiefs who had not previously made peace — Iron Star, Long Dog, Black Moon, Red Shield, Bearded Chin, Crow, Little Knife, and others — had come in, accepted terms, and joined the camp at Fort Peck. They were all drawing rations, and everything was quiet. By mid-January, Sitting Bull himself, with twenty to thirty lodges, was reported to be camped on Dry Creek, only about 40 miles from Fort Peck. The rest of his followers had joined the camp at the agency. The Lower Assiniboines, with the Santees and Yanktons, remained at Milk River Agency for the winter.[51]

New buildings to house Fort Peck Agency were constructed in 1873. Recognizing the impracticality of combining the two agencies, Simmons recommended that Milk River be continued; in July the creation of Milk River as a separate agency for the Upper Assiniboines and Gros Ventres was accomplished by executive order. The Lower Assiniboines, Santees, and Yanktons were officially transferred to Fort Peck. By June 15, 1873, Simmons could report that 1,260 lodges were already present at Fort Peck, representing all the Sioux bands as well as the Lower Assiniboines. He informed the Commissioner of Indian Affairs that in July the entire encampment would move up the Milk River to Beaver Creek, where they would have their summer buffalo hunt and cut new lodge poles in the Little Rocky Mountains. He expected them to return to the agency about the middle of September to form an encampment for the winter.[52]

During the summer of 1873 the Northern Pacific Railroad surveys continued. General Stanley headed an expedition of nearly two thousand men, including a corps of scientists, and spent three months marching westward from Fort Rice to the Yellowstone valley, down the Musselshell, and back by way of Glendive Creek. They were to survey the route for the railroad, collect scientific data, and intimidate the Indians. The flamboyant Lieutenant Colonel Custer, whose destruction of Black Kettle's village of Cheyennes on the Washita in 1868 had won him a reputation as an Indian fighter, was assigned to the Stanley expedition. On August 4, riding far ahead of the main column with two troops of the Seventh Cavalry, Custer was attacked by the Sioux near the mouth of Tongue River. Fighting them off, Custer charged the Indians, who scattered before his troops. On August 11, the Seventh Cavalry again skirmished with the Sioux on the north bank of the Yellowstone, below the mouth of the Big Horn, and pursued them 10 miles.[53]

It was not until January of 1874 that legal measures were taken to clarify the status of lands occupied by Indians in eastern Montana Territory. A congressional bill set aside the area from the boundary of Dakota Territory west to the Rocky Mountains and north of the Missouri River to the British line for the "use and occupation of the Gros Ventres, Piegan, Blood, Blackfoot, River Crow, and such other Indians as the President may, from time to time, see fit to locate thereon."[54] Although both Fort Peck and Fort Belknap fell within the boundaries of this reservation, neither was explicitly mentioned in the legislation. In September, Agent Simmons was replaced by William Alderson. The agency Indians learned a lesson in government bureaucracy; thereafter, frequent changes of agency personnel would be commonplace, always destroying continuity and setting back progress.

In his first annual report, Alderson estimated as "the lowest and most reliable list" the following Indians who were receiving supplies at Fort Peck Agency:

[Lower] Assiniboines	1,998
Santee and Sisseton Sioux	1,065
[Upper] Yanctonai	2,266
Uncpapa [Húnkpap'a] Sioux	1,420
Uncpatina [Húnkpat'ina (Lower Yanktonai)]	460
Mixed-bloods	98
Total	7,307

Alderson classified the Indians under his charge into three categories. First, the Assiniboines and Santee Sioux (including the Sissetons): "They appear to comprehend their situation and inevitable destiny to a much greater degree than any other uncivilized Indians on or near the upper Missouri." The agent suggested that, were it not for the availability of game, they would be ready at once to adopt civilization. Second, the Upper and Lower Yanktonais: Alderson noted a marked change in their attitude during the preceding ten months; at first disdainful of the power and authority of the government, they were coming to acknowledge their dependence on it: "Many express a desire to engage in agriculture, prominent among them those chiefs who visited Washington in September 1872." Third, the Hunkpapas: "Wild and ungrateful," they refused to stay on the reservation and still claimed interest in the lands through which the Northern Pacific Railroad would pass. Alderson believed that many of the Hunkpapas from his agency went to the Yellowstone country only to hunt, "but once there, they are restrained and overawed by Sitting Bull, his associate chiefs, and his formidable soldier lodge, so that they cannot return to the agency when they wish." Some 250 lodges of Hunkpapas had received annuities at Fort Peck during the autumn of 1873, and were fed there until January of 1874, when they set out on their winter hunt. Half of them had not returned as of September, although the agent anticipated that most of them would return before the end of the month.[55]

Although actual progress in the white men's ways was slight among the Indians at Fort Peck, Agent Alderson noted that six Indian houses had been built — a first step toward permanent homes and a settled way of life. The agent stressed that for real progress to take place it was essential to make haste slowly in the area of civilization. He mentioned with pride the Indians' acceptance of the new agency physician, Dr. Stone, who believed — doubtless incorrectly — that the Indians under his care were starting to abandon their belief in the efficacy of medicine men. More pragmatically, the Indians probably found that the doctor was effective in some areas of healing, and traditional means effective in others.

The establishment of Fort Peck Agency was more of a victory for the Sioux than for the Bureau of Indian Affairs. In defiance of the treaty makers of the 1860s, and in actual contempt of General Sherman and the military authorities, these displaced Sioux from Minnesota and Dakota Territory had managed to make good their takeover of Crow, Assiniboine, and Gros Ventres lands. Through sheer aggressiveness — and luck — they had convinced the government to recognize their claims to lands which, under the terms of the 1868 treaty, they had surrendered all right to occupy permanently, and to grant them an agency separated from, and independent of, the Great Sioux Reservation. When the Yanktonais had first come to Montana, Agent Simmons reported, they had called themselves "Chiefs of the Mountains and Plains."[56] And they had proven it.

In 1873 the Northern Pacific Railroad had reached the Missouri River at Bismarck. Economic depression following the Panic of 1873 postponed any immediate extension of the line west of the Missouri. Without the need to guard survey parties, the army in Dakota Territory could turn to other matters. General Sheridan contemplated establishing a military post in the heart of the Sioux hunting territory in order to keep the Indians in check. In the summer of 1874 he sent Lieutenant Colonel Custer, in charge of an expedition of some one thousand men, to explore the Black Hills and determine an appropriate site for a military post. Custer left Fort Abraham Lincoln, opposite Bismarck, on July 1, and he returned August 30 with reports of a region rich in grasslands and timber, producing as well "gold in paying quantities."[57]

Custer's report touched off a rush of fortune seekers to the Black Hills, an area within the boundaries of the Great Sioux Reservation, guaranteed by treaty to be off limits to all but the Sioux. Although the army was enjoined to prevent miners from entering the hills, it proved impossible to do so effectively or to remove them once they had slipped through. The next summer, 1875, the Secretary of the Interior ordered an exploration of the Black Hills by a scientific team headed by Walter P. Jenney of the New York School of Mines to assess the commercial potential of the region. Four hundred soldiers accompanied the four-month expedition as military escort. When newspaper reporters with the Jenney expedition publicized the findings, completely corroborating those of Custer the previous summer, the floodtide of prospectors and settlers was impossible to quell. The government had no choice but to treat with the Sioux for the relinquishment of the Black Hills.[58]

In the fall of 1875 the first Black Hills commission came to negotiate with the Sioux, asking for terms to buy or lease the area. In September they met representatives of the western Sioux near Red Cloud Agency. The talks went nowhere. The Indians' demands for payment were astronomical, and their requests for other compensation so complex — ranging from guns to cattle to bedsteads — that the commissioners simply gave up in defeat.[59] For the Sioux, the Black Hills was a special region, particularly sacred, the home of powerful spirit beings. Game was abundant there, and the slender pines necessary for making tipi poles could always be cut. Of the entire area demarcated within the boundaries of the Great Sioux Reservation, the Black Hills was the only region with a variety and abundance of natural resources. This, of all areas, they did not wish to surrender to the white men.

The Sioux were abiding by the treaty of 1868, some drawing rations at the agencies, others hunting in the lands reserved to them for that purpose by the treaty. In his annual report for 1875, the Commissioner of Indian Affairs estimated the entire Sioux population to be 49,546. Basing his report on information received from the Indian agents, he said that 35,454 of the Teton and Yanktonai Sioux were accounted for at the agencies on the Great Sioux Reservation; 11,092 were resident at seven other reservations: Crow Creek (Lower Yanktonais), Devils Lake (Sissetons, Wahpetons, and Cutheads), Sisseton, Flandreau (a colony of educated eastern Sioux), Santee (Mdewakantons and Wahpekutes), and Fort Peck (including representatives of almost every Sioux group). According to the Commissioner's calculations, this left only about three thousand "hostile" Sioux, who were reported to be scattered in western Dakota Territory. Given the limited supplies issued at each agency, it was essential that many of the Sioux hunt throughout the winter to support themselves, and this necessitated long trips to western Dakota and eastern Montana to find buffalo.[60]

The United States was less successful than the Sioux in abiding by the terms of the 1868 treaty. Growing tension over the Sioux situation had led the army, since the signing of the treaty, to establish a series of new military posts ringing the Great Sioux Reservation, each post paired with an Indian agency: Camp (later Fort) Robinson and Camp Sheridan guarded the Red Cloud and Spotted Tail agencies, respectively; Fort Hale was built near Lower Brulé; Fort Bennett near Cheyenne River; and Fort Yates at Standing Rock. Prepared as they were to control the Sioux, the army was not prepared to deal with non-Indian trespassers on the reservation. The military failure to remove white prospectors from the Black Hills violated both the spirit and letter of the treaty. As long as the situation remained unchecked, warfare seemed inevitable.[61]

The army clamored to be allowed to take over control of Indian affairs, following the original recommendation of the 1868 peace commission. The Interior Department refused, clinging to its right to oversee Indian affairs, and to the fast-fading hopes of Grant's Peace Policy. At last, on December 6, 1875, the Commissioner of Indian Affairs telegraphed orders to the Sioux agents that all the Indians belonging to the agencies on the Great Sioux Reservation must move within the reservation boundaries by December 31 or be considered hostile, to be dealt with as such by the army. The impracticality of the order must have been obvious to everyone involved; many of the scattered bands could not even have heard about the order before the end of December. It was a pretense, and a weak one at that, to mount the military campaign against the western Sioux that the army had postponed for a decade. Morality and legality faltered in the face of the inevitable military conflict.[62]

The failure of the 1875 Black Hills commission and the subsequent order that the Sioux must return to their agencies before the start of 1876 put the military machine in motion. The Dakota posts were under command of the Military Division of the Missouri, headed by Lieutenant General Philip H. Sheridan, who had no intention of putting the interests of Indians ahead of frontier development. But it was President Grant himself who decided that the army would make no further resistance to miners entering the Black Hills, and instead would focus its energies on forcing the western Sioux onto their reservation where they could be more easily controlled. Sheridan decided to mount a winter campaign, fearing that the Indians might obey the order to return, thereby cheating the army of the opportunity to chastise them. The plan paralleled the strategy he had used against the Indians of the southern plains in 1868 and 1874. Three separate columns of troops would converge on the "hostile" Sioux. Brigadier General Alfred H. Terry, commander of the Department of Dakota, and his subordinate, Lieutenant Colonel Custer, would lead a column westward from Fort Abraham Lincoln; Colonel John Gibbon, commander of the District of Montana, would march his troops eastward from Forts Shaw and Ellis; and Brigadier General George Crook, commander of the Department of the Platte, would approach from the south, starting from Fort Fetterman, Wyoming. The Sioux would be caught in the middle, defeated, and driven back to their reservation.[63]

Sheridan received authorization from the Secretary of the Interior on February 7, 1876, to begin his campaign against the Sioux. Crook's column of nearly nine hundred men left Fort Fetterman on March 1, braving severe snowstorms to reach the Powder River on March 16, where scouts reported a camp of Sioux. Crook ordered Colonel Joseph Reynolds, with three hundred men, to push ahead and attack. At dawn on March 17, Reynolds charged through the sleeping village, driving the people out into the snow and capturing the lodges and horse herd. The Indians, originally believed to be Crazy Horse's Oglalas, proved to be mostly Cheyennes who were on their way to Red Cloud Agency. In a counterattack the Indians recaptured their horses; Reynolds, losing his nerve, ordered the village burned and retreated to rejoin the main column. The Indians fled to Crazy Horse's camp, their intentions of moving to the agency abandoned. Infuriated with Reynolds' bungling of the affair, Crook returned to Fort Fetterman where he brought court-martial charges against Reynolds. Plans for a successful winter campaign evaporated.[64]

On April 3, Colonel Gibbon set out from Fort Ellis with over four hundred men and twenty-five Crow scouts, marching through deep snow down the Yellowstone valley to establish a supply camp at the mouth of the Big Horn. Terry and Custer, with over nine hundred men and some thirty-nine Arikara scouts, did not leave Fort Abraham Lincoln until May 17. Crook, with over a thousand men and more than two hundred Crow and Shoshone scouts, started from Fort Fetterman on May 29. Meanwhile, the numbers of Sioux in the hunting grounds of the Powder River country continued to swell as the Indians left their agencies for the summer buffalo hunts. Sheridan, in an effort to block the route from the agencies to the Powder River, dispatched a column of about eight hundred men of the Fifth Infantry, originally under command of Lieutenant Colonel Eugene Carr, but joined in the field on July 1 by its new commander, Lieutenant Colonel Wesley Merritt. These troops were to be held in readiness on the South Cheyenne River, west of the Black Hills.[65]

Despite the enormous size of the army in the field, things could not have gone much worse for the military. Unable to communicate easily with one another, each column groped about on its own, searching for the Indians. Sheridan had assumed that there would be no need for the columns to unite in the field. Only Terry had seemed concerned about the possible strength of the Sioux forces, but Sheridan had assured him of "the impossibility of any large number of Indians keeping together as a hostile body for even one week." On June 9, Terry met Gibbon (whose District of Montana was under Terry's command) on board the steamer *Far West* a few miles up the Yellowstone from the mouth of the Powder. Learning that the Sioux were camped on the Rosebud, and anticipating that Crook's column would drive them downstream to the Yellowstone, Terry ordered Gibbon to march his forces to the mouth of the Rosebud, remaining on the north bank of the Yellowstone to prevent the Indians from escaping in that direction. Terry immediately returned with the steamboat down the Yellowstone to establish his camp at the mouth of the Powder.[66]

While these military maneuvers were taking place, the Sioux and Cheyennes had gathered on the Rosebud River to hold their annual religious ceremonies. It was in this camp, during the Sioux Sun Dance, that Sitting Bull — now acknowledged as leader of the non-agency Sioux — had a vision of soldiers falling headlong into his camp, a portent of disaster for the army. Shortly after the ceremonies ended, on June 17, the Indians attacked Crook's forces on the Rosebud, forcing the soldiers to withdraw. Although the army claimed the victory, it was a hollow one. Crook retreated to his supply camp on Goose Creek, near what is now Sheridan, Wyoming, and waited for General Sheridan to send reinforcements. His Indian scouts returned home to look after their own interests.[67]

When Terry failed to hear any news from Crook, he was forced to devise a plan to reach the hostiles. Having moved downstream to the mouth of the Rosebud, on June 21 Terry again met with Gibbon on board the *Far West* to present his strategy. Custer, leading six hundred men of the Seventh Cavalry, would follow down the Rosebud, locate the Indians' trail westward, and continue south to the headwaters of the Tongue before marching down the Little Big Horn. This would give Gibbon time to bring his infantry down the Yellowstone to meet Terry's forces at the mouth of the Little Big Horn. June 26 was the target date. Custer would march down the Little Big Horn while Terry and Gibbon were coming up it; the Indians, caught in between, would be forced to fight. As well considered as the plan was, it failed. Custer pushed ahead to the Little Big Horn, anxious to be the first to strike the enemy. Locating the hostile encampment, and failing to appreciate its size, he divided his forces into three attack columns. In defense of their village, the Sioux and Cheyenne warriors killed Custer and the 215 men under his immediate command. The other columns, under Major Marcus A. Reno and Captain Frederick W. Benteen, managed to hold out until June 27, when the imminent arrival of the troops under Terry and Gibbon caused the Indians to scatter.[68]

Crook, meanwhile, unaware of events to the north, remained in camp at Goose Creek waiting for reinforcements.

On July 17, Colonel Merritt's Fifth Cavalry fought with a party of Cheyennes on Warbonnet Creek, only 25 miles northwest of Red Cloud Agency. He then led his troops northwest and joined Crook on August 3.[69]

News of Custer's demise galvanized the country, the first reports souring the Independence Day celebrations of that Centennial year. The threat of frontier warfare was sufficient to prompt Congress to appropriate the long-requested funds to build two military posts in the Yellowstone country. More troops were sent to reinforce Terry. Lieutenant Colonel Elwell S. Otis arrived on August 1 with six companies, and Colonel Nelson A. Miles arrived the next day with six more companies and 150 recruits. Terry and Gibbon's forces, now numbering 1,620 men, headed up the Rosebud River on August 8 and two days later met and joined forces with Crook's command, now numbering some 2,000 men. The unwieldly army swung east, following an Indian trail.[70]

After the Custer fight, the great Indian camp had begun to break up. It was impossible for such a large encampment to subsist indefinitely, and the time had come to provision themselves with dried buffalo meat for the winter. The Cheyennes headed off by themselves toward the Big Horn Mountains. Many of the Sioux straggled back to the agencies in small groups, while others remained in the Yellowstone region, scattering out for more efficient hunting, and keeping out of the soldiers' way. It became apparent to the army that a decisive battle with the Indians, allowing for a quick victory, had become impossible. General Sheridan decided to keep troops in the field during the winter, harassing any Indians that could be found, placing their hunting grounds under a state of siege. Meanwhile, he renewed his request for military control of the Sioux agencies, to prevent the hostiles from returning unnoticed. Authorization for the takeover came from the Secretary of the Interior on July 22. Sheridan's plan was to disarm and dismount the Sioux. "A Sioux on foot," the general wrote, "is a Sioux no longer." He transferred Colonel Ranald Mackenzie and six companies of the Fourth Cavalry from Oklahoma to Fort Robinson to take a census of the Indians at Red Cloud Agency, disarm and dismount them, and arrest hostiles as they returned to the agency.[71]

Realizing full well the ineffectiveness of their cumbersome military force, and no more able than the Indians to maintain such a large command, Terry and Crook parted ways. Terry ordered Colonel Miles' command to establish a cantonment on the Yellowstone near the mouth of Tongue River to serve as the winter base of operations. Gibbon's forces returned to Forts Shaw and Ellis, and Terry's to Fort Abraham Lincoln. Crook marched his men southeast to the Black Hills, struggling through the autumn rains and mud. On September 9, at Slim Buttes, a detachment of Crook's forces under Captain Anson Mills surprised and captured a

Minneconjou village, killing the chief. Other Sioux nearby, rallying to the aid of their relatives, forced Crook to withdraw. His men exhausted and nearly starving, reduced to eating their horses, Crook declined to pursue the Indians and continued on his way to the settlements in the Black Hills.[72]

Sheridan met with Crook and Mackenzie at Fort Laramie on September 21 to discuss strategy. He ordered Crook to return with his troops to the site of old Fort Reno (abandoned under the 1868 treaty) and establish a new cantonment there on the Powder River, from which it would be possible to control the area between the Black Hills and the Big Horns. Crook and Mackenzie would share the responsibility for occupying the Red Cloud and Spotted Tail agencies, while Terry would use the Seventh Cavalry to disarm and dismount the Standing Rock and Cheyenne River agencies. The horses taken from the Sioux would be sold and the proceeds used to buy cattle for the Indians.[73]

While the army settled in around the Great Sioux Reservation, Congress took steps of its own to resolve the Black Hills crisis that had precipitated the Sioux War. On August 15, a Congressional bill directed the president to appoint a commission to obtain the consent of the Sioux to the sale of the Black Hills, as well as all other lands lying outside their reservation. In addition, they were to agree to move the Red Cloud and Spotted Tail agencies to the Missouri River, and were to allow up to three roads to be built across the reservation. Until these conditions were met, Congress would make no further appropriations for their subsistence. During September the commissioners visited each of the agencies and dictated the terms to the Sioux; having no other choice, the leaders signed. The commission ignored article 12 of the 1868 treaty that required the signatures of at least three-fourths of all adult Sioux males to legalize any future land cessions; the Custer calamity, government officials reasoned, outweighed any legal claim the Sioux might have had to continued enforcement of the treaty.[74]

In October, Mackenzie surrounded the village of Red Cloud and Red Leaf, who had refused to bring their bands to Red Cloud Agency to be counted and receive rations, and confiscated their arms and ponies. General Crook, however, feared that following this course with all the Oglalas would only demoralize those who had remained faithful to the government, so he allowed the other bands at the agency to retain their arms and horses. Sheridan strongly disapproved, but Crook counted on the support of the friendly Sioux to tip the balance in defeating the hostiles.[75]

On November 15, Crook headed northward with nearly two thousand men, including a large number of agency Sioux enlisted as scouts. From the cantonment at old Fort Reno, he sent Mackenzie on to the Big Horn Mountains where, on November 25, his Indian scouts led him to the Northern Cheyenne camp of Little Wolf and Morning Star (Dull Knife). Taking the Cheyennes by surprise, Mackenzie destroyed the village, burning all the lodges, killing a reported forty warriors, capturing seven hundred ponies, and driving the survivors out into the snow to take refuge in the Sioux camps. Crook then retired his forces to winter quarters at old Fort Reno, leaving only Miles on the Yellowstone to worry the Indians throughout the winter.[76]

Based at his cantonment on the north bank of the Yellowstone, opposite the mouth of Glendive Creek, Colonel Miles with his force of less than five hundred men proved effective against the Indians. Skirmishes occurred throughout the winter, and from time to time, small groups of Sioux and Cheyennes came in to surrender. From their number, Miles recruited scouts to guide the soldiers in their search for fugitive Indians. On December 16, a delegation of Sioux chiefs came to council at the soldiers' cantonment and might have been able to bring about peace, but the Sioux were fired upon by the army's Crow scouts, and five of the chiefs were killed. On January 8, 1877, the soldiers turned their artillery on a force of five hundred Sioux and Cheyennes under Crazy Horse in an engagement known as the Battle of Wolf Mountain. Heavy snow called a halt to the fighting, and Miles' command returned to their cantonment. In the spring, some fifty lodges of Minneconjous under Lame Deer arrived in the Rosebud country to hunt buffalo. Miles attacked them in the Battle of Muddy Creek, May 7, and routed the camp. While apparently surrendering, Lame Deer seized his rifle and fired on Miles, who dodged the bullet. Lame Deer and Iron Star, head warrior of the camp, were both killed by the troopers.[77]

It was in the aftermath of the Custer disaster that Lieutenant Ogden B. Read came to Dakota Territory, transferred from Texas with Lieutenant Colonel George E. Buell's Eleventh Infantry and assigned to guard the Missouri River agencies. Read arrived in November of 1876 at the Post at Standing Rock, the northernmost agency on the Great Sioux Reservation. Originally established in 1869 at the mouth of the Grand River, and known as Grand River Agency, the agency was moved about 50 miles up the Missouri in the summer of 1873. A military post, known as the Post at Grand River Agency, had been built in 1870 adjacent to the original agency, and in 1874 it was moved to the new location. The name of the agency was changed to Standing Rock in 1874, taken from a local stone formation believed by the Indians to be a woman transformed into stone. The military post was known as the Post at Standing Rock Agency until 1878, when it was officially renamed Fort Yates.[78]

After the Grand River Agency was established in 1869,

its supervision was entrusted to the Roman Catholic Church, based on the missionary labors of Father Pierre-Jean DeSmet, who had baptized a large number of Sioux people along the Missouri. In 1870, DeSmet visited Grand River to prepare for the establishment of a mission at the new agency. The next summer, two Jesuit priests were sent for that purpose, but after witnessing the Sun Dance in Two Bears' camp of Lower Yanktonais and visiting the Hunkpapas as a guest in Sitting Bull's tipi, they returned to St. Louis, discouraged at the prospect of much success until the Indians had adapted themselves more fully to a sedentary lifestyle. It was not until 1876 that the Benedictine abbot Martin Marty came to Standing Rock to establish the first permanent mission and school.[79]

During its early years, the agency at Grand River and Standing Rock was under continual investigation for corruption and fraud, and relations between the agents (none of whom stayed for long) and the post military commanders were stormy. Each challenged the other's authority, and the Indians successfully played one side against the other. Young Indian men, dissatisfied with the agent, joined the army as scouts, thereby placing themselves beyond the agent's jurisdiction. The older leaders depended more heavily on the agent's good will to maintain their prestige; annuity goods and rations were distributed to the people in large piles through their chiefs, making it a political necessity for the chiefs to have the agent's support.

In his annual report for 1875, Agent John Burke — who had been at his job for only six months — reported the number of Indians at Standing Rock to be 7,322, as follows:

Lower Yanktonais	2,730
Upper Yanktonais	1,473
Hunkpapas	2,100
Blackfeet	1,019

Captain J. S. Poland, Sixth Infantry, commanding the military post, branded Burke's report an outright lie, asserting that no more than five thousand Indians were actually resident at the agency. Poland believed that the surplus rations issued to the Indians (based on the higher count) were being sent out to the camps of the hostile Sioux, thereby making it unnecessary for them to come to the agency. The result of Poland's complaints, which were far more vitriolic than might have been necessary, was to convince General Sheridan not only to see that Burke was replaced, but also to replace Poland. On August 30, 1876, control of the agency was assumed by Captain R. E. Johnston, who continued in this position after the arrival of the new commanding officer, Lieutenant Colonel W. P. Carlin.[80]

During the fall of 1876, the Indians were disarmed, dismounted, and carefully counted by the army, the assignment falling to Major Reno's command, fresh from their ordeal at the Little Big Horn. Some 1,650 horses and a mere 90 guns were confiscated.[81]

The agency was returned to civilian control in December, and the new agent, W. T. Hughes, started out on a good footing with Colonel Carlin. The revised census figures were revealing; the total was only 2,305, demonstrating the extent of depopulation at the agencies during this time:

Lower Yanktonais	768
Upper Yanktonais	462
Hunkpapas	513
Blackfeet	562

Hughes reported that the decline in population was the result of a general flight from the agency during the fall when the news was spread that the arms and ponies of the agency Indians were to be confiscated by the army. Hoping to preserve their property by going to other agencies, the Indians found the same policy in effect. Moreover, all Indians moving in to the other agencies were treated as surrendered prisoners and were not allowed to return to their proper agencies. Thus, there was considerable mixing up of band populations, some of which would never be sorted out.[82]

Despite the turmoil, the Indians who remained at Standing Rock were beginning to adapt to reservation life. The Indians had settled in camps within 15 miles of the agency, the Yanktonais choosing to locate along the Missouri, from north of Standing Rock to the Cannon Ball River; some of the lower Yanktonais had crossed the Missouri and planted gardens on the east bank. The Hunkpapas and Blackfeet were living south and southwest of the agency headquarters. The agent claimed that members of each of the bands were trying their hands at farming. Although the crops were destroyed by grasshoppers in 1876, the harvests in 1877 were good. Two of the headmen, Two Bears of the Lower Yanktonais and John Grass of the Blackfeet, had bought mowing machines for the use of their bands, paying for them with money from the sale of their share of the hides from the beef cattle slaughtered to provide their rations. Although the Indians as yet had no plows and few wagons, they seemed to the agent genuinely committed to making the reservation way of life work. In May of 1877, the Benedictines opened a boarding school, and the first class of thirty boys had their hair cut short, dressed in white men's clothes, and were learning the rudiments of English and of the white men's way of life.[83]

In the spring of 1877 Read's Eleventh Infantry, still under the command of Lieutenant Colonel Buell, was recalled from Cheyenne Agency and Standing Rock to assemble at Fort Abraham Lincoln in preparation for field duty. When

Two Bears. Lower Yanktonai. Photo by Alexander Gardner, Washington, D.C., 1872. Courtesy Bureau of American Ethnology Collection, National Anthropological Archives, Smithsonian Institution, neg. no. 3537.

the spring rise made steamboat travel possible on the Missouri and Yellowstone, the army began to ship men and supplies upriver for the two new posts being built in eastern Montana. On May 15, the Eleventh Infantry left Fort Lincoln, charged with construction of the post on the Big Horn River. Men and equipment were unloaded for the post being built at the mouth of the Yellowstone, and the supplies for the Big Horn post were unloaded on the bank of the Yellowstone near the mouth of the Big Horn, a supply depot subsequently known as Terry's Landing. Marching up the Big Horn, Buell selected the site for the new post on June 24, on the right bank of the river about 600 yards above the mouth of the Little Big Horn. By June 30, Buell had fortified his position, constructed two warehouses, and begun cutting timber for the post. Despite a setback in July, when a sudden rise washed away the cut logs being held in the river, the barracks and officers' quarters were ready for occupation before winter. On November 8, 1877, the Big Horn post was formally named Fort Custer, while the post at the mouth of the Yellowstone was named Fort Keogh (after Captain Myles W. Keogh of the Seventh Cavalry, who died with Custer on the Little Big Horn).[84]

Ogden B. Read remained at Fort Custer from its building until September, 1880, except for the period February to November, 1879, when he served with a detachment to guard the supply depot at Terry's Landing. Although this was a period that saw dramatic events in the history of relations between Indians and whites on the frontier, none of them took place near Fort Custer. In the fall of 1877, Chief Joseph of the Nez Percé tribe led his people on a flight from their homeland in western Idaho, across the mountains to Yellowstone National Park, and northward to the Bear Paw Mountains. Pursued from the west by troops under General O. O. Howard, the Nez Percés were finally headed off by General Miles and his troops from Fort Keogh. Following a sharp fight at the northern edge of the Bear Paws, the soldiers encircled the Nez Percé camp and prepared to wait them out. On October 5, after five days, Joseph surrendered his people to Miles. Just a year later, a group of Bannock Indians from Idaho left their reservation and followed the Nez Percé trail to Montana. Buell's forces from Fort Custer were called into the field to head the Indians off. Lieutenant Read went with Captain Erasmus C. Gilbreath and the pack train. Once again, Miles' troops from Fort Keogh arrived first on the scene and met the Bannocks on Clark's Fork. After three skirmishes, the Bannocks surrendered to Miles near Heart Mountain on September 4. Although the Eleventh Infantry saw no action against the Indians, Colonel Gilbreath recalled Lieutenant Read's prowess in catching mountain trout from the waters of Clark's Fork. Despite lack of opportunity for military distinction, Read received notification of his official promotion to Captain shortly after his return to Fort Custer.[85]

The hostile Sioux and Cheyennes, whose presence in Montana had brought the troops there to establish these new forts, had largely slipped away. During the spring of 1877 the Oglalas and other Sioux under Crazy Horse, as well as the survivors of the Northern Cheyennes from Mackenzie's attack, surrendered to the army at Fort Robinson and were settled at Red Cloud Agency. The Hunkpapas and other Sioux under Sitting Bull had chosen to move to Canada to escape the harassment of Miles' troopers.[86] The only Indians ordinarily seen near Fort Custer were the loyal Crows who served the army as scouts.

Events at Red Cloud Agency had exacerbated rather than soothed feelings of hostility between Indians and whites. In August of 1877, at the insistence of General Sheridan, the Northern Cheyennes were removed from the north and sent against their wishes to Oklahoma to live with their Southern Cheyenne relatives. At the end of August, General Crook visited Red Cloud to enlist Indian scouts to guide the army in the campaign against the Nez Percés. Crazy Horse, speaking for the recently surrendered hostile Sioux, stated that he would take his people north and fight — as the interpreter repeated it to Crook — "until not a white man was left." There seems little doubt that this was a mistranslation — perhaps a purposeful one — and that in fact he had said he would fight until not a Nez Percé was left. But General Crook was taking no chances and ordered the chief arrested. A few days later, on September 5, 1877, Crazy Horse was killed in a scuffle, bayoneted by a guard as the army attempted to imprison him at Fort Robinson. Shortly thereafter, the greater part of the surrendered Sioux fled north to join Sitting Bull in Canada.[87]

The Northern Cheyennes, meanwhile, suffered disease and death in Oklahoma and begged to be allowed to return north. At last, on September 9, 1878, they left their camp at Fort Reno and headed north. The desperate Cheyennes eluded military forces until they reached Nebraska. There they split, half of the people under Little Wolf going on to the Yellowstone country, the other half under Dull Knife heading for Red Cloud Agency, at Fort Robinson. The Cheyennes did not know that during their absence in the south the Red Cloud Agency had been removed; Dull Knife's people found themselves without support, surrendering to the military. They announced their resolve to die rather than be returned south. Although General Crook and other military authorities were disposed to permit the Cheyennes to remain on the Great Sioux Reservation, General Sheridan remained adamant: the Cheyennes' defiance was a threat to the stability of the entire reservation system. The Cheyennes were incarcerated at Fort Robinson and deprived of heat and food and water until they would agree to return to Oklahoma. After enduring this for five days, the Cheyennes broke out of their prison and attempted to escape; the soldiers hunted them down and killed over sixty. The survivors were captured and were eventually allowed to settle with the Sioux at Red Cloud Agency. The party under Little Wolf surrendered to Colonel Miles in Montana, who enlisted the men as army scouts and helped them remain in the north. Finally, in 1884, the Northern Cheyennes were granted a reservation in Montana contiguous to that of the Crows, and were allowed to consolidate their people.[88]

At the Fort Peck Agency the late 1870s was a period of relative tranquility. In the spring of 1876 Thomas R. Mitchell had replaced Alderson as agent. He arrived during the heavy spring rains, and his first recommendation was to move the agency some 75 miles downstream to Poplar River. The location of Fort Peck was disadvantageous for defense, and the river bank itself was being rapidly cut away by the current, endangering the agency buildings. The proposed new location at the mouth of Poplar River had many advantages. There the bottomland on the north bank of the Missouri was from 3 to 10 miles wide, extending many miles up and downriver. Grass was abundant, and could be easily cut to supply the new agency with hay. Timber abounded, allowing the new agency to be built cheaply. The Indians with whom he discussed the matter, including some of the chiefs, approved of the relocation. The Assiniboine subagency would remain at Wolf Point, 24 miles up the Missouri from Poplar River. There the Assiniboines had already built some houses and planted gardens, 45 miles downstream from old Fort Peck Agency. The removal of the agency, and of the Sioux who camped near it, to Poplar River would therefore locate the two tribes considerably closer to one another.[89]

In the latter part of May, 1876, the Sioux and Assiniboines of Fort Peck Agency left for their summer hunt, going as far west as the Little Rockies and Bear Paw Mountains, north to the Canadian line, east to the Dakota border, but staying north of the Missouri. Messengers kept the agent in weekly contact with the Indians. Hunting was good; Mitchell concluded that the Fort Peck Indians were peaceful and not in sympathy with the hostiles, even though, he wrote, "Sitting Bull's emissaries attempt to induce them to join him." The agency Indians' strongest complaint that summer was that the military ban on selling ammunition to Indians deprived them of sufficient supplies for hunting. This was particularly significant, for the Sioux of this period had practically abandoned the technology of flaking stone arrowheads and depended on their rifles for hunting. That winter Mitchell ordered hoop iron so that the Indians could cut metal arrowpoints for use in hunting.[90]

In March of 1877 the spring rise in the Missouri totally inundated the buildings at Fort Peck, and Agent Mitchell proposed that the agency be moved at once. The Commissioner of Indian Affairs agreed, but General Sheridan suggested that if it was moved at all, it should be relocated near Fort Buford, "on account of economy and a better control of the wild Indians." Sheridan dispatched Lieutenant Colonel James W. Forsyth to investigate the situation. He arrived at Fort Peck on May 26, but heavy rains, flooding, and impassable roads made personal investigation of the terrain impossible. However, Forsyth reported to Sheridan that he had been convinced that Poplar River was the only suitable site for an agency between Fort Peck and Fort Buford. The move was at last authorized in July.[91]

For the Indians, life at Fort Peck Agency was far from sedentary. In his annual report for 1877, Wellington Bird, who in March had replaced Mitchell as agent, noted that of the six to seven thousand Indians under his charge (including the Assiniboines and Gros Ventres at Fort Belknap, which was administratively consolidated with Fort Peck from 1876 to 1878), not over twenty families lived in any kind of permanent house. He wrote: "The rest live in teepees, moving about the reservation, occupying one place in summer, another in winter. For several months in summer and autumn they gather their effects and go out 50 or more miles among the buffalo and fix their hunting camp. When this is over they strike their tents and return." Thus, despite their belonging to an agency, the aboriginal hunting cycle dominated their lives. This was economic necessity since the Interior Department provided only a fraction of the supplies required to support the Indians throughout the entire year.[92]

The new agency buildings were ready in the fall, and Agent Bird moved his headquarters to Poplar River on October 18, 1877. Realizing that the supplies on hand could not provide for the agency during the coming winter, Bird asked his superiors to allow him to give the agency Indians limited quantities of powder, lead, and percussion caps with which to hunt buffalo. By letter of November 20, the Commissioner of Indian Affairs granted permission to sell ammunition to the agency Indians; by letter of December 3, the permission was withdrawn. With a touch of irony that reflected on the conflict between civilian and military authorities in Indian affairs, the agent wrote to the Commissioner on December 20 to acknowledge receipt of both letters by the same mail.

Unable to obtain ammunition at the agency, the Indians had no choice but to turn to the Métis traders. Bird reported in January of 1878 that seventy-five Red River carts and several hundred Métis had established winter headquarters on Milk River, intending to spend the season hunting buffalo and trading with the Indians.[93]

The question of potential relations between the hostile and agency Sioux was always a nagging one. In February, Captain Constant Williams, stationed at Fort Benton, learned from his Indian scouts that Long Fox, Black Tiger, and one other Yanktonai chief of equal importance were camped with their people on Lower Beaver Creek, above Tom Campbell's trading house. When some Sioux from Canada arrived at their camp, the chiefs had ordered the soldier lodge to whip them and expel them from the camp. Williams visited the Métis on Milk River, told them they had no right to hunt in the United States, and warned them about trading whiskey and ammunition to Indians. The Captain recommended that the Métis be removed by the army, but in early April, before his request got through military channels, the Métis broke their camp and most of them returned to Canada.[94]

By April of 1878, with agency supplies running very low, Agent Bird encouraged the Indians at Fort Peck to go on a buffalo hunt. They were not gone a week when thirty to forty families returned and reported that their horses had been stolen. Although it was first blamed on the Crows, the thiefs turned out to be from White Dog's band of Upper Assiniboines. The previous fall, Bird learned, a twelve-year-old Assiniboine boy had been murdered. His father, White Shell, and his kinsman, White Dog — a medicine man — blamed the murder on the Yanktonais, though without evidence. To soothe over the affair, the Yanktonais presented the father with one or two horses and some blankets. White Dog, however, urged retaliation, and perpetrated the theft of the horses. While the agency Sioux were out hunting, the Gros Ventres and Upper Assiniboines came to their camp, apparently for a peace parley. Several of the leading Yanktonai chiefs, including Black Catfish, Black Tiger, and Thundering Bull, harangued the camp to prevent bloodshed. They were overruled, however, by the younger men who wished to punish White Dog. A large war party gathered and in late June lay siege to Fort Belknap Agency, making nightly raids on the Indians' horse herds. Unfortunately for the Sioux, the Fort Belknap Indians were much better armed and were supplied with ammunition; when the Sioux finally left, three of their number were dead and four wounded.[95]

Mad Bear. Yanktonai. Photo by David F. Barry. Courtesy State Historical Society of North Dakota, no. A-3963.

Agent Bird blamed part of the trouble on lack of leadership. The Yanktonais had long recognized Medicine Bear as the leading chief, but he was now getting old and his influence had waned. In the environment of the agency, the agent wrote, "the biggest chief seems to be the one who can secure the largest amount of annuity goods or rations." He reported that there were over fifty chiefs at the agency, none of whom could claim a following of more than twenty lodges. This proliferation of chiefs occurred at all the agencies and seriously undermined the effectiveness of the traditional political system. Without strong chiefs to follow, the soldier lodges were ineffective. In an attempt to ease the transition from traditional political structures to the reservation system, the Bureau of Indian Affairs had called for the organization of agency police forces to maintain law and order. They were intended to give experience to promising Indians and provide an alternative political force to that of the chiefs. At the same time, a police force would give the agent some power over offenders, as well as protection in times of crisis. In 1878 Agent Bird organized a company of ten Indian police with a captain and two sergeants among the Assiniboines settled at Wolf Point. The Sioux, however, he did not judge ready for such an experiment.[96]

Game was abundant during the summer of 1878, but the lack of ammunition reduced the effectiveness of the Fort Peck Indians in killing sufficient numbers for their needs. As usual, supplies were short, and the agent worried about the possibility of actual starvation during the winter. Exacerbating the problem was the annual migration of Red River Métis. On October 3, Bird reported that some three hundred families of Métis were illegally living on the reservation between the Poplar and Milk rivers. "They are destroying the Buffalo as rapidly as an unlimited supply of Ammunition in their hands can do it," Bird wrote, "and our Indians with good reason complain bitterly."[97]

Agent Bird was not optimistic about the progress shown by the Sioux at his agency. In a letter of November, 1878, he wrote that the Yanktonais, since their return from the summer hunt, had "manifested a degree of recklessness and insubordination if not actual hostility never before witnessed since I came to the Agency." The Indians felt cheated by the government and complained of the lack of ammunition and the failure of the government to comply with promises to supply them with sufficient food and annuities. Bird blamed their attitude on the influence of the hostile Sioux, with whom the agency Indians were related by family ties, and on the increased number of war parties that had gone out from the agency during the preceding eight months. As though to support the Indians' complaint of unfair treatment, Bird closed his letter by noting that the agency stores contained only enough flour for six weeks and enough beef

Man Who Hides Under the Snow. Hunkpapa. Read Collection 1881.3.136.7.

for seven weeks — "and nearly 6 months of winter before we get additional supplies up the river."[98]

That winter White Dog continued his vendetta against the Sioux at Fort Peck. The Sioux lost thirty-five horses to White Dog and his raiders, but according to the Fort Belknap agent in a letter written in January of 1879, he had compelled the Assiniboines to return the stolen property. In terms of lost horses, the Indians at both Fort Peck and Fort Belknap lost more stock to Crow horse raiders than they did to one another.[99]

The winter began favorably, with warm weather and no snow and buffalo abundant on Milk River. This provided the Indians with meat to eat and hides to trade for sugar, tea, and other luxuries. Agent W. L. Lincoln at Fort Belknap reported that the reservation was being inundated by large numbers of Assiniboines and Crees from Canada, as well as Piegans, Blackfeet, and Chippewas. He wrote: "The Buf-

Fast Dog. Yanktonai. Photo by David F. Barry. Courtesy State Historical Society of North Dakota, no. Col. 22H73.

falo north of the Missouri River being confined principally to a section of country commencing about thirty miles below this Post, and extending some sixty or seventy miles further down Milk River, and through the Bear Paw Mountains," extreme pressure was being put on the dwindling herds, which could not be expected to sustain themselves.[100]

Early in January, Sitting Bull and his band were reported to be camped on Frenchman's Creek, only 60 or 70 miles from Fort Belknap. He sent word that his people were friendly and only wanted to hunt buffalo. Again, the Fort Belknap agent reported more Indians, including the Pend d'Oreilles, closing in on the herds. He cautioned, "So many Indians will soon kill or drive away all the game from this reservation." The presence of Sitting Bull on American soil did not escape the military authorities. A commission headed by General Terry had councilled with Sitting Bull in Canada only the previous October, offering the Sioux immunity if they would return to their reservation in the United States. The chief had been adamant, however, that he and his people would remain in Canada. But with the scarcity of game north of the line, they had no choice but to return to Montana to hunt buffalo. General Sheridan suggested that the Hunkpapas and other former hostiles be let alone as long as they remained north of the Missouri and committed no hostilities. In the spring the army planned to construct a new post, Fort Assiniboine, west of the Bear Paws, to strengthen the military presence in northern Montana.[101]

Spring of 1879 brought an increasing number of reports of Indian depredations, but Agent Bird took a level-headed view of the situation. On June 6, he wrote to Colonel Miles at Fort Keogh, sending his letter by John Bruyier as courier, to inform him of conditions on the reservation. He believed that Sitting Bull himself had crossed back into Canada toward the end of February, but Indians from his camps had been hunting buffalo from the mouth of Milk River to Wood Mountain (in Canada), and they were presently roaming on both sides of the Missouri, both on and off the reservation. Although the Assiniboines were peaceable and were making progress in farming, as were some of the Yanktonais leaders — notably Medicine Bear, Afraid of the Bear, and Thundering Bull — other chiefs — particularly Black Catfish and Black Tiger — using the power of their soldier lodges, were attempting to prevent them from farming. The agent recommended that the dissidents be disarmed.[102]

Bird's correspondence makes the frustrations of his job apparent. At last he resigned, and his replacement, N. S. Porter, arrived on July 7. But in mid-June, before Porter arrived, Sitting Bull's camps were on the upper Poplar River, only a day's journey from the agency. On June 15, Bird wrote to Fort Buford to ask for military protection. A detachment headed by Captain Thomas Britton arrived on June 24 to find that most of the hostile Indians had left, reportedly having returned to Canada. Britton learned that the single cause of dissatisfaction at the agency was the failure of the government to provide more than half of the rations due the Indians, but he hastened to add that the agent himself was not to blame.[103]

When the new agent arrived at Fort Peck in July, he found that Black Catfish and others of the Sioux chiefs had gone to Fort Keogh to visit Colonel Miles and air their grievances to him. They promised him to keep away from the hostiles, and in return Miles sent a letter back with Black Catfish to the agent recording their complaints about the shortage of food at the agency and the exorbitant prices charged by the trader. Porter promised to regulate the trader, but he could do nothing about the quantity of supplies furnished by the Indian Office.[104]

Many of the non-agency Sioux came to Fort Peck Agency

Rain in the Face. Hunkpapa. Read Collection 1881.3.136.2.

asking to be taken in and given rations. In July, Porter reported that he had already received 587 individuals, and that 93 more lodges were expected soon. He informed them that they would receive more food by surrendering to the soldiers, who would supply them with army rations, but the Indians preferred to be at the agency. Many of them were Oglalas and Brulés from Red Cloud and Spotted Tail agencies. Game was gone in Canada, and the Sioux were forced to come south of the line to hunt.[105]

The annual influx of Indians from other reservations and from Canada was repeated in the fall of 1879. The reservation Indians were forced to hunt south of the Missouri. They made a good hunt, then returned to Poplar River in November to receive their annuities; they were particularly anxious for the blankets. The number of Indians was greater than had been previously seen at the agency. Porter was anxious to get the distribution accomplished and send the Indians back on a hunt, but the weather failed to cooperate. Deep snow fell in November and stayed on the ground until the end of March, making travel impossible. The entire camp had to be fed from the agency supplies throughout the winter months.[106]

The invasion of the Fort Peck and Fort Belknap area by outsiders was the overwhelming concern of the winter of 1879–80. Lieutenant Colonel H. M. Black, commanding officer at Fort Assiniboine, reported that all the Sioux were south of the Canadian line, there being but few buffalo to be found north of the line. Black commented: "It is said there are more Half Breeds, hostile Sioux, Crees, Bloods and Blackfeet on this side of the line, who belong to the other, than were ever known before."[107]

At Fort Peck Agency, Porter reported some progress in adapting the Sioux to reservation life. After long opposing the establishment of an agency police force, the Sioux chiefs were finally persuaded to cooperate in selecting twenty men to serve on the force. Porter selected Stab Plenty as captain, a man he described as "one of the bravest and wildest Indians in the camp." Only a year before, he had been one of the soldier lodge members who had physically assaulted the Indian laborers in the fields; now he took his appointment as police captain with equal seriousness. In his annual report, the agent said of Stab Plenty, "He has been faithful and obedient, trying to live and act like a white man."[108]

During the winter, Sitting Bull's people again began to come to the agency. On January 28, forty families under the Hunkpapa chief White Gut arrived in destitute condition, surrendering ten ponies, twelve guns, and two revolvers. Agent Porter wrote to the Commissioner of Indian Affairs that White Gut was an influential man in Sitting Bull's camp, and that, like him, many of the others would come in if assured of good treatment. He added, "I think that with a little judicious Management the Whole question of the Sitting Bull Indians could be settled."[109]

On February 17, Agent Porter and Major Guido Ilges, on patrol from Fort Assiniboine, had an interview with Gall (*P'izí*, "gall"), one of Sitting Bull's principal men. The chief said that he had given up his ponies and guns several years before at one of the agencies, but he had left there because the people were starving. Again, over a year previous, he had given up his ponies to Captain Baldwin at Fort Peck Agency, and was sent back north to bring his people in. While they were returning to Fort Peck, they learned that the agent there had no food to issue to them, so they did not come. He had returned to Fort Peck only a month earlier, and Agent Porter had put his name on the ration list. He had come to see what the agency could do for his people. He said that if they were allowed to keep their ponies and arms, they would come in at once; or, if they believed there was enough food to feed them, they would agree to surrender their ponies and arms. But, Gall said, he could see that there was not enough food for even the agency Indians, so to come in and give up their ponies and arms seemed to him like facing starvation. The agent was inclined to agree with the chief, and suggested in his report to the Commissioner of Indian Affairs that if the government would only supply the Sioux with all the food needed to support them year round, instead of the current starvation policy, there would be no need for further expensive military campaigns.[110] But the army did not intend for the Bureau of Indian Affairs to claim any credit for the eventual surrender of Sitting Bull. He was a military problem, first and foremost.

By the end of April, 1,116 individuals from the non-agency Sioux had come to Fort Peck and had surrendered forty-three ponies, forty guns, and seven revolvers. The addition of these people raised the total number receiving rations at the agency to seven thousand. In May, Agent Porter reported that the Indians were suffering terribly from hunger. "They are getting more anxious for food every day," he wrote. At last, on June 5, a shipment of flour was received and immediate issues were made to avert starvation. Indian Inspector McNeil also arrived in June and confirmed Agent Porter's reports. He informed the Secretary of the Interior that the Indians at Fort Peck "had eaten their ponies when they were only skin and bone and were existing on wild turnips, flagroot and such small game as chance brought them."[111]

In his annual report dated August 12, 1880, Agent Porter attempted to emphasize the positive accomplishments of the previous year at Fort Peck Agency. He noted progress in house building and farming. He commended the Indians' labor in cutting and selling wood to the steamboats. But on this same day he dispatched a letter to Colonel Miles asking that troops be detailed to remove the "turbulent element" from the agency camp. The Yanktonais had just returned from their summer hunt, and with them had come a large number of hostile Sioux, the agent wrote, who would like to stay at the agency and eat corn and potatoes. The agency police force was incapable of driving them away. In the interest of the agency Indians, Porter requested that troops be stationed near Fort Peck; troops at Fort Buford and Fort Keogh were too far away to be of practical assistance. The hostile Sioux customarily crossed the Missouri between Fort Peck Agency and the mouth of the Milk, providing a corridor through which they could pass unmolested from the lower agencies in Dakota Territory to the north and back again.[112]

Such a drastic measure probably seemed unnecessary to Colonel Miles, who, on August 19, reported that 830 hostile Sioux had surrendered at Fort Keogh, with one thousand more said to be on the way. The next day, Miles telegraphed his superiors that Rain in the Face and his people were at Poplar Creek, "silent and sullen." Porter, telegraphing from Fort Buford, confirmed that no less than a thousand hostile

Scout E. H. Allison. Courtesy State Historical Society of North Dakota, no. A-4287.

Sioux under Rain in the Face were at the agency, living off produce from the gardens and rations issued to the agency Indians.[113]

In response to communications from officers in the field, General Sherman decided that for the present there would be no additional troops sent to Dakota and Montana. If Fort Peck Agency needed military protection, it would have to be provided by General Terry's Department of Dakota. Sherman expressed his judgment that the Fort Peck Agency should not exist at all, and that the Indians there should be moved within the limits of the Great Sioux Reservation of 1868.[114]

Prospects for a quick end to the Sioux problem were not bright. Sitting Bull sent word that he had no intention of surrendering but agreed to leave the soldiers alone if they would leave him alone. The presence of the Sioux in Canada was a continual embarrassment to the United States, and a military solution was impossible. In September, Major Brotherton, at Fort Buford, proposed to send E. H. Allison, the post interpreter, to visit Sitting Bull and the other non-agency Sioux, assure them of fair treatment, and per-

Camp Poplar River, Officers' Quarters, 1895. Courtesy Bureau of Indian Affairs, Fort Peck, Montana.

suade them to surrender to the army under the same terms as the rest of their people. General Terry approved, and Allison set out on his mission. He held an initial council with Sitting Bull on October 3 in which he learned that the Indians believed arrangements were being made for them to settle permanently in Canada. After consulting with Canadian officials at Wood Mountain, Allison informed the Sioux that their belief was unfounded and that they had no choice but to return to the United States. Sitting Bull spoke of the dread his people had of the United States Army, and his fear of what the soldiers would do to them if they surrendered. He asked for time to think the matter over, pledging in the meanwhile to maintain peace. Allison believed that many of Sitting Bull's people were ready to surrender but were prevented from doing so by the soldier lodge. After reporting to Brotherton on October 12, Allison returned to the Sioux camps and worked throughout the winter to bring in the last of the hostile Sioux.[115]

Responding to Agent Porter's request, on September 22, 1880, General Terry authorized the commanding officer at Fort Custer to send two companies of troops to Poplar River. On October 1, Captain O. B. Read, commanding the detachment, was ordered to establish a cantonment at Fort Peck Agency. He was informed that the Yanktonais camp from the agency was at the moment moving slowly up the Redwater, accompanied by a camp of hostile Sioux. The latter were reported to be heading for Fort Keogh to surrender. The Captain was ordered to take extreme caution not to mingle with Indians, not to allow any ammunition to pass into Indian hands, and to make every effort not to disturb game on the reservation; while marching from the Yellowstone to the Missouri, the detachment was not to be allowed to discharge arms except in case of attack. "The object of your movement and command," the orders issued Read instructed, "is to sustain the authority of the Agent at Poplar River and to keep the hostile Indians away from the agency."[116]

As Captain Read's command marched northward, they passed near the large Sioux village on the Redwater. Two hundred lodges were under the leadership of Spotted Eagle, and the remaining three hundred lodges were agency Sioux. About a mile from the village, the column was met by a small party of Indians bearing a flag of truce. Since the Indians displayed no sign of hostility, Read passed them by without stopping. On October 11, Spotted Eagle came to Read's camp and remained with the column until it reached Poplar River. Then he returned to his people, stating that he would take them to Fort Keogh to surrender.[117]

Read sent a courier to Fort Buford on October 19 to telegraph Terry the news that two hundred lodges under Black Moon and Rain in the Face were heading for the agency and should arrive in a few days. Read requested full instructions. Terry's reply of October 21 probably failed to satisfy the captain. On the one hand, he was instructed, his purpose for being there was to protect the agent, the agency employees, and the agency property: "Your action must, in a great degree, be determined by the policy which the agent sees fit to pursue. For this reason no precise instructions can be given you." On the other hand, the captain was told that after consulting with the agent, he must use his own judgment. If the Indians attempted to negotiate with him, he should tell them that the terms remained unchanged: they must surrender unconditionally, agree to go to whichever of the Sioux agencies the government might assign them, and give up their arms and all ponies except such as were necessary to transport them to the agencies to which they would be assigned. The surrendered ponies would be sold and the proceeds invested in cattle for the Indians' benefit. Moreover, Read was further instructed that his post was part of the District of the Yellowstone and he must therefore obey the orders of Colonel Miles at District Headquarters, Fort Keogh.[118]

That same day Miles telegraphed Read (via the telegraph station at Fort Buford) that Spotted Eagle's camp of eighty lodges was at the head of Cherry or Cedar Creek. Rain in the Face was with them. Miles warned that Read should under no circumstances allow the hostiles within rifle range of his own camp. No Indians were to be allowed in the cantonment, and no soldiers were to be allowed in the Indian camps.[119]

On the evening of October 26, 1880, Captain Read sent for Black Moon and Little Knife, leaders of the Hunkpapas camped at the agency, and dictated to them the terms of surrender. Then he added:

> When I came here I was told the hostile Indians had 30 days in which to surrender. The 30 days are all gone but 4. After those 4 days the troops will be in the field and may attack them whenever they find them.
>
> If you want to surrender you should do it now. If not you must be prepared to fight whenever you meet troops, and you are likely to meet them wherever you go.

Black Moon replied that he was ready to surrender, but he wanted to remain at Fort Peck Agency. He and Little Knife each had ten lodges nearby. Read replied that he could not grant their request, but would communicate it to Colonel Miles. The reply came from Fort Keogh the next day: the Indians must come to Miles himself to surrender and must spend the winter at Fort Keogh. Then the Colonel would recommend that Black Moon and Little Knife be assigned to Fort Peck Agency. In the meantime, Read sent a copy of the speech he had read to Black Moon to the hostile Sioux camped on the Redwater with the Yanktonais.[120]

The winter of 1880–81 was unusually snowy and severe, a factor that undoubtedly played into the hands of the army. On October 31, Spotted Eagle, Rain in the Face, and Charge the Eagle, with five hundred people, surrendered at Fort Keogh.[121]

On November 4, Captain Read learned that a party of hostile Sioux was heading for the agency despite his instructions that they must go to Keogh. The captain sent them word again, warning them to stay away. If they had been told that the agent wanted them to come there, it was not so. Joseph Culbertson, a prominent half-breed, was with the camp and sent a note to Read on the 5th in behalf of the Indians. Read replied the same day, bluntly stating that he could not change the orders issued to him and that the Indians must stay away. Culbertson sent another note, saying that the headman of the group was Lame Deer's son, and asking Read to talk to the Indians. They wished to see the captain and Culbertson suggested they could meet him at his house, if the captain found it convenient. For Read, this raised suspicions that the interest of the traders was the force drawing the hostile Sioux to the agency. The Indians followed Read's orders and went into camp on the south bank of the Missouri across from the agency. Black Moon and Black Horn were with them.[122]

On November 26, Read reported to District Headquarters that Gall arrived that day from Sitting Bull's camp at Wood Mountain with twenty-three lodges. They were armed with Winchesters and had plenty of ammunition. The captain characterized Gall's behavior as "impudent as usual." The chief refused to answer questions, claimed that the country belonged to him and that he would go where he pleased, and asserted that neither he nor Sitting Bull had any intention of surrendering. Read was incensed, and frustrated by what he no doubt felt were overly restrictive orders. If authorized to do so, he proposed to attack the hostile camp, asking for reinforcement from two additional troops. He wired to headquarters: "Would attack them tonight if I felt I would be sustained in doing so." He felt he could depend on support from about two-thirds of the Yanktonai camp. The hostile Indians had been warned that if they failed to surrender by October 30, the troops would attack them. The loss of credibility caused by failing to live up to the threat, Read believed, would eventually precipitate a fight at the agency. Gall claimed the right to purchase unlimited ammunition from the agency trader; Read countered by ordering the trader to turn over to the military his entire stock of ammunition.[123]

The next day, Colonel John W. Davidson, the new commander of the District of the Yellowstone (Miles having relinquished command on November 20 to assume the rank of Brigadier General and take command of the Department of Columbia), asked authorization from his superiors to comply with Read's request for reinforcements; General Terry at department headquarters refused on the grounds that troops could not be sent to Poplar River in sufficient numbers to justify offensive movements against the Indians. He ordered instead that a detachment of thirty picked men under a lieutenant be sent from Fort Buford. Major Brotherton, the commanding officer at Buford, persuaded Terry to rescind the order, fearing that it would jeopardize Allison's negotiations for the surrender of Sitting Bull. Angrily, the District of the Yellowstone requested the Department of Dakota to withdraw Camp Poplar River from its command, inasmuch as they were unable to protect it. The request was granted on November 30, and Read was ordered to report thereafter directly to General Terry at department headquarters in St. Paul as an independent post. The military politics centering on who would have the honor of accepting the surrender of the hostiles — especially Sitting Bull — clearly took precedence over the mundane issue of getting the job done. Major Brotherton was explicit in his last dispatch of November 29 to Read: "Do not receive the surrender of any Indians, but direct them to Fort Buford or Keogh." The rationale behind this could only be political.[124]

The number of Sioux at Fort Peck Agency was growing steadily. On November 30, Gall's camp consisted of seventy-three lodges by actual count. Although the hostiles complained about the prohibition on ammunition sales, Read reported that they were well supplied with ammunition and were able to get more in the vicinity of the agency. The captain believed that the Indians intended to stay at the agency unless removed by force. Gall declared that if any attempt were made to remove them, they would fight. In Read's opinion, the situation called for action. On December 9 he wrote to Brotherton:

> What I could have done ten days ago with my own command will now require three times the number, and I respectfully recommend that either the troops be entirely withdrawn from this Agency or a sufficient force be sent here to enforce any order that may be given.

Such a force, Read suggested, should be large enough to compel the hostiles to surrender or to drive them across the line into Canada and prevent their return.[125]

On December 11 General Terry acquiesced and instructed Major Ilges, with five companies of the Fifth Infantry from Fort Keogh, to reinforce Camp Poplar River. Ten picked men from each infantry company at Fort Buford, under a lieutenant, were also ordered to proceed to Poplar River, under escort of Captain Bell's company of the Seventh Cavalry.[126]

Major Brotherton, at Fort Buford, continued to fret about the effects that these movements of troops would have on the negotiations for Sitting Bull's surrender. Allison had been expected to leave Wood Mountain on December 11, escorting Sitting Bull and his band to Fort Buford. Terry agreed that precautions were essential to avoid alarming the Indians, and telegraphed to Ilges on December 14, emphasizing his concern that the troops avoid any conflict with the Indians.[127]

Captain James Bell's cavalry detachment arrived at Camp Poplar River on December 15. The captain did not find the situation alarming. Although Gall had collected a large number of followers from Sitting Bull's camp, and had spoken in threatening language, it seemed apparent that he had no intention of attacking either the agency or the military post.[128]

On the evening of December 19, Allison arrived at Camp Poplar River with a delegation from Sitting Bull's camp. Captain Bell decided to have a talk with Gall and the other headmen from his camp in Allison's presence, in order to ascertain their true disposition. Bell sent a dispatch to Brotherton recommending that after Major Ilges' arrival, the hostiles be compelled to surrender at Poplar River. This would destroy Gall's influence and set the stage for Sitting Bull's surrender. Allison concurred that such a move would not alarm Sitting Bull's people.[129]

In his reply to Bell, Brotherton suggested that perhaps too much importance was being placed on Gall. Brotherton preferred to wait before making any recommendation. He reminded the captain that Terry's objective was to avoid a winter campaign if possible, and therefore nothing should be done that might prevent Sitting Bull's surrender. Accordingly, Bell reported that he had met with Gall on December 20, talking to him "kindly but plainly and firmly," informing him that his surrender could not be accepted at Poplar River, and that he must go to Fort Buford or Keogh before any permanent arrangement could be made for him. Bell concluded his dispatch: "The key to the whole process is here — force the Gall's surrender and the rest will follow as a natural sequence."[130]

Major Ilges and the Fifth Infantry arrived at Poplar River on the evening of December 24 and camped, in Ilges' words, "upon the high plateau lining Poplar River and to the west of the cantonment proper. The camp of the hostile 'Sioux' was plainly visible on the opposite shore of the Missouri River situated in a heavy growth of Cottonwood timber filled with thick underbrush and in an elbow formed by the river." The camp numbered about one hundred lodges — totaling about four hundred people.[131]

On Christmas morning, with some sixty of his warriors, Gall came to talk with the major. He claimed that he was ready to surrender to Ilges, but that his people would not surrender until spring, when they would decide whether to stay at Fort Peck Agency or to go to Fort Buford or Keogh. The chief asked for transportation and an escort in order to visit Buford. Ilges refused the request and told the Indians that they must go to Buford immediately. He would wait three days for their answer.

Later in the day, Crow, another of the Hunkpapa Sioux chiefs, accompanied by twelve headmen, requested a talk with Ilges. In the major's words, the Indians "stated that they wanted to await the action of 'Sitting Bull' who was their only Chief and that he and his followers were ready and willing to do whatever this Chieftain advised."[132] While

Crow King. Hunkpapa. Read Collection 1881.3.136.5.

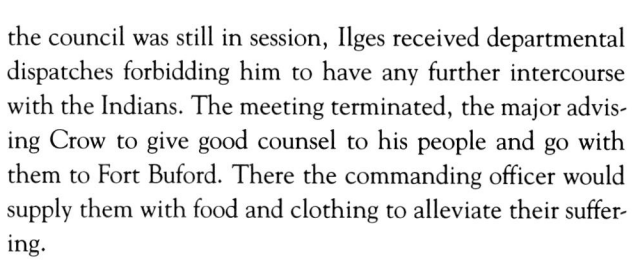

Crow. Hunkpapa. Photo by David F. Barry. Courtesy State Historical Society of North Dakota, no. C-229.

the council was still in session, Ilges received departmental dispatches forbidding him to have any further intercourse with the Indians. The meeting terminated, the major advising Crow to give good counsel to his people and go with them to Fort Buford. There the commanding officer would supply them with food and clothing to alleviate their suffering.

On December 28 Terry changed his tactics. He telegraphed to Ilges revoking former instructions and authorizing him to compel the surrender of Gall and his people by whatever means suitable. On the basis of these new orders, Ilges reopened negotiations with the hostile camp. On December 31 he assembled the headmen in a room at the agency headquarters. Bear Hat, Black Moon, Crow, Crow King, and Gall were all present, as were Allison and the two emissaries from Sitting Bull's camp, now on their way back from Fort Buford. Joseph Culbertson and George Fluery served as official interpreters.

Ilges opened the meeting by requesting Crow King, head soldier from Sitting Bull's camp, to tell the gathering about his visit to Fort Buford. Crow King told the council that he had just come from Buford, where he had heard good words spoken. When he returned, he told the Indians that he was going to be at peace with all the Americans. The people had said *Hau!* to express their agreement. Crow King said: "I want to go where these good words were spoken to me: I speak for Sitting Bull: all these Indians have said how [*hau*]: he wants them to move near Buford so as to be fed."[133] Crow King told Ilges that the Indians all intended to go to Buford, but because of the cold and the deep snow they wished to travel slowly, hunting along the way in order to provide skins for the women and children, who were suffering from lack of clothing. He asked that the agent provide them with powder and ammunition to enable them to hunt and requested clothing and provisions as well.

In response to the Indians' requests, Major Ilges offered to transport the people to Buford in wagons and to provide them with food to sustain them along the way. Crow, one of the headmen from Gall's camp, refused, stating that they preferred to travel at their own pace, without military guard. After some subdued argument, Ilges commented: "The Great Father has not sent me here with all these soldiers for nothing." After further argument, Crow said: "We want to wait for Sitting Bull, and go with him." Ilges was apparently losing patience. He told Crow that he should do what was best for his people. The council terminated, Ilges urging the headmen to go to their camp and talk the matter over.

In his official report, written a month later to department headquarters, Ilges asserted that at the conclusion of this conference the Indians "fully understood my demand for removal on the 2d instant [January 2, 1881], and also, that I would move against them on that day to compel surrender with force in case of refusal on their part."[134] However, if Ilges did make this clear to the headmen, it is not reflected in the transcript of the council.

On the evening of January 1, Crow went to the house of Joseph Culbertson, who was serving as the army's interpreter, and sent a message to Major Ilges which the officer paraphrased in part as follows:

> that he and his people would not move until spring[;] that he was tired of talking with me[;] that the soldiers were cowards and afraid to fight[;] that they cried in winter and could not handle a gun[;] and that if I attempted to interfere with his people there would be trouble[;] that he was ready to fight me if I wanted [to] fight.[135]

That same evening Gall warned Henderson, the post trader, that he and his employees should leave the agency immediately. According to Ilges' report, Gall told Henderson: "To-morrow we will fight and wipe out the soldiers and kill everybody at the soldier camp."[136]

Major Ilges' conclusion from these reports was unequivocal: "It then occurred to me most forcibly that further delay in bringing these hostiles to terms should cease and that action against them should be prompt and most decisive."[136] On the morning of January 2, Ilges prepared to attack the Indians without giving further warning. Leaving behind a small force to protect the cantonment, Ilges mounted 12 commissioned officers, 272 enlisted men, 19 Indian scouts and volunteers, and 2 citizen volunteers. Armed with a good map of the terrain upon which the Indian camps were located, Ilges planned an effective strategy.

Captain Read, with fifty-eight officers and men and a 3-inch Rodman Gun, was ordered to take up a position on the north bank of the Missouri River to the east of the Indian encampment. Major Ilges led the rest of the column, taking along a Hotchkiss Gun, across the Missouri to the south bank, west of the Indians' position. Passing through a slough thickly fringed with willows, they came upon a Minneconjou village of some thirty-two lodges. With the exception of "a few superannuated bucks," who came running out of the woods toward Ilges' column "and deposited a few worthless muskets on the ground," the village was deserted.[137] A search of the tipis turned up sixteen rifles or guns and two pistols, all of which the soldiers burned.

Scout Joseph Culbertson. The X in the background marks the site of Major Ilges' attack on Gall's camp, January 2, 1881. Courtesy Montana Historical Society, no. 941-831.

Moving east, the column came upon Gall's village of some forty lodges. Ilges reported, "Here perfect silence reigned and not an Indian could be seen. I then directed Lieut. Woodruff to place the field gun in position and to send a few shells into the woods for the purpose of convincing the hostiles gathered in the timber to the rear that I was in earnest." After the first shot a solitary Indian came out of a tipi and walked slowly away from the soldiers. Ilges ordered Captain Hargous, commanding Company C, Fifth Infantry, to advance on the village. As they did so, Ilges reported, a shot rang out from one of the tipis. The soldiers returned the fire, killing one man and wounding a man and a woman.[138]

At this point, Read's command crossed the river and took up a position on Ilges' right. The major ordered them to fire on some Indian men who were seen running from the rear of the Minneconjou village toward the river, where they dropped out of sight in the willows. Apparently they were heading for the agency. Ilges called for cease fire and sent Joe Culbertson into the trees to call out to the Indians and ask them to surrender. The only answer was an occasional yell. Ilges then resumed firing shells into the woods and ordered the destruction of the tipis.

Soon Culbertson reported seeing a white flag. Ilges with his scouts went to the spot, a clearing about 75 yards square located in front of the eastern side of the village. Although ordered repeatedly to do so, the Indians would not emerge from the woods and surrender. Ilges brought up his field guns and informed the Indians that they had ten minutes to surrender, after which he would fire upon them again. Before long the soldiers observed some of the tipis being taken down as the warriors emerged from the woods in quick succession, laying their guns on the ground in front of Major Ilges. While the soldiers watched, the Indians carried their baggage across the Missouri, heading for the military camp. All the tipis that the Indians left standing were burned by the soldiers. Captain Bell was dispatched with his company to confiscate the pony herd; more than two hundred animals were captured.

The next day the soldiers counted the prisoners and found over three hundred; only thirty-one tipis had been salvaged. The others, looted and burned by the soldiers, were the source of many souvenirs, a number of which Captain Read obtained for his collection. In his official report, Ilges noted that the army had suffered no casualties in the engagement, whereas eight Indians were killed in the fight or died later of their wounds. He estimated that some sixty of the Sioux escaped. Some of the captured guns and ponies were given to the Yanktonais scouts who aided Ilges' command.

On the morning of January 3, Major Ilges led his column, including the field guns, toward the Yanktonais camp on the Redwater, 15 miles from Camp Poplar River. He had received reports that the escaped hostiles had taken refuge there, and he was determined to force them to surrender. Agent Porter accompanied the command. When they were about halfway to the camp, they were met by the Yanktonais chiefs Medicine Bear and Skin of the Heart who begged Ilges to return to Poplar River. They feared trouble if the soldiers came to their camp, and they said they did not want to fight. The major stated that he, too, had no desire to fight, but that the hostiles must surrender. Agent Porter interceded in the Yanktonais' behalf, and the agency Indians promised to bring the hostiles to the soldiers' camp the next day. The column turned back to Poplar River, and the next day, Ilges wrote, the Yanktonais fulfilled their promise "to a greater extent than I had any reason to expect."[139]

On January 6, Ilges sent the prisoners on their way to Fort Buford, guarded by Captain Bell's company of the Seventh Cavalry. They arrived there on the 9th, and the Indians went into camp as prisoners of war.[140]

General Terry congratulated Major Ilges on his success and on January 14 suggested that if Allison failed to bring Sitting Bull in, Ilges would be ordered to move against him. Meanwhile, Allison was with the Hunkpapa camp on Milk River, heading for Wolf Point. Perhaps in reaction to reports

Group photo taken after a dinner honoring Major Ilges. Back row (left to right): Lieutenant F. W. Sibley, 5th Infantry; Lieutenant E. S. Avis, 5th Infantry; middle row: W. D. Knight, Yellowstone Journal; Maj. Guido Ilges, 5th Infantry; Joseph Culbertson, scout; front row: Lieutenant Thomas Defree, 5th Infantry; L. A. Huffman. Photo by L. A. Huffman, Miles City, Montana. Courtesy Montana Historical Society, no. 981-831.

of Ilges' attack on Gall's camp, Sitting Bull, with forty-three lodges, broke away and escaped again across the Canadian line. Allison escorted Crow King, with fifty-one lodges, about three hundred people, to Wolf Point, where they were met by a detachment from Camp Poplar River bringing wagons to hasten the Indians' move. They arrived at Ilges' camp on January 31; and Captain Read, with a detachment from his Company F, Eleventh Cavalry, was detailed to conduct them to Fort Buford. A few days earlier, on January 29, Iron Dog, with eight lodges — sixty-four people — surrendered at Poplar River, having come directly from Wood Mountain. These Indians reported that there was no game to be found in Canada and that Royal Canadian Mounted Police had advised them to surrender to the American army. Ilges characterized the Indians as being "in a most pitiful condition for want of food and clothing[;] they having eaten nearly all of their ponies on the journey."[141]

Early in February the Yanktonai camp moved back to the agency. On February 8, Ilges began to arrest hostile Sioux

Little Assiniboine. Hunkpapa. Photo by David F. Barry. Courtesy State Historical Society of North Dakota, no. Col. 22H100.

hiding in the agency camp. The Missouri had risen to flood stage owing to unseasonably warm weather, making it impossible for the Indians to escape. Ilges' action resulted in the capture or surrender of 185 non-agency Sioux, who were sent on February 12, under guard, to Fort Buford. Ilges commended the Yanktonais for their cooperation: "The Yanktonais were at first disposed to object to my visit with military force to their camp, but they have since submitted with grace to the inevitable." Their work completed, Ilges and his troops left for Fort Keogh on February 12, turning command of Camp Poplar River back to Captain Read.[142]

From late winter until early the next summer, much of the activity at Poplar River centered around small parties of Sioux coming down from the north and being sent to Fort Buford to surrender. By May 26, 1881, the prisoner camp at Buford numbered 1,125 individuals; on that day they were boarded on steamboats and sent downriver to Fort Yates. On June 13, an additional 1,641 Sioux prisoners were sent by steamers from Fort Keogh. On July 22, all these prisoners were turned over to the agent at Standing Rock; those belonging to other agencies were later allowed to return to their relatives.[143]

At last, on July 19, Sitting Bull himself, with 187 of his people, arrived at Fort Buford and surrendered to Major Brotherton. Canadian officials had refused to give the Hunkpapas a reserve; the buffalo had disappeared from the Canadian plains; Sitting Bull had no choice but to surrender. Although he may well have expected to be killed by vengeful soldiers, he and his people were treated well. On July 29 they were sent by steamer to Fort Yates, where they found their relatives already established. However, military authorities were concerned that Sitting Bull and his immediate band receive some special punishment; accordingly, they were sent on September 10 down the Missouri to Fort Randall, where they established their camp as prisoners of war. (In 1883, the army, no longer willing to pay the bill for feeding them, returned Sitting Bull and his people to Standing Rock.)[144]

The year 1881 was an important one for other reunions as well. The Bureau of Indian Affairs authorized the transfer to Pine Ridge Agency of the four hundred Northern Cheyennes living in Oklahoma; they arrived there in December.[145]

At Camp Poplar River, Captain Read busied his command with garrison routine, the building of new quarters, and construction of a military telegraph line from Fort Buford. Sitting Bull and the hostile Sioux who followed him, refusing to return to their agencies on the Great Sioux Reservation, had been the force that drew the military to eastern Montana. With the Sioux back on their reservation, it may have seemed that the drama on the northern plains was over. But one more act remained to be played out that would mark the end of an era in frontier life: the extermination of the northern buffalo herds.

When Captain Read wrote his annual report in September, 1881, he was optimistic about the progress of the Indians at Fort Peck Agency. In June, when they were in a starving condition and there were no provisions left to issue them, Agent Porter and Captain Read had been able to convince the Indians to remain at the agency for one more week to hoe the 250-acre farm they had planted. Then they left on their summer buffalo hunt, returning in September "with plenty of meat and skins to find an abundant harvest awaiting them." The Indians' own efforts, therefore, were able to provide them with the necessities of life that, supplemented by the annuities and subsistence supplies issued at the agency, ensured their existence.[146]

During the summer and fall of 1881 there was again an inundation of outsiders drawn to northeastern Montana by the last of the buffalo herds. By executive order in July of

1880, much of the region south of the Missouri River had been opened to white settlement. Hide hunters came to make a living from the herds, and other white men settled on the Missouri — many taking Indian women as wives. They made their livelihood by illegally chopping the Indians' timber and selling wood to the steamboats during the summer, and hunting, trapping, and trading with the Indians during the winter. On March 2, 1881, Agent Porter wrote to the Commissioner of Indian Affairs asking for military assistance to remove these intruders. The Bureau of Indian Affairs transmitted the agent's request to the Secretary of the Interior, who duly sent it on to the Secretary of War, and thence down the military chain of command.[147]

At last, on July 18, General Terry ordered two mounted companies from Fort Keogh to Camp Poplar River to assist the agent. On July 25 Terry clarified his orders by telegraphing to say that if the intruders were not guilty of any crime other than being on the reservation, they were to be conducted off but not turned over to the civil authorities. That day, Captain Robert McDonald, with Companies D and K, Fifth Infantry, left Fort Keogh and arrived seven days later at Poplar River. There he found that his small force was insufficient to carry out the agent's requests. Porter telegraphed to Terry on August 1, explaining that a steamboat would be required to remove the intruders, as their locations on the river were inaccessible by land because of swamps and dense underbrush. Terry telegraphed Sheridan's office on August 4, stating that the steamboat required to transport the troops and enable them to bring the intruders downriver to Fort Buford would cost an estimated $10,000. Sheridan delayed a reply, waiting until September 12 to disapprove the expense. On September 17 Captain McDonald was ordered to return to Fort Keogh, his expedition aborted. The incident is illustrative of the difficulty Indian agents experienced in obtaining military cooperation.[148]

McDonald's report of his return trip provides a vivid portrayal of the work of the white hide hunters:

> Returning I was deeply grieved to find many parties on the range outside the reservation slaughtering the buffalo, simply for the hide for which they get in Miles City from $1.00 to $1.25 per skin[,] occasionally cutting out the tongue [the choicest piece of meat] and, by this quibble, avoiding responsibility and, with these exceptions, leaving the hills covered with slaughtered buffalo.... Sooner or later the Yanktonais[,] indignant at this waste[,] will jump the ruthless rascals, who will then, doubtless, howl for troops and protection.

This report was sent to department headquarters in St. Paul, where General Terry forwarded it to division headquarters in Chicago, adding an endorsement that the killing off of the game would result in greater government expenditures to feed the Indians. Although it would "solve the Indian problem," Terry commented, "the slaughter of animal life in such a way is abhorrent to me." Sheridan returned the report, adding his own endorsement: "If I could learn that every buffalo in the Northern herd were killed, I would be glad. The destruction of this herd would do more to keep Indians quiet than anything else that could happen." The army would not protect the buffalo.[149]

White hide hunters were not the reservation Indians' only competitors for the buffalo herds. In July, Agent W. L. Lincoln, at Fort Belknap, reported more than five hundred lodges of Canadian Crees and Blackfeet camped at the big bend of Milk River, headed for the Cypress Hills. He sent them warning that if they came by way of the agency, he would call for help from the troops at Fort Assiniboine. In August, Lincoln reported that buffalo were only about 30 miles from Fort Belknap, and that a large group of Canadian Indians was attempting to drive the animals away. He applied to Fort Assiniboine for military assistance, and General Terry ordered a force to be sent into the field to tell the foreign Indians that they must return to Canada, and to prevent them from driving the buffalo out of reach of the agency Indians. An expedition set out from Fort Assiniboine on August 20 under command of Captain Martin E. O'Brien, Second Cavalry, marching down Milk River. Starting out with 5 officers and 90 men, reinforcements were later sent to raise the command to 10 officers and 163 men. The Canadian Indians found it easy to stay out of the column's way; after O'Brien's force had passed Fort Belknap, a group of Crees and Métis came down from Canada and were running buffalo only 25 miles from Fort Belknap.[150]

Meanwhile, Captain Read reported from Poplar River on September 30 that there were said to be five hundred white hunters between his post and the Yellowstone, "who are organized for defense and determined not to allow Indians to run Buffalo." The agency Yanktonais had moved their camp to the Redwater for their fall hunt, and the Indians feared there would be a collision between their young men and the white hunters. In response to this report, Captain Simon Snyder, with three mounted companies of the Fifth Infantry, set out from Fort Keogh for the Redwater. There they found the Sioux hunting camp, but very few white hunters. The captain stated that the white hunters were anxious to avoid meeting Indians, and that they denied the existence of any organization to interfere with the Indians' hunt. Snyder believed that rather than five hundred, there were no more than fifty hunters within 25 miles of the Yanktonais' camp. "The white hunters are slaughtering the Buffaloes at a fearful rate," he wrote, "the prairie in places being literally strewn with skinned carcasses, but all this is taking place far beyond the limits of Fort Peck Indian Reservation." While the reports may have been exaggerated, the situation they portrayed was not. The Indians at Fort Peck and Fort Belknap found themselves hemmed in by white buffalo hunters to the south and by Indian and Métis hunters to the north.[151]

A larger force was deemed necessary to drive the intruders from the reservation. On October 8, 1881, a column under command of Captain Kline, consisting of 12 officers and 239 men, left Fort Assiniboine on a scout through the Milk River country. On October 17 they found twenty-six lodges of Métis and nine lodges of Crees; on October 20, two hundred lodges of Crees; and on October 24, thirty-two lodges of Crees. The camps were broken up and the offenders removed north of the Canadian line. But the effect was only temporary. In early January, 1882, Captain Read undertook a personal reconnaissance to ascertain the numbers and location of the intruders. He wrote, "I found wherever I went on Milk River, Half Breeds and Crees in every point, all in comfortable log huts, clustered together in groups of from two or three, to a dozen or more." He estimated their numbers at two hundred families, averaging six to eight persons per family. There were also large camps of Crees and Chippewas on Rock Creek and Beaver Creek. The main buffalo herd was above the Canadian intruders, near the big bend of the Milk. "Driven north of the Missouri by white hunters, the buffalo fall into the hands of these trespassers, who take good care to keep between [the buffalo] and the Agency Indians, thus depriving the latter of an important part of their subsistence." Read complained that an illicit trade in whiskey and ammunition was flourishing, and that the Crees were accused of frequent thefts of horses. He recommended the use of military force to drive the intruders back to Canada, but General Terry demurred, awaiting Sheridan's approval.[152]

The winter hunt for the Indians of Fort Peck Agency was a failure. Agent Porter reported that they had taken few robes, and that they had taken most of their meat from the carcasses of buffalo killed by white hunters.[153]

It was not until March that troops were again sent out from Fort Assiniboine to break up the Métis settlements and usher them and the Canadian Indians back across the boundary. The expedition, consisting of some three hundred men, was prompted not out of concern for the interests of the reservation Indians, but in response to reports of the intruders' "hostile attitude." The expedition had the desired effect, and the intruders were once more reported to have returned to Canada. But on March 31, Captain Read informed departmental headquarters that only a portion of the Métis had left, and that the Crees were still on Beaver Creek. Military scouts in early May failed to find any of the Métis or Crees.[154]

In June there were reports that two hundred lodges of Crees had started out from Fort Walsh to hunt buffalo, and would likely come south to the Milk River. On June 27, General Terry ordered a detachment of two troops of cavalry and four of infantry to march from Fort Assiniboine and establish a temporary summer camp on the south side of the Milk, near the big bend. Their purpose was to warn Canadian Indians and Métis to return to their own country, and to force them to do so if they refused. The detachment, headed by Captain E. R. Kellogg, went into camp on the Milk a mile above Medicine Lodge Creek on July 9. On the way there, they met a party of Crees and Métis hunting buffalo. When told to leave, "they refused and were insolent." As the column marched toward them, they fled; the soldiers overtook them 4 or 5 miles north of the river, confiscated their weapons and cartridges as well as some horses "presumed stolen," and sent them across the line.[155]

Early in June, Agent Porter called the agency chiefs together and informed them that they must take their people out on the hunt. The problem of food shortage at the agency was, as usual, critical. They went, although, Porter wrote, many were reluctant to do so. The grass west of the agency and as far as Milk River was burnt off; the buffalo herds were small and scattered. Their crops failed from drought. In October, Captain Read commented that "the buffalo are becoming more and more scarce every day." The captain complained that the amount of food provided by the Commissioner of Indian Affairs for the Indians of Fort Peck Agency averaged a mere 30 ounces per person per week, or about 97 pounds per person per year. Combined with the scarcity of buffalo and the failure of the crops, the situation for the winter looked grim. General Sheridan wrote that the effect would be to starve the Indians at Fort Peck: "The practical result of the Commissioner's order will be a cruelty to individuals who have shown a desire to help themselves but who as yet have been unable to do so."[156]

With the arrival of winter and the troops back in quarters at Fort Assiniboine, Canadian Indians and Métis began once again to enter the reservation in search of buffalo. Captain Read sent out Sergeants Neeland and Bobst, with two Indian scouts, to investigate. On December 2, they found a camp of Métis and Crees near Tom Campbell's house on Milk River; the Canadians fled with their horses, leaving behind fifty-eight Red River carts and harnesses, two hundred hides, and sixteen thousand pounds of meat, as well as other property. Scout Culbertson reported that not only was the Milk River country overrun with Crees and Métis, but that white hunters were also nearby.[157]

Captain Read sent out repeated detachments during the winter to drive away intruders. On December 21, at the request of Agent Porter, Read himself, with Sergeants Neeland and Bobst and Yellow Eagle, an Indian scout, left Camp Poplar River for the Milk River. Although they found the trails of many Canadian Indians, and on Christmas day surprised and scattered a Métis camp, most of the intruders were back over the Canadian line. Read heard that they would return to the reservation after New Year's: "They must come to buffalo or starve." Read wrote: "What few buffalo are left are on the North [side] of the Missouri and on Indian reservations. The white hunters from the south and the half Breeds and Indians from the North are constantly trespassing upon the reservation." The effect on the reservation Indians was devastating: "The Indians who alone are entitled to hunt in this locality are kept out of it from fear of a collision with the intruders and are themselves suffering for food." Agent Porter was equally impressed with the gravity of the situation. He wrote to Captain Read on January 5, 1883, officially requesting that all the intruders be driven from the reservation.[158]

Despite the good intentions of military officers in the field, the army would not authorize a full-scale campaign against the intruders. Writing on January 3 in reply to a formal request from the Secretary of the Interior that something be done to protect the interests of the reservation Indians in northeastern Montana, General Sherman commented:

> We have not troops enough to follow these Arabs of the Prairie nor are the laws in force there specific enough for us to use violence. Indeed it is the judgment of most military men that the buffaloes are doomed and the sooner they are gone & replaced by meat cattle, the sooner will the Indians be found to rear cattle and labor for their own subsistence.
>
> The buffaloes are ferae naturae, the property of all mankind, the whites as well as the Indians. The hides are worth from 5 to 8 dollars a piece, and this will tempt hunters to kill and cure the hides as robes. What right have we to prevent the killing of these buffalos? — except to remove trespassers on Indian Reservations.
>
> The Indian Reservations north of the Missouri are not well defined, and our troops cannot tell what is, and what is not Indian Territory.

General Sherman, who had not approved of settling the Indians on reservations in this part of Montana, was not willing to send troops out into the severe winter weather to protect them now. The Secretary of War commented in his reply to the Secretary of the Interior that after a conversation with General Sherman, he was convinced that to send troops on a winter campaign in Montana "would be unjustifiable cruelty to our soldiers."[159]

Small military detachments continued to make forays from Camp Poplar River and Fort Assiniboine to keep reservation intruders in check. In January, Captain Read made a tour of Milk River and reported that the buffalo had moved north and were located on Frenchman's Creek, near the Canadian border. The Métis were camped in Canada, at Wood Mountain, and were sending their hunting parties out against the herd. The captain found no intruders on the reservation with the exception of four white hunters, whom he brought back to Camp Poplar River. Late in February, Scout Culbertson surprised and disarmed a camp of

Yellow Eagle and His Two Wives. Yanktonai. Read Collection 1881.3.136.8.

nine lodges belonging to Big Bear's Canadian Crees. He reported that about two weeks earlier there had been thirty lodges of Crees at the big bend of Milk River; they were ordered away by troops from Fort Assiniboine. Read sent out a detachment to aid Culbertson; following orders from department headquarters, the soldiers returned the Crees' weapons and sent them across the boundary. The detachment followed them by wagon as far as possible "to protect them from the Yanktonais who were determined to kill them."[160]

The winter of 1882–1883 was a cold and snowy one. The Indians of Fort Peck Agency spent the season camping along the Missouri River west of Wolf Point. From this location they could hunt buffalo on the Milk and exchange the hides at the trading houses south of the Missouri, just across the reservation boundary. When they returned to the agency in the spring, they planted some one thousand acres. Then they went off on their summer hunt, which proved a failure. Back at the agency, they found that their crops had again been destroyed by drought.

During the summer, Agent Porter was replaced by S. E. Snider. The new agent was not a newcomer to Fort Peck, however. He had spent the previous two years as superintendent of the agency boarding school. In his annual report, written in August, Snider stated: "The buffalo are a thing of the past in this Northwest. Neither the Department nor the Indians anticipated such a sudden disappearance of the game; therefore no adequate provision has been made for their subsistence during the present fiscal year." The situation had reached crisis proportions: "The wolf of hunger is in every lodge." Captain Read, in his annual report dated in September, corroborated Snider's portrayal. The Indians, he wrote, "are in a most deplorable condition with starvation staring them in the face." Supplies at the agency would last them only two months. "The Indians fully understand this, and many of them have gone to Standing Rock in the hopes of doing better."[161]

While the present outlook was grim, Agent Snider expressed hope for the future. He looked to irrigation as the key to successful agriculture in eastern Montana. The Indians were well disposed and, the younger men at least, "show an inclination to abandon the former customs and habits of their forefathers and adopt the better ways of the white man." They appreciated the importance of agriculture for securing their future; for them it was no longer a disgrace to wear white men's clothes and work in the fields. But when Inspector C. H. Howard visited the agency in October, he was not so sanguine about progress. Howard was outraged to learn that Agent Porter had allowed the Assiniboines and Sioux to hold their Sun Dances during the previous summer. "It leaves the Indians in an excited state," he wrote, "inflames all the old passions and carries the whole tribe back irresistibly to savagery." Moreover, the inspector complained, "The medicine men keep up their incantations every night. Their drums can be heard far into the night. Their influence is solidly against all civilized habits and steady work." The old economy of buffalo hunting had become a thing of the past; now the Bureau of Indian Affairs wanted to root out the religion and customs of old times and transform the people into agrarian citizens, Christian in belief and civilized in habit.[162]

Agent Porter had maintained excellent rapport with Captain Read, providing a model instance of cooperation between the civilian and military branches of administering an Indian agency. Agent Snider, on the other hand, was antagonistic toward the military from the start. In his first annual report to the Commissioner of Indian Affairs he suggested that the military presence was demoralizing to the Indians, and he accused the soldiers of prostituting the Indian women. The sale of intoxicating liquors was a further demoralizing force: "Where and how it gets into the Indian camps seems to be, as yet, an impenetrable mystery." But in a letter to the Commissioner of Indian Affairs dated September 7, Agent Snider's reference to "drunken soldiers" around the agency and the Indian camps left little doubt as to his opinion of the source of at least some of this alcohol. The agent requested that Camp Poplar River be abandoned on the grounds that it was no longer required for the security of the agency.[163]

In early October, Captain Read reported that nearly all the Indians had left the agency, gone south of the Missouri, and were camping along the Yellowstone. Black Catfish's band of Yanktonais had crossed the Yellowstone, intending to hunt on the Little Missouri on their way to Standing Rock. In November, Scout Culbertson was sent out to notify Indians leaving the agency without permission that if they did not return, soldiers would be sent after them. The Indians apparently returned, since there is no record of troop movements from Camp Poplar River at that time.[164]

The gloomiest predictions of hardship came true at Fort Peck during the winter of 1883–84. In January, Captain Read visited the Assiniboines at Wolf Point, in the company of Agent Snider, to investigate rumors of starvation. They visited most of the families living around the sub-agency. The captain reported: "In one [household] we found a good supply of horse meat, but with this exception, not one of them had a single mouthful of anything to eat, as we learned from personal examination, and all stated that they had had nothing for from three to four days." Rations were issued weekly, and the amount was sufficient to last for only two or three days. "Some said that members of the family had died of starvation," Read wrote. The Yanktonais camped around the Fort Peck Agency were found to be only slightly less destitute. The captain concluded his report to departmental headquarters with this plea:

> I could not sit quietly by and see these people starve without reporting it and feel that I had done my duty, and if not strictly within my province to make such a report, I do it in the cause of humanity, and in the hope that in some way the subject will be brought to the attention of the authorities that something will be done to alleviate the sufferings of these wretched people.[165]

Captain Read's letter had a good effect. Forwarded through proper channels, it eventually reached the Commissioner of Indian Affairs. A special appropriation of funds to feed the Fort Peck Indians finally solved the problem, and in the meantime, disaster was averted by General Terry's directive to Read to issue subsistence supplies from Camp Poplar River as necessary to prevent actual starvation.[166]

As they faced the new year, 1884, the Sioux and Assiniboines of Fort Peck found themselves in a period of baffling and disorienting change. Although the Bureau of Indian Affairs would never again force the Indians at Fort Peck to endure a winter of starvation like the one they had just passed, neither would they again have the opportunity to provide for themselves by hunting. In the summer of

Fort Abraham Lincoln. View by David F. Barry. Courtesy State Historical Society of North Dakota, no. C-247.

1884, the Bureau of Indian Affairs' ban on the Sun Dance was enforced at Fort Peck; neither tribe held their annual sacred ceremonies. As much as anything else, this interference with their religious life signaled the enormity of the changes that were upon them and the gravity of the decisions that they would have to make in the years ahead in order to create a life for themselves on the reservation. Encroached upon from every side, in 1888 their reservation was reduced to a fraction of the lands they had hunted over for the past half-century, and the days of traveling in tribal groups through the country, guided by familiar landmarks, were over.[167]

On June 16, 1884, Captain Read and his two companies of the Eleventh Infantry boarded the steamer *Helena* at Camp Poplar River and set out for Fort Abraham Lincoln, three days downriver. Camp Poplar River had already fulfilled its intended mission and might easily have been abandoned, but the wheels of the military bureaucracy turn slowly, and the post continued in operation until 1893, when the flag was lowered for a last time and the soldiers marched away for good.[168]

Changing conditions on the western frontier affected whites as much as Indians. In 1884 Fort Abraham Lincoln was no longer essential to military operations in Dakota. But situated at the juncture of the Northern Pacific Railroad and the Missouri River, the fort oversaw an important ordnance depot; this, and the political pressure of the neighboring city of Bismarck, which profited from servicing the post, were the main reasons for its continued existence. First established in 1872 on a bluff overlooking the west bank of the Missouri about 4½ miles south of Bismarck, it was originally an infantry post named Fort McKeen. In 1873, the post became regimental headquarters for the Seventh Cavalry, new facilities were constructed in the bottomlands south of the infantry buildings, and the name was changed to Fort Abraham Lincoln. Protection of the survey crews for the Northern Pacific Railroad was the original purpose for locating a military installation near the growing city of Bismarck, east-river terminus of the Northern Pacific Railway and, since 1883, capital of Dakota Territory. After Custer's death, the military strength of Fort Abraham Lincoln reached nearly nine hundred men as reinforcements were brought to Dakota from other areas of the country. When Captain Read was transferred there in 1884, the command at Fort Abraham Lincoln had declined to fewer than two hundred men, the cavalry were gone, and the post was garrisoned by two companies of the Eleventh Infantry and two companies of the Seventeenth.[169]

In August of 1886, after two uneventful years at Fort Abraham Lincoln, the two companies of the Eleventh Infantry were transferred some 70 miles downriver to Fort Yates, the military post at Standing Rock Agency. Although the Indians there gave the army very little trouble, Fort Yates had developed into a major military installation, with a garrison in 1886-87 of nearly three hundred men. The concentration of personnel resulted from the abandonment of many smaller posts and the consolidation of troops at larger ones. Once again, O. B. Read found himself at Standing Rock Agency.[170]

Conditions at Standing Rock had changed a great deal since Captain Read's departure in 1877. In the aftermath of the fighting with the army, the Sioux population had sorted itself out at the various agencies, reuniting social groups that for twenty years or more had been separated over the issue of dealing with the white men. In 1886 the Commissioner of Indian Affairs set Thursday, September 30,

Fort Yates. Parade Ground and Officers' Row. Photo by David F. Barry. Courtesy State Historical Society of North Dakota, no. C-246.

as the date to begin a definitive census of the Great Sioux Reservation, directing agents to ensure that all the Indians under their jurisdiction were assembled at their respective agencies. The commissioner very pragmatically authorized a three-day feast to motivate the Indians to cooperate. The results of the census were reflected in the agents' annual reports for 1887. The total population of Standing Rock was 4,545 individuals: 705 Upper Yanktonais, 1,400 Lower Yanktonais, 1,736 Hunkpapas, 584 Blackfeet, and 120 mixed bloods. Many of these Sioux people had been resident at Standing Rock since its establishment; others had returned there after surrendering to the army in Montana. Sitting Bull and his band had been returned to the agency in 1883 after two years of life at Fort Randall as prisoners of war. Wiser and sadder, the chief accepted the inevitable and actively sought to adapt his people to reservation life.[171]

After a succession of agents whose careers at Standing Rock had each ended in scandal or suspicion, Agent James McLaughlin had taken over in 1881 and had provided a consistency of direction to running agency affairs. The Indians had abandoned their large tipi encampments near the agency and settled in communities along the Missouri, Cannon Ball, and Grand rivers, each settlement representing a band. Tipis were fast giving way to log houses, at least for winter habitation. The Yanktonais remained in the northern portion of the area, the Hunkpapas and Blackfeet to the south. By 1886 they had begun to engage seriously in agriculture, cultivating a total area of 3,500 acres. Unfortunately, the crops that summer were largely destroyed by hail and drought. Despite the loss, McLaughlin reported that the Indians were not discouraged; the crops of neighboring white farmers fared no better, if not worse. The Indians supplemented their income by cutting some 1,500 cords of dead and fallen cottonwood, which they sold to whites for an average of four dollars per cord.[172]

Education was flourishing at Standing Rock. Over a thousand students attended the two government boarding schools, five government day schools, and one mission school. An additional fifty-four students were attending off-reservation boarding schools.[173]

The effects of Christian missionary groups were strongly felt at Standing Rock. The Roman Catholics, to whom the agency had been assigned under the Grant Peace Policy, had three resident priests in 1886 (five in 1887), who operated four mission stations. Many of the Indians were baptized in the church, and each year a few marriages were solemnized. The Benedictine fathers had run a boarding school at Standing Rock since their arrival in 1877; although the school was transferred to government control in 1883, it continued to be staffed largely by Catholic religious. The official policy established under the Grant administration to limit missionary activities at each agency to a single religious denomination was rescinded in 1882, allowing other churches to establish missions at Standing Rock. While living in the prison camp at Fort Randall, Sitting Bull's son had joined the Episcopal Church, and the chief thereafter was kindly disposed toward the "white robes," as the Sioux called the Episcopals to distinguish them from the "black robes" (Catholics). The Protestant Episcopal Church established its first mission station on Oak Creek; in 1887 this station, St. Elizabeth's, was headed by the Rev. Philip J. Deloria, a Yankton Sioux who had been ordained as an Episcopal deacon (later priest). St. Elizabeth's developed into a thriving boarding school to which Deloria gave his life's work. The Dakota Mission of the American Missionary Association established a mission station on Grand River, under the direction of Thomas L. Riggs. The Indians' acceptance of Christian religions may have had more to do with the appeal of the organizational and social aspects of church life than with religious belief; whatever the cause, Agent McLaughlin welcomed it as a sign of the Indians' advancement toward becoming "a Christian body of useful citizens."[174]

McLaughlin was proud of his Indian police force, consisting of about thirty men. The authority of the police was sustained by a Court of Indian Offenses, which met biweekly at the agency. John Grass, the Blackfeet chief, served as chief judge, and the two officers of the police force served as associate judges. The court was empowered to levy fines and prison sentences. Surviving court records from this period reveal that most cases involved relations between the sexes. For example, on January 13, 1886, the court found three parties guilty of crimes: one man was fined $10 for deserting his wife; another was fined $10 and sentenced to eighteen days' confinement for deserting his wife and stealing someone else's wife; a third man was fined $20 for "Returning to Divorced wife." Polygyny, an acceptable social practice for men of high status in traditional Sioux culture, became a crime. On August 29, 1885, a man was fined $16.50 and given five days' confinement for taking a second wife. That same day, a man was fined $4 and given five days' confinement for "Insulting his Sister-in-law." (Obligatory sexual joking between siblings-in-law of the opposite sex was an integral part of proper Sioux kinship etiquette, but under the new system it became a crime.) The court also enforced respect for the law, as in the case of a man who was fined $2 on September 30, 1885, for "Disrespectful language to Police Judges."[175]

The police and court system functioned very much like

Gall. Hunkpapa. Read Collection 1881.3.136.3.

the soldier lodge in traditional Sioux political life. Certainly, McLaughlin played the role of chief, but so did John Grass and the other judges. The success of the system seems to have been a sharing of authority between the agent and some of the leading Indians. In his autobiography, McLaughlin wrote of the efforts he made to develop friendships with Grass, Gall, and Crow King — all important leaders. By the time Sitting Bull returned in 1883, the system was already well on its way to becoming routinized, and although McLaughlin seems to have at first attempted to integrate Sitting Bull into it, he soon gave him up as "non-progressive." In his annual report for 1887, McLaughlin boasted that the Court of Indian Offenses had extended its authority even over Sitting Bull:

> This court is no respecter of persons, as, having recently had the conceited and obstinate Sitting Bull before them for assault, the tomahawk with which he attacked his antagonist Shell King, was confiscated by the court, as was also Shell King's knife, with which he had attempted to strike Sitting Bull.

McLaughlin may have considered that such authority over

chiefs was novel to the reservation situation, but the old soldier lodges had always extended their authority to all offenders, regardless of status.[176]

The garrison at Fort Yates during the mid-1880s was little more active than that at Fort Abraham Lincoln. During the year that he was stationed at Fort Yates, Captain Read served as the military inspector of annuities and supplies at Standing Rock Agency. The army had the responsibility of detailing officers to witness the delivery of goods to the agency and the issue of annuities to Indians by the civilian agents of the Bureau of Indian Affairs, a formality intended to check possible fraud. This brought Read into regular contact with the agency and apparently allowed him to come to know some of the Indians well. Surely, he renewed acquaintances with many of the Hunkpapas he had first met when they surrendered to the army in Montana several years before. Gall had developed from an outspoken partisan of the hostiles to an equally outspoken advocate for the whites and for the organization of agency life at Standing Rock. He allowed his picture to be taken on several occasions by David F. Barry, the Bismarck photographer, and the chief did a lively business by selling copies of his likeness. There are two of these photos in the Read collection, along with a typed copy of a letter the captain received from Gall after leaving Dakota Territory for far-off New York. It reads as follows:

Standing Rock, D.T.
March 31, 1888

Capt. O. B. Read

Dear Sir:

As I have the opportunity I thought to drop you a few lines and inform you that I am still among the living and sincerely hope that these few lines may find you the same. When you was stationed here every month, as we came up to receive our rations, you always gave me everything that I could wish for, and since you have left, I must say that I have missed you very much, and Cap't I don't think that I shall ever forget you. I have remembered a great many times since, Dear Brother, as I am not able to do my own writing I will have to close, by saying Good-bye and my kindest regards to yourself and Mrs. Read and the children.

I remain as ever
Your friend,
Gall — Pizi

Appended to the letter is a note that attests to the sincerity of Gall's friendship: "When the Read family left Dakota territory Gall rode three days and nights on his pony to say good-bye to [the] family."[177]

As the Sioux who had been at war with the United States returned to their agencies in the period from 1876 to 1881, they faced a world in which many of their fundamental understandings no longer held true. Some of the people clung fiercely to the old beliefs and old religious practices; others rejected them and embraced the religious beliefs and practices of the white men's Christianity. Most Sioux, like most people everywhere, made no unshakeable commitment and embraced something of both religious traditions, making sense of the world as they saw it. Spiritual by nature, the Sioux sought meaning in the ways of the white men just as they did in their old ways.

The government, through its representatives — the Indian agents and military officers — pressured the Sioux, like other tribes, to abandon all their traditional ways. Most disturbing to the whites were the old religious practices, potent symbols of what whites feared most: the heathen savage, fierce, primordial, unremitting. During the 1880s the Sun Dance was outlawed; those found guilty of participating in or attending the ceremony were punished by having their rations cut off. To the Sioux, the suppression of the Sun Dance was a significant spiritual blow, for the Sun Dance was an annual religious festival that embodied the power and spirit of the Sioux as a people. Babies had their ears pierced that they might hear as human beings and be members of the tribe; young men and women met during the big encampment, which provided a time for courting and the arranging of marriages; both men and women participated in the Sun Dance itself in sacrifice that their prayers be heard and that the people prosper; religious dreamers performed their special ceremonies to cure the sick and bring blessings on the people. In short, the Sun Dance renewed all life in a spiritual sense. After public celebration of the Sun Dance was prohibited, life at the agencies ceased to have any meaning derived from religious traditions; the people were cut off from their past.

Also prohibited were the give-aways of property held a year after a person's death to insure that the soul of the deceased was properly ushered to the land of the dead. Judged inimical to household economy, the practice was outlawed without regard to its moral implications. Similarly, dancing of all kinds was frowned upon, the Indian agents setting the days when such social celebrations could occur. The effect of these measures was to drive native Sioux religious practices into the sphere of private family life, weakening the effectiveness of traditional religion to draw the Sioux together as a people.[178]

In 1888, only a year after Read's departure from Dakota Territory, commissioners from Washington again visited the Sioux, this time to seek their assent to surrendering 9,000,000 acres of land, breaking up the Great Sioux Reservation and accepting in its place five smaller ones centered around the old agencies: Standing Rock, Cheyenne River, Pine Ridge, Rosebud, and Lower Brulé. Whites in Dakota Territory saw the Sioux reservation as a vast barrier to progress, whose opening to homesteading would attract more settlers, allow the development of roads and railroads, and bring increased economic prosperity. Adhering now to the treaty of 1868, the government sought to record the signatures of three-fourths of the adult Sioux males before the land cession could be ratified by Congress. The Sioux had no desire to sell the land, their last asset, and stood firm. In 1889 another group of commissioners came, headed this time by General Crook. They cajoled and threatened the Sioux by turns, and when the commissioners had completed their work, they left with more signatures than needed to carry the agreement. The question of what had changed the Indians' minds seems not to have concerned government officials at the time. It was the year of statehood for North and South Dakota, Montana, and Washington, and western boomerism paid no heed to the concerns of Indians. Today, fair assessment of the Crook Commission accuses it of fraud and misrepresentation, sometimes intentional, sometimes not. The commissioners had been sent out to do a job and they had done it.[179]

Only months after the commissioners left, an economy-minded Bureau of Indian Affairs made severe cuts in the funds for rations on the new Sioux reservations. The Indians soon felt the pinch of hunger, then faced actual starvation. The situation was grim, as it had been during the year the buffalo disappeared. The reservation Sioux had progressed in the ways of the whites; they had embraced the white men's ways of making a living and they had embraced the white men's religions, but rather than life improving for their children, conditions only worsened and the children died of hunger and disease.

During that cold and hungry winter of 1889–90, word reached the Sioux on their reservations of a messiah, an Indian Christ come to earth to rescue the Indian people from the wrongs they had suffered at the hands of the whites. The spirits of the dead would return, and a new earth would be created where all would live eternally in a paradise of buffalo and other game. If the people would dance the Ghost Dance, praying for the return of the ghosts, the day of deliverance would come. The Sioux and many other Plains tribes quickly adopted the new ceremony, sending delegates to Nevada to learn from Wovoka, the prophet himself, the teachings of the new religion. Perhaps it would be the salvation of the Indian people.

Agent McLaughlin saw in the Ghost Dance only the desperation of a people driven by hunger and despair; let alone, the movement would die on its own when the new world failed to materialize. But the white settlers of the Dakotas were nervous about Indians dancing; in the old pioneer tales, whenever Indians danced, war and pillage followed. They clamored for military protection.

Responding to public pressure, the Commissioner of Indian Affairs authorized the arrest of the Ghost Dance leaders. On December 15, 1890, Sitting Bull was shot and killed by the Standing Rock Indian Police as they attempted to arrest him. Panic spread among the Ghost Dancers. A band of Minneconjous from Cheyenne River, led by Big Foot, fled south to seek refuge among the Oglalas at Pine Ridge Agency. Intercepted by the Seventh Cavalry, they went into camp on Wounded Knee Creek the evening of December 28. The next morning, while the army attempted to disarm them, a shot rang out and the soldiers turned their fire on the Indian men, women, and children, chasing them along the crooked creek bed. A count of bodies numbered 146 Indian dead; the actual total was undoubtedly higher. The massacre at Wounded Knee formed the final chapter in the history of the Sioux wars with the United States Army. Neglected in the literature that recounts the military events of this long conflict between the Sioux and the United States are the moral issues raised by this unhappy period of history.[180]

After the bloodshed at Wounded Knee, few of the Sioux people maintained faith in the Ghost Dance. It was for them a kind of spiritual betrayal. Like the Oglala holy man, Black Elk, who regretted in the long years following 1890 that he had relied on his Ghost Dance visions instead of the visions derived from old Sioux culture that he had received as a boy, many of the Sioux sensed that the Ghost Dance had betrayed the old ways. Some of the religious leaders of the people faced the future with equanimity, unable to abandon the past, but also unwilling to bequeath it to their children. Little Wound, the Oglala chief, voiced this sentiment to James R. Walker, the medical doctor at Pine Ridge who, at the turn of the century, devoted himself to making a record of the traditional Oglala religion. The chief had completed telling Walker sacred secrets that he would not pass down to younger members of his own tribe, and he said:

> My friend, I have told you the secrets of the *Hunkayapi*. I fear that I have done wrong. But the spirits of old times do not come to me anymore. Another spirit has come, the Great Spirit of the white man. I do not know him. I do not know how to call him to help me. I have done him no harm, and he should do me no harm. The old life is gone, and I cannot be young again.[181]

In the years following Wounded Knee, the Sioux experienced their first real encounter with the modern world. The old ways truly were gone forever, and soon all those who had lived those days were also passed beyond. The remembered past, a legacy of legend, history, and myth, departs ever more from the past as it was lived. The Sioux, like all other Americans, have faced the modern world sometimes boldly, sometimes timidly. They have fought in America's wars, conquered modern technology, and transformed many of the values from the past into social practices for the present. Old customs like the Sun Dance live again, replete with new meanings and new relevance. Indian people return to their past to make sense of the present, to answer the gnawing questions of self-identity and self-significance. At the same time, non-Indians, too, are drawn to the Indian past, a way of life tied intimately to the American land and rooted in the primordial concerns of spiritual strength and harmony. The fundamental humanity that lies beyond our Western cultural heritage is as fascinating to us today as it was repellent to our progenitors of the last century. Through the material remains of that way of life — collections like that of Captain Read, embodiments of Plains Indian tradition — we can all seek understanding of the past, strength for the present, and wisdom for the future.

Acknowledgements

The author wishes to acknowledge with gratitude the help of the following individuals, each of whom contributed to the work on which this essay is based: Loretta K. Fowler, Steven D. Frangos, David R. Miller, Douglas R. Parks, Joanna C. Scherer, and S. Douglas Youngkin.

Special Abbreviations

AG	Adjutant General
AAG	Assistant Adjutant General
ARCIA	Annual Report of the Commissioner of Indian Affairs
ARSW	Annual Report of the Secretary of War
CIA	Commissioner of Indian Affairs
LRCIA	Letters Received by the Commissioner of Indian Affairs
M	Microcopy No.
NARS	National Archives and Record Service
RG	Record Group No.

Notes

1. Francis Paul Prucha, *The Great Father: The United States Government and the American Indians*, 2 vols. (Lincoln: University of Nebraska Press, 1984), provides the best and most thorough introduction to the history of relations between the United States and the American Indian tribes. The most useful introductions to eastern Sioux history are Roy W. Meyer, *History of the Santee Sioux: United States Indian Policy on Trial* (Lincoln: University of Nebraska Press, 1967) and Gary Clayton Anderson, *Kinsmen of Another Kind: Dakota-White Relations in the Upper Mississippi Valley, 1650–1862* (Lincoln: University of Nebraska Press, 1984); for introductions to western Sioux history, see George E. Hyde, *Red Cloud's Folk: A History of the Oglala Sioux Indians*, rev. ed. (Norman: University of Oklahoma Press, 1957) and James C. Olson, *Red Cloud and the Sioux Problem* (Lincoln: University of Nebraska Press, 1965); for the best introductions to the military encounters between the United States and the Sioux, see Robert M. Utley, *Frontiersmen in Blue: The United States Army and the Indian, 1848–1865* (New York: Macmillan Publishing, 1967) and Utley, *Frontier Regulars: The United States Army and the Indian, 1866–1891* (New York: Macmillan Publishing, 1973). For perspectives on changing religious values among the western Sioux, see James R. Walker, *Lakota Belief and Ritual*, ed. Raymond J. DeMallie and Elaine A. Jahner (Lincoln: University of Nebraska Press, 1980) and Raymond J. DeMallie, "The Lakota Ghost Dance: An Ethnohistorical Account," *Pacific Historical Review* 51 (1982): 385–405.

2. Richard Irving Dodge, *The Plains of the Great West and Their Inhabitants...* (New York: G.P. Putnam's Sons, 1877), p. 3; *Proceedings of a Board of Commissioners to Negotiate a Treaty or Treaties with the Hostile Indians of the Upper Missouri* (Washington, D.C.: GPO, 1865), p. 25.

3. Dee Brown, *Bury My Heart at Wounded Knee: An Indian History of the American West* (New York: Holt, Rinehart & Winston, 1970) and Evan S. Connell, *Son of the Morning Star* (New York: Harper & Row, 1984) are the best of the recent popular histories of the Indian wars.
   Turner's "The Significance of the Frontier in American History," presented in 1893 to the American Historical Association, is reprinted in Frederick Jackson Turner, *The Frontier in American History* (New York: Holt, 1920), pp. 1–38.

4. See the entry "Dakota" in Frederick Webb Hodge, ed., *Handbook of American Indians North of Mexico*, Smithsonian Institution, Bureau of American Ethnology, Bulletin 30, 2 vols. (Washington, D.C.: GPO, 1907, 1910) 1:376–80. Material on Sioux social and linguistic divisions draws from Raymond J. DeMallie, "Teton Sioux Kinship and Social Organization" (Ph.D. diss., University of Chicago, 1971).

5. The earliest full discussion of the Seven Fireplaces appears in William H. Keating, *Narrative of an Expedition to the Sources of St. Peter's River, Lake Winnepeek, Lake of the Woods, &c., Performed in the Year 1823 by the Order of the Hon. J. C. Calhoun, Secretary of War, under command of Stephen H. Long, U.S.T.E.*, 2 vols., rpt. ed. (Minneapolis: Ross and Haines, 1959) 1:392–404.

6. For lists of Sioux social divisions, see Stephen Return Riggs, *Dakota Grammar, Texts, and Ethnography*, ed. James Owen Dorsey, Contributions to North American Ethnology 9 (Washington, D.C.: GPO, 1893), pp. 156–64.

7. For material on Sioux social and political organization, see Jeanette Mirsky, "The Dakota," in Margaret Mead, ed., *Cooperation and Competition in Primitive Society* (New York: McGraw-Hill, 1937), pp. 382–427; Ella Deloria, *Speaking of Indians* (New York: Friendship Press, 1944), pp. 24–49; and James R. Walker, *Lakota Society*, ed. Raymond J. DeMallie (Lincoln: University of Nebraska Press, 1982), pp. 3–67.

8. For the "soldier lodge," or *akíc'ita*, see Riggs, *Dakota Grammar, Texts, and Ethnography*, pp. 195–96, 200–202, and Walker, *Lakota Society*, pp. 28–34.

9. The best recent study of the fur trade and its effects on Plains Indians is Arthur J. Ray, *Indians in the Fur Trade: Their Role as Trappers, Hunters, and Middlemen in the Lands South of Hudson Bay, 1660–1870* (Toronto: University of Toronto Press, 1974). For the role of the eastern Sioux in the fur trade, see Anderson, *Kinsmen of Another Kind*, chaps. 2–4.

10. Texts of treaties between the Sioux and the United States are printed in Charles J. Kappler, comp. and ed., *Indian Affairs, Laws and Treaties*, 4 vols. (Washington, D.C.: GPO, 1904–1929).

11. Hyde, *Red Cloud's Folk*, chaps. 1–4.

12. Meyer, *History of the Santee Sioux*, chaps. 2–3; Anderson, *Kinsmen of Another Kind*, chap. 7.

13. Meyer, *History of the Santee Sioux*, chaps. 4–5; Anderson, *Kinsmen of Another Kind*, chaps. 9–11; Hyde, *Red Cloud's Folk*, pp. 64–67; Raymond J. DeMallie, "Touching the Pen: Plains Indian Treaty Councils in Ethnohistorical Perspective," in Frederick Luebke, ed., *Ethnicity on the Great Plains* (Lincoln: University of Nebraska Press, 1980), pp. 38–53.

14. Edwin Denig, *Indian Tribes of the Upper Missouri*, ed. J. N. B. Hewitt, Smithsonian Institution, Bureau of American Ethnology, Annual Report 46 (Washington, D.C.: GPO, 1930), p. 397. Material from the 1865 treaty commission is taken from *Proceedings of a Board of Commissioners*; quotation from Two Lances, p. 58; from Running Antelope, p. 102; from Lone Horn, p. 24.

15. *Missouri Republican*, November 9, 1851, quoted in DeMallie, "Touching the Pen," p. 45.

16. *Proceedings of a Board of Commissioners*, pp. 25, 29.

17. Hyde, *Red Cloud's Folk*, pp. 72–81.

18. Meyer, *History of the Santee Sioux*, pp. 97–101; Anderson, *Kinsmen of Another Kind*, pp. 216–21.

19. Meyer, *History of the Santee Sioux*, chaps. 6–7.

20. Donald J. Berthrong, *The Southern Cheyennes* (Norman: University of Oklahoma Press, 1963), pp. 207–23; Father Peter John Powell, *People of the Sacred Mountain: A History of the Northern Cheyenne Chiefs and Warrior Societies 1830–1879 With an Epilogue 1969–1974*, 2 vols. (New York: Harper & Row, 1981) 1:299–310.

21. Prucha, *The Great Father* 1: chaps. 19–21.

22. Hyde, *Red Cloud's Folk*, pp. 140–49; Olson, *Red Cloud and the Sioux Problem*, chap. 4.

23. Olson, *Red Cloud and the Sioux Problem*, chap. 5.

24. Prucha, *The Great Father* 1:527–33.

25. The text of the 1868 treaty is printed in Kappler, *Indian Affairs* 2:998–1007, and the text of the treaty (without the names of the signers) also appears in Olson, *Red Cloud and the Sioux Problem*, pp. 341–49.

26. Olson, *Red Cloud and the Sioux Problem*, p. 78.

27. ARCIA 1869:27–29; Hyde, *Red Cloud's Folk*, chaps. 10–11; Olson, *Red Cloud and the Sioux Problem*, chaps. 7–9.

28. Prucha, *The Great Father* 1:512–19.

29. Lt. G. Cusick to Lt. J. M. Marshall, Nov. 14, 1868, Fort Buford, Letters Sent, RG 393, NARS.

30. Alf. Sully, Helena, M.T., to CIA, Sept. 23, 1869, in ARCIA 1869:289–93; A. S. Read, Fort Browning, M.T., to Supt. Sully, Sept. 12, 1869, Records of the Montana Superintendency, RG 75, NARS, M833, roll 2:373–76.

31. Bvt. Brig. Gen. Henry A. Morrow to AAG, Dept. of Dakota, Sept. 8 and Sept. 14, 1869, Fort Buford, Letters Sent, RG 393, NARS.

32. For relations among the Sioux bands, see Rev. Samuel William Pond, "The Dakotas or Sioux in Minnesota as They were in 1834," *Collections of the Minnesota Historical Society* 12 (St. Paul, 1908), pp. 320–22.
   For the 1868 treaty commission, see *Papers Relating to Talks and Councils Held with the Indians in Dakota and Montana Territories in the Years 1866–1869* (Washington, D.C.: GPO, 1910).

33. *Papers Relating to Talks and Councils*, p. 98.

34. James Owen Dorsey, *Siouan Sociology*, Smithsonian Institution, Bureau of [American] Ethnology, Annual Report 15 (Washington, D.C.: GPO, 1897), p. 218, reports the Sioux tradition for the origin of the Assiniboines.
   For the 1866 peace commission's meeting with Medicine Bear and Red Stone, see "Proceedings of a Board of Commissioners Appointed to Negotiate a Treaty or Treaties with the Hostile Indians of the Upper Missouri, [1866]," RG 75, NARS, entries for July 7 and 13.

35. Lt. Col. Henry A. Morrow to AAG, Dept. of Dakota, Oct. 28, 1869, and reply, Nov. 2, 1869, Fort Buford, Letters Received, RG 393, NARS; copy of letter from Col. D. S. Stanley, Fort Sully, to AAG, Dept. of Dakota, Feb. 12, 1870, ibid.

36. Lt. Col. Henry A. Morrow, [Memorandum on] "Indians," June 14, 1870, Fort Buford, Letters Received, RG 393, NARS; Acting Agent A. S. Read, Gros Ventres and River Crow Agency, to Supt. Alfred Sully, ARCIA 1870, p. 201.

37. Black Eye, Poplar River, M.T., to Lt. Col. C. C. Gilbert, Fort Buford, Letters Received, RG 393, NARS.

38. Agent F. D. Pease, Crow Agency, Fort Parker, M.T., to Supt. J. A. Viall, Helena, [Dec. 1870], LRCIA 1871–V2, RG 75, NARS, M234, roll 491: 402–409.

39. J. A. Viall to CIA, Dec. 24, 1870, ibid.

40. Lt. Col. C. C. Gilbert to AAG, Dept. of Dakota, March 17, 1871, Fort Buford, Letters Sent, RG 393, NARS; "Statement of Flying Crow [Arikara scout]," Fort Buford, D.T., Feb. 1871, Fort Buford, Letters Received, ibid.

41. Special Agent A. J. Simmons, Milk River Agency, Fort Browning, M.T., to CIA, May 12, 1871, LRCIA, Montana Superintendency, 1871–V78, RG 75, NARS, M234, roll 491:631–52.

42. Supt. J. A. Viall, Helena, M.T., to CIA, May 20, 1871, ibid.; Viall to CIA, May 21, 1871, LRCIA, 1871–V80, ibid.; Viall to CIA, July 17, 1871, LRCIA, 1871–V123, ibid.

43. Agent A. J. Simmons, Milk River Agency, Fort Browning, M.T., to Supt. J. A. Viall, Aug. 31, 1871, Records of the Montana Superintendency, RG 75, NARS, M833, roll 2:382–3.

44. For the 1871 Northern Pacific Railroad survey, see Mark H. Brown, *The Plainsmen of the Yellowstone: A History of the Yellowstone Basin* (New York: G.P. Putnam's Sons, 1961), pp. 196–97.
   Special Agent A. J. Simmons, Milk River Agency, Fort Browning, M.T., to Supt. J. A. Viall, Dec. 5, 1871, enc. in Viall to CIA, Dec. 23, 1871, LRCIA 1871–V222, RG 75, NARS, M234, roll 492:636–63.

45. Sec. of War to Sec. of Interior, Aug. 10, 1871, in ARCIA 1871, pp. 433–34.

46. "Report of Hon. B. R. Cowen, Assistant Secretary of the Interior, Hon. N. J. Turney, and Mr. J. W. Wham, commissioners to visit the Teton Sioux at and near Fort Peck, Montana," in ARCIA 1872, pp. 456–60.

47. "Indian Delegations Visiting Washington During the Year," ibid., pp. 97–98; "Report of Hon. B. R. Cowen," ibid., p. 460.

48. For the 1873 Northern Pacific Railroad surveys, see Brown, *Plainsmen of the Yellowstone*, pp. 197–203.
   Agent A. J. Simmons, Fort Peck, M.T., to Gen. B. R. Cowan [Cowen], Ast. Sec. of the Interior, Dec. 8, 1872, LRCIA 1873–S465, RG 75, NARS, M234, roll 495:751–67.

49. Agent A. J. Simmons, Fort Peck, M.T., to CIA, Dec. 1, 1872, LRCIA 1872–S439, ibid., roll 495:740–44; Simmons to Hon. N. J. Turney, Dec. 15, 1872, LRCIA 1872–S465, ibid., roll 495:751–67.

50. Simmons to Cowan [Cowen], Dec. 8, 1872.

51. Agent A. J. Simmons, Helena, to CIA, Jan. 11, 1873, LRCIA 1873–S408, RG 75, NARS, M234, roll 495:732–33.

52. Agent A. J. Simmons, Fort Peck, M.T., to B. R. Cowen, Ast. Sec. of the Interior, June 15, 1873, LRCIA 1873–S181, ibid., roll 495:836–39.

53. For the 1873 Northern Pacific Railroad survey, see Brown, *Plainsmen of the Yellowstone*, pp. 203–10; William H. Goetzmann, *Exploration and Empire: The Explorer and the Scientist in the Winning of the American West* (New York: Alfred A. Knopf, 1967), pp. 415–19.

54. "Indian Reservation in Montana," 43rd Cong. 1st sess., House Ex. Doc. No. 38 (ser. set no. 1606).

55. Agent William W. Alderson, Fort Peck, to CIA, Sept. 1, 1874, in ARCIA 1874, pp. 265–69.

56. A. J. Simmons to CIA, May 12, 1871.

57. For Custer's 1874 Black Hills expedition, see John W. Bailey, *Pacifying the Plains: General Alfred Terry and the Decline of the Sioux, 1866–1890* (Westport, Conn.: Greenwood Press, 1979), pp. 94–103; Goetzmann, *Exploration and Empire*, pp. 419–21.

58. For the 1875 Jenney Black Hills expedition, see Goetzmann, *Exploration and Empire*, pp. 421–24; Walter P. Jenney, "Report of Geological Survey of the Black Hills," ARCIA 1875, pp. 181–83.

59. W. B. Allison, et al., "Report of the Commission Appointed to Treat with the Sioux Indians for the Relinquishment of the Black Hills," ibid., pp. 184–201; Olson, *Red Cloud and the Sioux Problem*, pp. 201–13.

60. ARCIA 1875, pp. 90–94.

61. Lt. Gen. Philip H. Sheridan's annual report of Nov. 23, 1875, in ARSW 1875 1:55–69, presents his philosophy for settling the Indian problem by transferring jurisdiction of Indian affairs to the army; the accompanying report of Brig. Gen. Alfred H. Terry lists the distribution of troops at the various posts in the Department of Dakota.

62. See Lt. Gen. Philip H. Sheridan's account in ARSW 1876 1:440; Paul Andrew Hutton, *Phil Sheridan and His Army* (Lincoln: University of Nebraska Press, 1985), pp. 298–300; John S. Gray, *Centennial Campaign: The Sioux War of 1876* (Fort Collins, Colo.: Old Army Press, 1976), chap. 3; Bailey, *Pacifying the Plains*, pp. 120–24.

63. Gray, *Centennial Campaign*, chap. 4; Hutton, *Phil Sheridan and His Army*, p. 301.

64. Gray, *Centennial Campaign*, chap. 5.

65. Ibid., chaps. 7–8; Hutton, *Phil Sheridan and His Army*, pp. 302–15.

66. Gray, *Centennial Campaign*, chap. 9; Bailey, *Pacifying the Plains*, pp. 138–49; Hutton, *Phil Sheridan and His Army*, p. 312.

67. For the Sioux Sun Dance on the Rosebud, see Stanley Vestal, *Sitting Bull: Champion of the Sioux*, rev. ed. (Norman: University of Oklahoma Press, 1957), pp. 149–51; Powell, *People of the Sacred Mountain* 2:951–52.
   For Crook's fight on the Rosebud, see Gray, *Centennial Campaign*, chap. 10.

68. Gray, *Centennial Campaign*, chaps. 11–15; Powell, *People of the Sacred Mountain* 2:1009–1033.

69. Gray, *Centennial Campaign*, chap. 17.

70. Ibid., chap. 18; Hutton, *Phil Sheridan and His Army*, pp. 315–21; Bailey, *Pacifying the Plains*, pp. 160–66.

71. Hutton, *Phil Sheridan and His Army*, pp. 322–23; the quote from Sheridan is printed in Bailey, *Pacifying the Plains*, p. 167.

72. Gray, *Centennial Campaign*, chap. 21; Bailey, *Pacifying the Plains*, pp. 167–68.

73. Gray, *Centennial Campaign*, pp. 255–60; Hutton, *Phil Sheridan and His Army*, pp. 323–25.

74. Olson, *Red Cloud and the Sioux Problem*, pp. 224–30; Gray, *Centennial Campaign*, pp. 260–64.

75. Olson, *Red Cloud and the Sioux Problem*, pp. 230–35; Hutton, *Phil Sheridan and His Army*, pp. 325–26.

76. Powell, *People of the Sacred Mountain* 2:1056–71; Hutton, *Phil Sheridan and His Army*, p. 326.

77. Utley, *Frontier Regulars*, pp. 276–80.

78. Francis Paul Prucha, *A Guide to the Military Posts of the United States, 1789–1895* (Madison: State Historical Society of Wisconsin, 1964), pp. 76, 118.

79. Sister Mary Claudia Duratschek, *Crusading Along Sioux Trails: A History of the Catholic Indian Missions of South Dakota* (Yankton: Grail, 1947), pp. 60–72.

80. *ARCIA 1875*, p. 244; Capt. J. S. Poland, Post at Standing Rock, to AAG, Dept. of Dakota, July 14, 1876, Military Division of the Missouri, Special Files, "Sioux War, 1876," no. 1876–4883, RG 393, NARS; copy of Sec. of War to Sec. of the Interior, Aug. 7, 1876, ibid., no. 1876–5415.

81. Figures of horses and guns confiscated are from Lt. Col. W. P. Carlin to AAG, Dept. of Dakota, Dec. 8, 1876, Fort Yates, Letters Sent, no. 1876–484, RG 393, NARS.

82. *ARCIA 1877*, pp. 71–72.

83. Ibid., *1876*, pp. 38–40; ibid., *1877*, pp. 72–75.

84. *ARSW 1877*, 1:517–20, 550–51.

85. Ibid., pp. 7–15; ibid., *1878* 1:66–67; Erasmus Gilbreath's memoirs are printed in Richard Upton, comp. and ed., *Fort Custer on the Big Horn, 1877–1898: Its History and Personalities as Told and Pictured by Its Contemporaries* (Glendale, Calif.: Arthur H. Clark, 1973), pp. 48–50.

86. Olson, *Red Cloud and the Sioux Problem*, pp. 235–41.

87. Ibid., pp. 242–46.

88. Hutton, *Phil Sheridan and His Army*, pp. 333–37; Powell, *People of the Sacred Mountain* 2:1158–1261.

89. Agent Thomas J. Mitchell, Bismarck, D.T., to CIA, June 6, 1876, LRCIA, Montana Superintendency, no. 1876–M448, RG 75, NARS, M234, roll 505:320–28.

90. *ARCIA 1876*, pp. 90–92.

91. Agent Thomas J. Mitchell, Fort Peck Agency, M.T., to CIA, March 27, 1877, LRCIA, Montana Superintendency, no. 1877–F86, RG 75, NARS, M234, roll 507:57–61; copy of Lt. Col. James W. Forsyth, Chicago, to Lt. Gen. P. H. Sheridan, June 11, 1877, with endorsement by Sheridan, June 12, ibid., roll 508:829–35.

92. *ARCIA 1877*, pp. 137–39.

93. *ARCIA 1878*, p. 89; Agent W. Bird, Fort Peck Agency, Poplar River, M.T., to CIA, Dec. 20, 1877, LRCIA, Montana Superintendency, no. 1878–B22, RG 75, NARS, M234, roll 509:116–17.

94. Capt. Constant Williams, Fort Belknap, M.T., to Acting AAG, District of Montana, Feb. 23, 1878, ibid., 1878–W564, roll 512:81–96.

95. *ARCIA 1878*, p. 91.

96. Ibid., pp. 91–92.

97. Agent W. Bird, Fort Peck Agency, M.T., to CIA, Oct. 3, 1878, LRCIA, Montana Superintendency, no. 1878–B1521, RG 75, NARS, M234, roll 509:487–90.

98. Agent Bird to CIA, Nov. 16, 1878, ibid., no. 1878–B1702, roll 509:577–81.

99. Agent Bird to CIA, Dec. 5, 1878, ibid., no. 1878–1789, roll 509:648–50; Agent W. L. Lincoln, Fort Belknap Agency, M.T., to CIA, Jan. 21, 1879, ibid., no. 1879–L37, roll 514:374–82.

100. Agent Lincoln to CIA, Dec. 9, 1878, ibid., no. 1878–L870, roll 511:268–73.

101. Agent Lincoln to CIA, Jan. 7, 1879, ibid., no. 1879–L9, roll 514:342–48; endorsement by Lt. Gen. P. H. Sheridan, Chicago, Feb. 8, 1879, on telegram from Lt. Col. John R. Brooke, Fort Shaw, M.T., to AAG, Department of Dakota, Feb. 1, 1879, ibid., no. 1879–W514, roll 515:589–92; Vestal, *Sitting Bull*, pp. 214–20.

102. Agent Bird, Fort Peck, to Gen. Nelson A. Miles, Fort Keogh, June 6, 1879, LRCIA, Montana Superintendency, no. 1879–W1570, RG 75, NARS, M234, roll 515:777–87.

103. *ARCIA*, *1879*, p. 95; Agent Bird to Col. D. Huston, Fort Buford, June 15, 1879, LRCIA, Montana Superintendency, no. 1879–W1503, RG 75, NARS, M234, roll 515:744; Capt. Thomas Britton, Camp at Poplar River, M.T., to Adjutant, Fort Buford, June 24, 1879, Fort Buford, Letters Received, RG 393, NARS; Capt. Britton to Adjutant, Fort Buford, June 28, 1879, ibid. (copy in LRCIA, Montana Superintendency, no. 1879–W1682, RG 75, NARS, M234, roll 515:801–806).

104. Agent N. S. Porter, Fort Peck Agency, M.T., to CIA, July 19, 1879, transmitting copy of letter from Gen. Miles, July 19, 1879, LRCIA, Montana Superintendency, no. 1879–772, RG 75, NARS, M234, roll 514:882–91.

105. Agent Porter to CIA, July 14, 1879, ibid., no. 1879–P627, roll 514:853–56.

106. *ARCIA 1880*, p. 112.

107. Endorsement by Lt. Col. II. M. Black, Fort Assiniboine, M.T., Dec. 5, 1879, on letter of Agent A. R. Keller, Crow Agency, M.T., to Adjutant, Fort Custer, M.T., Nov. 7, 1879, LRCIA, Montana Superintendency, no. 1880–W95, RG 75, NARS, M234, roll 518:10–15.

108. *ARCIA 1880*, p. 113.

109. Agent N. S. Porter, Fort Peck Agency, M.T., to CIA, Feb. 6, 1880, LRCIA, Montana Superintendency, no. 1880–P394, RG 75, NARS, M234, roll 517:291–94.

110. Agent Porter to CIA, Feb. 17, 1880, ibid., no. 1880–P398, roll 517:299–303.

111. *ARCIA 1880*, p. 113; Agent Porter to CIA, May 20, 1880, LRCIA, Montana Superintendency, no. 1880–P736, RG 75, NARS, M234, roll 517:373–76; Inspector John McNeil, Fort Peck, to CIA, June 7, 1880, ibid., no. 1880–I395, roll 516:342–45.

112. *ARCIA 1880*, pp. 111–13; Agent Porter to CIA, Aug. 12, 1880, ibid., no. 1880–P1074, roll 517:450–52.

113. Gen. Nelson A. Miles, Fort Keogh, to AAG, Dept. of Dakota, Aug. 19, 1880, ibid., no. 1880–W1788, roll 518:385–86; AAG, Dept. of Dakota, to Comdg. Officer, Fort Buford, D.T., Aug. 21, 1880, repeating telegram from Col. Miles of Aug. 20, Fort Buford, Letters Received, RG 393, NARS; Agent Porter, Fort Buford, to CIA, Aug. 24, 1880, LRCIA, Montana Superintendency, no. 1880–P1065, M234, roll 517:445–48.

114. Gen. W. T. Sherman, Washington, D.C., to Gen. W. D. Whipple, Military Division of the Missouri, Aug. 26, 1880, LRCIA, Montana Superintendency, no. 1880–W1878, RG 75, NARS, M234, roll 518:390–92.

115. Maj. D. H. Brotherton, Fort Buford, to AAG, Dept. of Dakota, Aug. 23, 1880, Dept. of Dakota, Letters Received, no. 1880–3120, RG 393, NARS; *ARSW 1881* 1:100; E. H. Allison, Fort Buford, to Commanding Officer, Oct. 12, 1880, Dept. of Dakota, Letters Received, no. 1880–3827, RG 393, NARS.

116. Lt. E. Rice, AAG, District of the Yellowstone, Fort Custer, M.T., to Capt. O. B. Read, Oct. 1, 1880, Camp Poplar River, Letters Received, RG 393, NARS.

117. Capt. O. B. Read to AAG, Dept. of Dakota, Oct. 14, 1880, Camp Poplar River, Letters Sent, RG 393, NARS.

118. Capt. Read to AAG, Dept. of Dakota, Oct. 19, 1880, ibid.; Brig. Gen. Alfred H. Terry, St. Paul, to Capt. Read, Oct. 21, 1880, Camp Poplar River, Letters Received, ibid.

119. Col. Nelson A. Miles, Fort Keogh, M.T., to Capt. Read, Oct. 21, 1880, ibid.

120. Capt. Read to AAG, District of the Yellowstone, Fort Keogh, Oct. 27, 1880, ibid.

121. Lt. E. Rice, AAG, District of the Yellowstone, Fort Keogh, to Capt. O. B. Read, Nov. 1, 1880, ibid.

122. Capt. Read to "Uncapapas Indians now enroute to Poplar Creek Agency," Nov. 4, 1880, Camp Poplar River, Letters Sent, ibid.; Capt. Read to Joseph Culbertson, Nov. 5, 1880, ibid.; Joseph Culbertson to Capt. Reid [sic], Nov. 5, 1880, Camp Poplar River, Letters Received, ibid.; Capt. Read to AAG, District of the Yellowstone, Nov. 5, 1880, Camp Poplar River, Letters Sent, ibid.

123. Capt. Read to AAG, District of the Yellowstone, Nov. 26, 1880, ibid.

124. Col. John W. Davidson, Fort Custer, M.T., to AAG, Dept of Dakota, Nov. 27, 1880, Dept. of Dakota, Letters Received, no. 1880-4322, RG 393, NARS; AAG, Dept. of Dakota, St. Paul, to Comdg. Officer, Camp Poplar River, Nov. 27, 1880, Camp Poplar River, Letters Received, ibid.; Maj. D. H. Brotherton, Fort Buford, D.T., to AAG, Dept. of Dakota, Nov. 27, 1880, Dept. of Dakota, Letters Received, no. 1880-4323, ibid.; AAG, Dept. of Dakota, to Comdg. Officer, Fort Buford, Nov. 28, 1880, District of the Yellowstone, Letters Received, ibid.; Col. Davidson, Fort Custer, to Capt. Read, Camp Poplar River, Nov. 29, 1880, Camp Poplar River, Letters Received, ibid.; AAG, Dept. of Dakota, to Comdg. Officer, Camp Poplar River, Nov. 30, 1880, Camp Poplar River, Letters Received, ibid.

125. Capt. Read, Camp Poplar River, to Commanding Officer, Fort Buford, Dec. 9, 1880, quoted in Maj. D. H. Brotherton, Fort Buford, to AAG, Dept. of Dakota, Dec. 11, 1880, LRCIA, Montana Superintendency, no. 1880-W2741, RG 75, NARS, M234, roll 518:443-54.

126. Ibid.

127. AAG, Dept. of Dakota, to Maj. Guido Ilges, Fort Custer, Dec. 14, 1880, LRCIA, ibid., roll 518:438-42.

128. Maj. Brotherton, Fort Buford, to AAG, Dept. of Dakota, Dec. 17, 1880, Dept. of Dakota, Letters Received, no. 1880-4635, RG 393, NARS; Capt. James Bell to AAG, Dept. of Dakota, Dec. 23, 1880, Camp Poplar River, Letters Sent, ibid.

129. Capt. James Bell to Maj. Brotherton, Fort Buford, Dec. 19, 1880, Camp Poplar River, Letters Sent, ibid.

130. Maj. Brotherton, Fort Buford, to Capt. Bell, Camp Poplar River, Dec. 19, 1880, Camp Poplar River, Letters Received, ibid.; Capt. Bell to Maj. Brotherton, Dec. 20, 1880, Camp Poplar River, Letters Sent, ibid.

131. Maj. Ilges' report of his actions at Camp Poplar River, on which the following account is based, is printed in *ARSW 1881* 1:101-106.

132. Ibid., p. 101.

133. The transcript of this meeting is enclosed in Maj. Ilges, Camp Poplar River, to AAG, Dept. of Dakota, Dec. 31, 1880, Fort Buford, Letters Received, RG 393, NARS.

134. *ARSW 1881* 1:102.

135. Ibid.

136. Ibid.

137. Ibid., p. 103.

138. Ibid. Joseph Culbertson later claimed that the Indians on that day did not fire a single shot. Frank Delger, *Joseph Culbertson: Famous Indian Scout Who Served Under General Miles in 1876-1895* (Wolf Point, Montana, 1958), p. 21.

139. *ARSW 1881* 1:104.

140. Ibid.

141. Ibid., pp. 104-105.

142. Ibid., p. 106.

143. Ibid., p. 107; Maj. Ilges, Fort Keogh, to AAG, Dept. of Dakota, June 15, 1881, Military Division of the Missouri, Special File, "Sioux Indian Papers, 1881," no. 1881-3887, RG 393, NARS.

144. *ARSW 1881* 1:107-108; ibid., *1883* 1:113; Vestal, *Sitting Bull*, pp. 231-38.

145. *ARCIA 1881*, pp. 44-45.

146. Capt. O. B. Read to AAG, Dept. of Dakota, Sept. 19, 1881, Camp Poplar River, Letters Sent, RG 393, NARS.

147. *ARCIA 1880*, p. 226; ibid., *1881*, p. 120.

148. Agent Porter, Fort Peck, to CIA, March 2, 1881, LRCIA, no. 1881-4792, RG 75, NARS; AAG, Dept. of Dakota, to Comdg. Officer, Camp Poplar River, July 18, 1881, Camp Poplar River, Letters Received, RG 393, NARS; AAG, Dept. of Dakota, to Comdg. Officer, Fort Keogh, July 25, 1881, LRCIA, no. 1881-13628, RG 75, NARS; Agent Porter, Poplar River Agency, to AAG, Dept. of Dakota, Aug. 1, 1881, with reply dated Aug. 4, 1881, LRCIA, no. 1881-14506, ibid.; AAG, Dept. of Dakota, to AG. Military Division of the Missouri, Aug. 4 and Sept. 6, 1881, LRCIA, no. 1881-17141, ibid.

149. Capt. R. McDonald, Fort Keogh, to Post Adjutant, Sept. 26, with endorsement by Brig. Gen. Terry, St. Paul, Oct. 7, and by Lt. Gen. Sheridan, Chicago, Oct. 13, LRCIA, no. 1881-18715, ibid.

150. Agent Lincoln, Fort Belknap Agency, to CIA, July 4, 1881, LRCIA, no. 1881-12359, ibid.; Comdg. Officer, Fort Assiniboine, to Acting AAG, District of Montana, Aug. 12, 1881, and reply from AAG, Dept. of Dakota, Aug. 15, 1881, LRCIA, no. 1881-14999, ibid.; Comdg. Officer, Fort Assiniboine, to AAG, Dept. of Dakota, Aug. 20, 1881, and attached correspondence, LRCIA, no. 1881-15459, ibid.; Agent Lincoln, Fort Belknap Agency, to CIA, Sept. 1, 1881, LRCIA, no. 1881-16451, ibid.

151. Capt. Read, Camp Poplar River, to AAG, Dept. of Dakota, Sept. 30, 1881, LRCIA, no. 1881-18340, ibid.; Capt. S. Snyder, Fort Keogh, to Post Adjutant, Oct. 23, 1881, Dept. of Dakota, Letters Received, no. 1881-6722, RG 393, NARS.

152. *ARSW 1882* 1:84; Capt. Read, Camp Poplar River, to AAG, Dept. of Dakota, Jan. 14, 1882, LRCIA, no. 1882-3202, RG 75, NARS.

153. *ARCIA 1882*, p. 111.

154. *ARSW 1882*, 1:86; Capt. Read to AAG, Dept. of Dakota, March 31, 1882, Camp Poplar River letterbook, Robert Hull Fleming Museum, The University of Vermont; Capt. M. E. O'Brien, Fort Assiniboine, to Post Adjutant, May 5, 1882, LRCIA, no. 1882-11672, RG 75, NARS.

155. Comm. A. G. Irvine, Fort Walsh, to Comdg. Officer, Fort Assiniboine, June 21, 1882, Camp Poplar River, Letters Received, RG 393, NARS; AAG, Dept. of Dakota, to Comdg. Officer, Fort Assiniboine, June 27, 1882, ibid.; Capt. E. R. Kellogg, Camp on Medicine Lodge Creek, to Post Adjutant, Fort Assiniboine, July 10, 1882, LRCIA, no. 1882-14490, RG 75, NARS.

156. *ARCIA 1882*, p. 111; Capt. Read, Camp Poplar River, to AAG, Dept. of Dakota, Oct. 21, 1882, with endorsement by Lt. Gen. Sheridan, Chicago, Oct. 18, 1882, LRCIA, no. 1882-19467, RG 75, NARS.

157. *ARSW 1883* 1:110; Capt. Read to AAG, Dept. of Dakota, Dec. 4, 1882, Camp Poplar River letterbook, Robert Hull Fleming Museum, The University of Vermont.

158. Capt. Read to AAG, Dept. of Dakota, Jan. 5, 1883, Camp Poplar River, Letters Sent, RG 393, NARS; Agent Porter, Fort Peck Agency, to Comdg. Officer, Camp Poplar River, Jan. 5, 1883, Dept. of Dakota, Letters Received, no. 1883-475, ibid.

159. Sec. of War to Sec. of Interior, Jan. 5, 1883, including endorsement by Gen. Sherman, Jan. 3, 1883, LRCIA, no. 1883-452, RG 75, NARS.

160. Capt. Read, Camp Poplar River, to AAG, Dept. of Dakota, Jan. 30, 1883, ibid., no. 1883-4421; Capt. Read to AAG, Dept. of Dakota, March 1, 1883, Dept. of Dakota, Letters Received, no. 1883-1476, RG 393, NARS; Capt. Read to Col. Thomas H. Ruger, District of Montana, Helena, March 27, 1883, Camp Poplar River letterbook, Robert Hull Fleming Museum, The University of Vermont.

161. Capt. Read to AAG, Dept. of Dakota, Jan. 30, 1883, Camp Poplar River, Letters Sent, RG 393, NARS; ARCIA 1883, p. 103; Capt. Read to AAG, Dept. of Dakota, Sept. 3, 1883, Camp Poplar River, Letters Sent, RG 393, NARS.

162. ARCIA 1883, p. 103; Inspector C. H. Howard, Fort Peck, to Sec. of Interior, Oct. 24, 1883, Indian Inspection Reports, no. 1883-26651, RG 48, NARS, M1070, roll 14:945-1009.

163. ARCIA 1883, p. 104; Agent S. E. Snider, Fort Peck Agency, to CIA, Sept. 7, 1883, LRCIA, no. 1883-17264, RG 75, NARS.

164. Capt. Read to Comdg. Officer, Fort Buford, Oct. 9, 1883, Camp Poplar River letterbook, Robert Hull Fleming Museum, The University of Vermont; Capt. Read to Scout Joseph Culbertson, Nov. 17, 1883, Camp Poplar River, Letters Sent, RG 393, NARS.

165. Capt. Read to AAG, Dept. of Dakota, Jan. 14, 1884, ibid. (copy in LRCIA, no. 1884-2342, RG 75, NARS).

166. Lt. James E. Pilcher, Post Surgeon, Camp Poplar River, to Post Adjutant, Feb. 29, 1884, with endorsement by Brig. Gen. Terry, Feb. 29, 1884, LRCIA, no. 1884-6094, RG 75, NARS.

167. ARCIA 1884, p. 117; "Reduction of Indian Reservations," 50th Cong., 1st sess., House Ex. Doc. no. 63, ser. set no. 2557.

168. ARSW 1884 1:112-13; Prucha, A Guide to the Military Posts of the United States, p. 98.

169. Arnold O. Goplen, "The Historical Significance of the Fort Lincoln State Park," North Dakota History 13 (October, 1946):151-221.

170. ARSW 1887 1:148.

171. J. D. C. Atkins, CIA, to Agent James McLaughlin, Aug. 5, 1886, Standing Rock Reservation, Letters Received, RG 75, Federal Archives and Records Center-Kansas City; ARCIA 1887, p. 48.

172. ARCIA 1886, pp. 86-88.

173. Ibid., pp. 88-91.

174. Duratschek, Crusading Along Sioux Trails, pp. 75-89; ARCIA 1886, p. 91; ARCIA 1887, pp. 51-52; McLaughlin quote is in ARCIA 1886, p. 92.

175. ARCIA 1886, pp. 91-92; "Transcript of Records of the Court of Indian Offenses held at Standing Rock Indian Agency, D.T.," March 31, 1886, and Sept. 10, 1885, Records of Standing Rock Reservation, RG 75, Federal Archives and Records Center-Kansas City.

176. James McLaughlin, My Friend, the Indian (Boston: Houghton Mifflin, 1910), pp. 34-35; ARCIA 1887, p. 53.

177. D. F. Barry to Agent McLaughlin, April 13, 1885, Standing Rock Reservation records, RG 75, Federal Archives and Records Center-Kansas City; Gall to Capt. Read, March 31, 1888, Read Collection, Robert Hull Fleming Museum, The University of Vermont.

178. For the Sun Dance, see James R. Walker, "The Sun Dance and Other Ceremonies of the Oglala Division of the Teton Dakota," American Museum of Natural History, Anthropological Papers 16 (pt. 2), 1917; for a historical account of forced changes in Sioux religious life, see DeMallie, "The Lakota Ghost Dance."

179. Hyde, A Sioux Chronicle (Norman: University of Oklahoma Press, 1956), chaps. 7-8.

180. Ibid., chaps. 9-12; DeMallie, "The Lakota Ghost Dance."

181. For Black Elk's experience with the Ghost Dance, see Raymond J. DeMallie, ed., The Sixth Grandfather: Black Elk's Teachings Given to John G. Neihardt (Lincoln: University of Nebraska Press, 1984), pp. 256-82; the quote from Little Wound is in Walker, Lakota Belief and Ritual, p. 198.

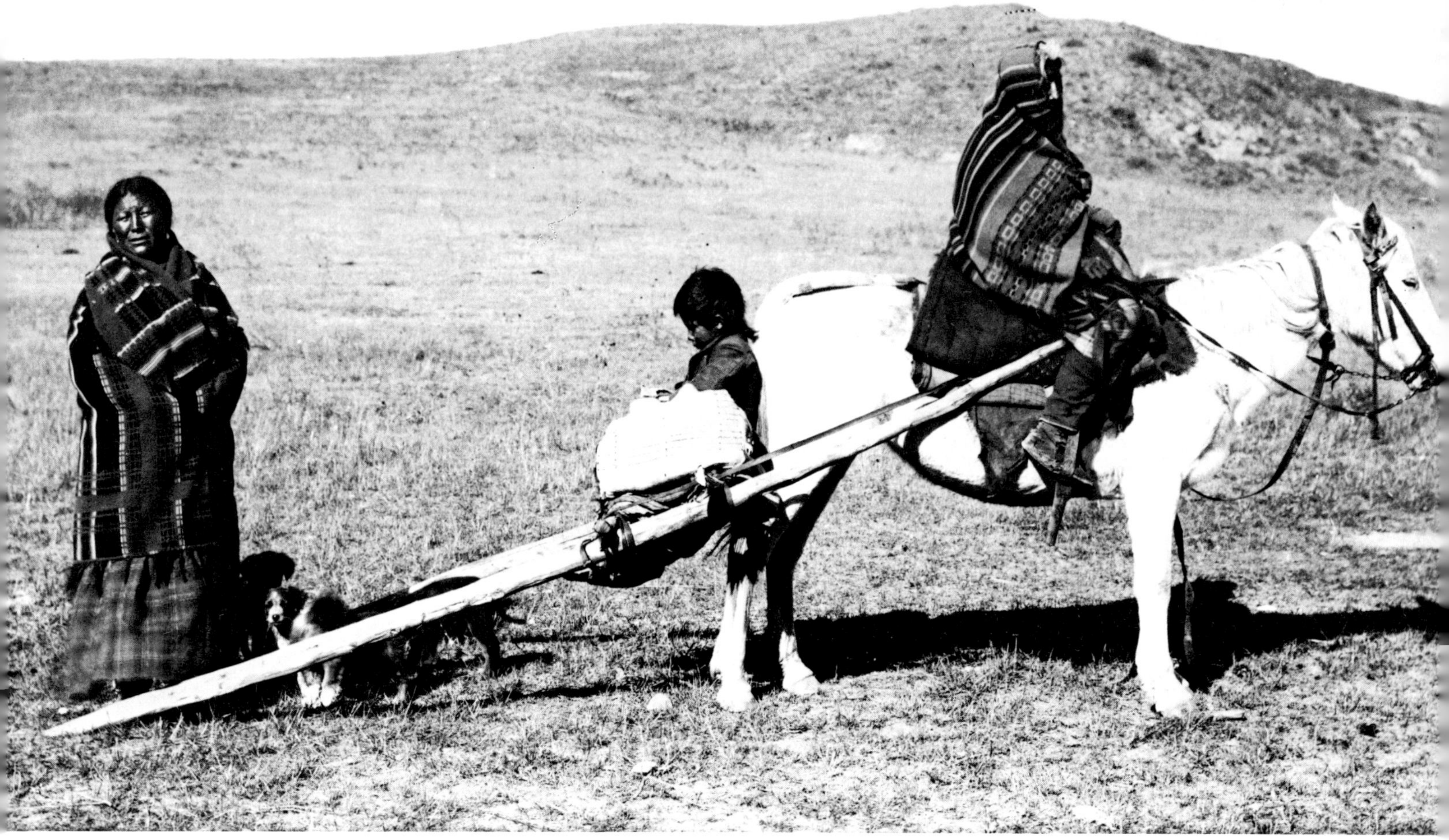

The Culture of the Sioux

In 1850, the realm of the Teton Dakota, or Lakota Sioux, reached from the banks of the Missouri River to the Big Horn Mountains, and from the shores of the Platte north to the Heart River. To the east lived the Yankton and Yanktonai, or Nakota Sioux, whose territory stretched east of the Missouri to the headwaters of the Red River.[1]

These warlike buffalo hunters dominated the Central Plains, where they carried on a constant warfare, capturing horses and conquering territory from their nomadic enemies (the Crow and Plains Cree, the Cheyenne, and the Kiowa) and from the sedentary farming people (the Mandan and Hidatsa, the Arikara, and the Pawnee). By 1815 the Sioux had wrested the Black Hills from the Kiowa and Cheyenne, with whom they later made treaties of friendship; and by 1823 they had won the Big Horn Mountains from the Crow, with whom they never made peace. They were at war also with the Shoshone of the Rocky Mountains, from whom they continually stole horses and took scalps.

The Sioux had not always been so powerful. Prior to the introduction of the horse from the southwest in the mid-eighteenth century and of firearms from the northeast in the early nineteenth century, these Indians had consisted of small bands of wandering hunters. They eked out an existence on the Eastern Plains in search of buffalo and small game. The advent of the horse immediately increased the Sioux's mobility. From hunters tracking game on foot, they became mounted horsemen who could surround and outrun the buffalo, killing great numbers at a time. From footsoldiers trekking mile upon mile to raid an enemy village, they became cavalrymen capable of sudden attack and quick retreat. The fortuitous possession of both guns and horses placed the Sioux at a great advantage. Their enemies to the north and east had firearms but few horses; the tribes to the south and west had horses but few guns.

The Teton Sioux were composed of seven divisions, each occupying an area within the overall Sioux territory. (See page 21 for a listing.) Each division included a varying number of bands, or *t'iyóšpaye*, extended families under the leadership of a man recognized for his ability as a wise counselor. This leader was a man whose responsible authority led the people to prosper and assured them a sense of security. He was generally a proven hunter or warrior with an outstanding record for bravery, whose reputation for generosity in giving to the poor and elderly was unparalleled. Frequently a patriarch, he often bequeathed his position to a qualified son.

It was customary for the bands to congregate in the summer months for a celebration of the Sun Dance and other ceremonies by the entire division. This was the time when the full council of *nacás* met and new officers were appointed. The government of the Sioux consisted of a council composed of retired headmen or chiefs of the various bands, venerable hunters, renowned warriors, and retired shamans, or priests — a congress of elders. From among themselves they appointed a group of up to ten males, called *wic'áša itánc'ans*, to act as an executive committee. Such men interpreted and made practical the broad policies of the *nacás*. It was they who decided when a communal hunt was to be undertaken, when war should be declared or peace entered into. The *wic'áša itánc'ans*, in turn, chose two to four younger men whose outstanding war records, acts of generosity, and potential for leadership made them eligible for the office of *wi'cášas*, or "Shirt Wearers." Each was invested with a special shirt as a badge of office. As the executive officers of the tribe, they were called upon to decide matters of tribal concern, reconcile quarrels, and negotiate diplomatic relations between foreign nations. The people's welfare was their chief responsibility, one which included providing bountiful hunting and good camp grounds. They were the supreme counselors.

In addition to the selection of the *wic'ášas*, the *wic'áša itánc'ans* appointed from among the *nacás* two to four *wakíc'unzas*, or "Pipe Bearers," usually older men. Each was presented with a highly ornamented ceremonial pipe and tobacco bag as a badge of his office. Among their responsibilities was the "Making of Brothers," or peace ceremony. It was also their duty to organize all camp moves and to appoint the *akíc'ita*, or police. The *wakíc'unzas* assigned camping locations to the bands and families, and determined the halts or rests when the camps were moving. It was they who gave the orders for large tribal hunts. As leaders of the march, they walked in advance of the procession, all the while directing the activities of the *akíc'ita*, who flanked the main body of the caravan, keeping order, prodding stragglers, and guarding against possible enemy attack.

Among the various divisions, there were a number of young men's societies, such as the Kit Foxes, the Badgers, the Brave Hearts, and the Crow Owners, which boys as young as sixteen might be invited to join. Besides the conviviality, these groups gave their members a team spirit in warlike adventures. Officers were expected to exhibit such virtues as bravery and fortitude. Should one of the members be killed in battle, the entire membership was pledged to avenge his death. Each of the societies vied for recognition by the tribal elders, hoping to be appointed as *akíc'ita* by the *wakíc'unzas*. In this capacity, they would serve as the police force for a year. Sioux government was not only well conceived and logically organized, it demanded of its leaders the most qualified of men, thereby maintaining a standard of excellence that the people respected.

The smallest unit of Sioux society was the conjugal one of man and wife. It was also the least permanent, subject to dissolution by divorce or death. A young man, finding the girl of his choice, properly offered horses to her brothers. If the bride price was acceptable, a feast would be arranged by the bridegroom's family. The bride's brothers escorted her to the feast on one of the horses they had received. When the feast was finished, the marriage was consummated. The newlyweds set up their tipi near the groom's parents, and the bride became part of his family.

The Sioux practiced polygamy. Often at the suggestion of the first wife, a man would marry her younger sister. This younger sister would assume many of the household chores, leaving the older wife time for handiwork, club meetings, and parties. Divorce was simple: were a man to tire of his wife, all he need do was appear at a meeting of his warrior society, beat on a drum, and announce, "You can have her, I don't want her, she's too mean for me." Since the tipi and all its contents belonged to the woman, the divorcée usually took these and often the children, as well, to her family's camp. The husband collected his belongings — weapons, medicines, and clothing — and moved in with his mother.

The Sioux system of kinship was one in which children referred to their mother and her sisters as "mother" (*iná*), and to their father and his brothers as "father" (*até*). A father's sister was called "aunt" (*t'unwín*), a mother's brother, "uncle" (*lekší*). Thus, at the loss of a parent through divorce or death, children still had people with whom they interacted as mother or father. These extended families offered a security to children with the knowledge that, in effect, they had many parents. Moreover, there was a permanence which went beyond the conjugal family. Children belonged not so much to their parents as to their parents' families.

The buffalo was the mainstay of the Sioux economy. Not only were the Indians dependent upon these great animals for food, but from them they also obtained hides for tipi covers and robes, parfleches and moccasin soles, packing cases and tobacco bags, as well as sinew for threads, horns for spoons and cups, and hair for ropes. Even the skull was used — as an altar.

Communal buffalo hunts were organized when a herd was discovered. Most frequently, scouts were sent in search of buffalo and, when successful, they reported their discovery to the leaders at the council lodge. If the herd was at some distance, the entire village might be ordered to break camp and move in order to be closer to the kill. One of the police societies was assigned the authority to keep the mounted hunters in line. Surprise was all important. The men were usually divided into two groups in order to surround the herd. When the signal was given to charge, the entire force surged in upon the animals. Once the buffalo were surrounded, each hunter was on his own. Anyone found starting before the signal, however, was apprehended by the *akíc'ita*. Those who jumped the gun might be sorely beaten and perhaps have their tipi destroyed as well.

The hunters guided their ponies as close to the buffalo as possible, shooting their arrows into the left side of the animal, the side closest to the heart. Good hunters selected two-year-old cows for their mark, as their meat was most tender and their hides made the best robes. Chasing the buffalo was dangerous: ponies were gored; men were thrown from their mounts and trampled. Hunters were reputed to have jumped from falling mounts and run over the backs of the fleeing herd to save themselves from being crushed.

Each hunter marked his arrows with identifying painted bars so that after the kill he could claim the animals that were his. After the hunt, old men or men who were unsuccessful at hunting might enter the field and tie knots in the tails of the fallen buffalo. In this way, they laid a claim to part of the carcass, which the rightful owner was obliged to honor. Such men, known as "tail tiers," were disdained; however, they did give the successful hunters a chance to be generous. Onto the field along with the "tail tiers" came the women, equipped with their sharp knives, to begin the butchering. They brought with them the pack horses and the travois and dog teams. First, the hides were removed; then the quarters were cut and loaded, along with the hides, onto the travois and horses to be hauled back to camp. The entrails, kidneys, liver, heart, pancreas, brains, and tongue were packed in the paunch of the slaughtered animal. Liver, considered a great delicacy, was sometimes eaten raw on the spot.

Although buffalo was the staple, all manner of smaller game was hunted — deer and antelope, elk and bighorn sheep, rabbits, racoons, and porcupines. Individual hunters, small teams of men and, occasionally, families set out in search of game. Sometimes they stalked their prey; at other times they set traps, consisting of either nooses placed along trails or camouflaged pits. For the Sioux, hunting was not a recreation; it was work — hard, arduous work requiring patience, skill, and endurance. Successful hunters were respected for their ability to provide for their families and to share meat with the less fortunate, the elderly, and the indigent. By common agreement, those men with the fastest horses generally occupied the largest tipis. The Sioux had every reason to tap this bountiful resource and they did so most effectively.

Efficient hunters, the Sioux were also exploitive predators. Such a tendency was not surprising for men who believed that their natural resources, especially the buffalo, were inexhaustible. Buffalo roamed the plains in countless millions and replenished their numbers each spring with newborn calves.

If the men were the force that sustained the exploitive economy, it was the women who fostered the productive aspects of the system. In addition to the preparation of food, they tanned the hides for tipi covers and liners, robes, and clothing. They tailored the garments and made the moccasins, decorating them with paint or porcupine-quill embroidery. Women also made the containers, both painted rawhide parfleches and quilled or beaded soft packing bags.

Preparing a buffalo hide was a strenuous and tedious task that demanded strength, skill, and patience. The first step was the removal of the flesh and gristle by staking the hide out and scraping away the tissue with a chisel-like implement fashioned from a bone and tipped with a blade. Stooping over the skin, the woman pulled the blade toward her, removing the particles. The hide was then allowed to dry in the sun, perhaps for several days, before being scraped to an even thickness with a short hoe-like tool. The hide was then turned over to remove the hair, a process usually carried out with a scraper. At this point the rawhide was stiff and hard. After soaking in water for about two days, the hide became soft and pliable and was ready for final curing. Mixtures of brains, liver, fats, and sometimes red grass were rubbed thoroughly into the skin, and then allowed to dry. Next the skin was stretched and finally worked back and forth over a twisted rawhide thong to break down the tissue completely. Though minor variations in techniques might be employed, tanning was a tedious process that might take one woman as long as ten days.

As many as ten to twelve of these tanned buffalo hides were required to make a tipi cover. They were sewn together, generally using an old tipi as a pattern. It was customary for a woman of unquestioned morality to be invited to sew the smoke flaps; if an immoral woman were chosen, the tipi would smoke. Eighteen to twenty peeled pine poles about 15 feet tall were needed for the average tipi. Furnishings included a tipi liner, or "dew cloth," a pair of backrests made of willow rods for each bed, a stake from which to hang the water paunch, a small altar consisting of a buffalo skull placed behind the fire pit, a pipe rack, and a ceremonial pipe arranged on a bed of sage. Buffalo robes served as floor covering. Dew cloths, hung around the inside perimeter of the lodge to a height of about 5 feet, served as insulators. These liners were often decorated by the women with horizontal bands of quillwork or beading. The council lodge, situated in the center of the camp, was painted red. However, most tipis were undecorated save for a row of quilled pendants on either side of the pins securing the tipi at the front. Often, four quilled medallions were spaced equidistant around the cover at eye level to give a pleasing effect. A scalp might be hung from atop one of the tipi poles.

Architecturally, the tipi was an ingenious dwelling. Its conical shape saved heat in the winter, as the volume of warm air was progressively reduced toward the top. The Indian literally lived in his chimney. In summer, the sides of the tipi could be rolled up so that it became a cool parasol. The smoke flaps, too, could be adjusted in accordance with the wind and weather so that the optimum smokeless draft might be obtained.

The woman owned the tipi and all its contents. She was responsible for putting it up and taking it down. In all, it required about an hour to set one up with the furnishings in place and the packing bags stowed away. A tipi could be dismantled and its contents packed on the travois and ready to move in fifteen minutes.

Quilling was probably the highest attainment in the female arts. Unlike the process of tanning, which required much brawn, quilling demanded delicate dexterity. The

Sioux woman graded her quills into four sizes and stored them in bladder pouches according to size and color. By boiling roots or berries, she obtained various colors and hues. For instance, Blue Whirlwind, a Sioux quillworker active in the 1880s, derived red from the snakeberry root, yellow from the huckleberry root, and a purplish black from the fox grape. Green dye was acquired from an unknown root, while blue was obtained from clay secured through trade. Blue Whirlwind soaked the white quills briefly in water before immersing them in the dye; they were allowed to remain in the dye only a short time lest the core of the quill be worked out. When the color was satisfactory, the quill was placed on a piece of bark to dry in the sun.[2]

In quilling, the Sioux woman first softened about six quills in her mouth, with the points extending just beyond the corner of her lips. In decorating moccasins, the woman marked two guidelines on the hair side of the skin with the point of her awl. At the heel she punched two holes parallel to the surface of the skin and the guidelines. Through these holes she ran pointed sinew threads, tying a knot in the end of each to hold them fast. All sinew sewing was done through the surface of the hide so that no stitching was visible from the underside. Next she would tie a long strand of sinew to a little stick and secure the stick by stepping on it or by placing it in her moccasin. She tied the loose end of the sinew to the upper thread already stitched at the point of the knot. The thread of sinew, stretched to her foot, acted as a guide.

After the quill was split, and the butt flattened over the side of the overgrown nails of the thumb and forefinger, it was laid under the lower sinew at the starting point and turned over tightly. Then a stitch was taken with the sinew exactly the width of the flattened quill and secured by a half hitch or loop stitch. The quill was then turned under the lower thread and a similar stitch was taken, and so on, with new quills spliced in until the desired length was reached. The quills might be used alternately from upper and lower threads. When opposing colors were used, a pleasing plaited effect resulted. This stitch, the most widely used, was called "quilling with tied sinew," but the same effect could be had by the use of parallel rows of stitches with the tied sinew.

At least nine different quilling techniques were employed, all having special names and many reserved for special tasks. Thus, the quilling of the rawhide fringe of a pipe bag involved a wrapping technique; the embellishing of a pipe stem required plaiting. Fine lines for use in narrow designs, called "one-quill quilling," were produced with only one thread around which the quills were twisted.

The Plains Indians used two different methods of beading, one referred to as the lazy stitch, the other called the overlay, or spot stitch. After punching a hole in the surface of the skin with her awl, the beadworker tied a knot at the end of a strand of sinew and threaded it through the hole. Next, the woman threaded from five to nine beads on the strand and, after punching another hole in the skin, secured the thread. Then she added the same number of beads and secured the thread in the same fashion. Continuing, she produced a band of beads for whatever distance the design required. Overlay beading was accomplished by threading enough beads on the sinew thread to complete the entire length of the desired design. A second thread was stitched over every three or four beads to secure them.

Among the Plains Indians, three different styles of design have been isolated and named the Crow, the Blackfeet, and the Sioux, after the tribe which used them. The Crow preferred the use of massive diamonds, triangles, and hourglasses, often bordered with white against a background of red flannel. Lavender and pale blue were favorite colors, although green, yellow, and dark blue are found. The overlay stitch was most commonly employed. The Shoshone and Utes also used this technique to a degree.

Like the Crow, the Blackfeet style was composed of large diamonds, triangles, and hourglasses. However, the designs were often composed of many small squares, frequently set against a background of white. The Blackfeet preferred the spot stitch. The Plains Cree, Flathead, and Sarsi also used this technique.

The Sioux employed the same geometric designs, but on a much smaller scale. Thin straight lines — crossed, terraced, or forked — extended from the basic geometric forms, which, in turn, were layered out over a solid background, most often of white or pale blue. The Sioux used the lazy stitch exclusively. The Arapaho and Cheyenne also used this technique, as did the Assiniboine, Gros Ventre, and Ute, although on a much more limited scale.

Men's clothing consisted of a buffalo robe, leggings, a breech cloth, and moccasins. Shirts were worn on occasion and for special purposes. Women wore robes, dresses of elkskin which reached below the knee, short leggings which tied above the calf, and moccasins. For daily wear, clothing was undecorated and rather drab, but for special occasions highly ornamented garments were fashionable. Robes were embellished with bands of quillwork or beads, or painted with complex geometric forms. Men's robes displayed the "black bonnet" design: a series of concentric circles composed of lozenge-shaped figures representing feathers. Men also wore robes with painted figures depicting their warlike exploits. Women favored a geometric border-and-box design which was, in fact, a stylized image of a buffalo. An hourglass figure symbolizing the spider was also popular. Robes were worn with the hair side in during the winter; for summer wear, robes with the hair removed were often preferred. Elkskin robes were popular with women. Robes bearing horizontal quilled or beaded bars interspersed with medallions, later known as blanket strips, were worn by both sexes.

Shirts were poncho-like garments with open sleeves, usually made of deerskin, although elk and antelope were not uncommon. These were decorated with wide bands of quillwork over the shoulders and down the arms. A large medallion or a triangular tab of quillwork was placed below the neck. Some shirts were painted with protective symbols to be worn in battle. Tribal executives, or *wic'ášas*, were invested with hair-fringed shirts painted either blue and yellow or red and green symbolizing, respectively, the gods of Sky and Rock, or of Sun and Earth. Locks of hair attached to the shoulders and sleeves represented the people of the tribe for whom the "Shirt Wearers" were responsible. Such locks were donated by female relatives and were not scalps, as often assumed.

Leggings were often embellished with bands of quilling along the sides. Some might display horses' hooves indicating the number and color of captured horses; others were emblazoned with symbolic crosses, circles, and dragonflies. These ornamented leggings might be worn in battle as protection — quick and evasive, the dragonfly was considered especially hard to kill. The *wic'áša yatapícas*, or Supreme Chiefs, were entitled to wear leggings with locks of hair in addition to hair-fringed shirts.

Most Sioux moccasins were of two pieces: a soft upper piece sewn to a rawhide sole. However, one-piece, soft-soled moccasins, especially fur-lined buffalo footwear, were made for winter use. Hard-soled moccasins were decorated with quills and beads in a variety of patterns.

Women's elkskin dresses consisted of a large open-sleeved yoke sewn to a loosely fitted tubular skirt. Early dresses were decorated with bands of quills or beads along the outer seams of the sleeves, across the neck, over the seam attaching the yoke to the dress, and around the hemline. Later, fully beaded yokes became fashionable, replacing the use of simple beaded banding. Rows of elk's teeth, dentalium shells, and even coins were used to decorate the yokes. No dress was complete without a belt. In later years, harness leather ornamented with brass upholstery tacks or disks of German silver became fashionable.

Women's leggings were ornamented with a bar of beading at the outside seam where they were tied. Their moccasins, like men's, were often elaborately embroidered with quills or beads. Probably no people displayed a more colorful footwear than the Indians of the Plains. The arduous work of tanning, the skill of painting, and the dexterity of quilling attest to the industry and aesthetic insight of these Plains Indian women. Their works still stand as a colorful contribution to American heritage.

Men, too, contributed to the productive economy, manufacturing goods mostly for their own use, however. Their special achievements were in wood and stone carving, feather work, and painting. Painted decorations on robes and tipi liners consisted of scenes with human figures commemorating the artist's warlike exploits in hand-to-hand combat. The tipi itself might be decorated with similar scenes or with symbols of the owner's power, which he received in visions from the supernatural. Men made their own weapons, including bows and arrows, lances, and clubs. Shamans made shields from fire-hardened buffalo hide with covers of soft deerskin painted with mystical figures and designs. It was the magical power of the design, rather than the thickness of the hide, which protected the owner from harm. Pipes were also the man's specialty: stems of ash wood were equipped with carved pipe bowls of catlinite, a soft red stone which hardened upon exposure to air. For ceremonial use, pipe stems were ornamented with plaited porcupine quills, a decorative technique which the women contributed. Musical instruments — drums, whistles, flutes, and rattles — were fashioned by the men. Shamans made eagle-feathered headdresses to be worn in battle as magical protection against arrows and bullets.

Warfare for the Plains Indian was the reason for life. Men waged war to avenge the death of a relative or a society brother, to acquire new territory or defend the homeland, or to capture horses from the enemy. When a man was killed in battle, it was the responsibility of his brothers to satisfy this wrong. Frequently, the members of the victim's police society would be asked to help. War parties usually set out before dawn. They were often accompanied by one or two twelve-year-old boys whose duties were to water the horses and to feed the warriors ritually (by offering them morsels of food and sips of water) before their entry into battle. These boys would guard the animals until the combat was over, at which time they would rendezvous with the warriors.

The object of such an expedition was threefold: first and foremost, to bring home a scalp, thereby avenging the death of a tribesman; second, to build one's war record by striking, or "counting coup," upon the enemy; and third, to capture enemy horses and thus increase one's wealth. All of these accomplishments brought honor to the warrior.

Each man rode a horse and, if he owned one, led his war pony. The group might travel by day at first, but as they approached enemy country, they would travel by night, hiding in timbered bluffs or river bottoms by day. The war leader, usually a man who had dreamt of wolves and who was thus equipped with the power to see around mountains and over hills, could locate an enemy camp. Once the site of the enemy village was determined, the war party would seek a vantage point from which to observe the camp — checking the size of the pony herd, the lay of the land, and the best route for attack and escape. All day the men would lay their plans; at night they would eat a cold supper, since no fires were permitted.

By dawn the men would be preparing themselves. They would apply war paint to their faces and bodies as magic protection. Some would put on their finest attire in order to present a pleasing appearance to their ancestors and gods in the event of death in battle. Others preferred to fight naked, unencumbered by clothing. Those who owned war bonnets or had protective medicines, or *wótawes*, would wear them. Men also painted their war horses and blew medicine into the animals' nostrils to give them speed and stamina. Finally, the war leader donned his wolfskin mask and led the party to the enemy.

The Sioux launched their attacks in the early morning, when the horses were customarily let out to graze. Surrounding as much of the herd as possible, they would drive the animals away from the village toward the site selected for rendezvous. Upon discovering their loss, the enemy would pursue. Only when the enemy's mounts had tired and they were strung out would the main body of the Sioux turn and engage their pursuers in combat, while two or three of the men continued to drive the horses.

With bows and arrows, clubs and lances, the warriors attacked their adversaries. Striking an enemy with a club, a quirt, or a bare hand earned coup counts for the warrior. Killing and scalping an enemy earned no points, although the scalp as a trophy was proof of one's fortitude. The battle might last until the Sioux found themselves outnumbered. Having killed and scalped two or three of the enemy, the warriors would then retreat, riding hard for the rendezvous with their own ponies and the stolen herd. They would continue to canter their war-horses as long as the animals lasted; then they would change mounts and ride on toward home.

A successful war party planned to re-enter their village in the early morning. In preparation, they worked red ochre and grease into the enemy scalps, which they displayed suspended on willow poles, and painted their own faces black, as a sign of victory. They rode into the village as if making an attack. After circling the camp with their trophies in full view, the warriors would dismount and report to the red council lodge, where they would tell the elders all about the expedition, "biting the knife" as proof of their veracity. In the evening, a victory dance might be held in celebration of the event. At this time the warriors would present the enemy scalps to the mothers or sisters of the slain relative in whose honor the war party had been organized: "Here is your son; rejoice for he is again as one." The people would dance until late at night, honoring the warriors with songs.

For the Sioux man, "power" was the most important of all attributes. It was the force, the inner strength, that enabled men to accomplish great deeds. With it, men could count many coups, capture many horses, and kill many buffalo. Power enabled men to cure the sick, to find lost articles, and to make *wótawes* to protect themselves in battle. Men with power became leaders and priests; men without it merely existed.

Power was acquired in visions received from the realm of the supernatural, which consisted of a complex hierarchy of gods. For the Sioux, the ultimate source of power was *Wakan Tanka*, the Great Mysterious, who was one deity, yet four: the Chief God, the Creator, the Great Spirit, and the Executor. *Wakan Tanka* also comprised the Superior Gods: the Rock, the Earth, the Sky, and the Sun. Rock, as the ancestor, was a symbol of authority and the patron of the arts. His color was yellow. Earth, the All Mother, was the protector of the household. Her color was green. Sky, the source of power and force, was the chief adjudicator. His color was blue. Sun, the first in rank among the gods, was all powerful. He was defender of the four virtues: bravery, fortitude, generosity, and fidelity. His color was red.

In addition to the Superior Gods, *Wakan Tanka* represented the four Associate Gods: Moon, Wind, *Whope*, and Winged. Moon, the wife of Sun, set the time for important undertakings. Wind, kin to Sky, controlled the seasons and admitted spirits to the Spirit Trail or Milky Way. *Whope*, daughter of Sun and Moon, was the mediator and patron of harmony and pleasure. It was she who came to earth, bringing with her the sacred pipe to be used in sanctifying peace among men and nations. She appeared to the people as a beautiful woman and, after delivering her message, departed as a white buffalo, thus earning the appellation "White Buffalo Maiden." Winged, associate of Rock, was the patron of cleanliness. His form was that of an eagle.

In the Sioux pantheon, *Wakan Tanka* also consisted of the four Subordinate Gods: the Buffalo, the Bear, the Four Winds, and Whirlwind. Buffalo was the patron of hunters, ceremonies, industry, and fecundity. Bear was patron of wisdom, medicine, and curing. The Four Winds determined the weather and directions. Whirlwind sponsored games and courtship.

The Gods-Like, forces resembling gods, were possessed by every individual and again were four in number: the Spirit, the Ghost, the Potency, and the Spirit-Like. The Spirit was an individual's personality: that assemblage of traits which set one apart from others. The Ghost was a vitality such as observed in one's breath and shadow. The Potency was the power that an individual possessed to accomplish things. The Spirit-Like was one's essence as witnessed in the continued growth after death of fingernails and hair. For the Sioux, hair was symbolic of life everlasting. The scalped warrior was an incomplete being who could not enter the World of the Ancestors. Like murderers and homosexuals, his spirit remained in limbo. Only when an enemy scalp was presented to a close female relative of the victim might the body be made complete and the Spirit enter the Spirit World.

The world of the supernatural was not without its malevolent forces. *Iya*, the Tornado, was the chief of all evil. *Iktomi*, son of Rock, was the trickster, while *Waziya*, the Old Man, and his wife *Wakanda*, the Witch, were pervasive forces of evil. Their daughter, *Anog Ita*, was the double-faced woman — one side beautiful, the other horrible. In addition, there was Crazy Buffalo, who caused wrongdoing, and *Miniwatu*, or maggots, which caused aches, pains, and suffering. But the powers of good, fortunately, were more potent than those of evil. Shamans, through ritual, prayer, and song, could thwart evil and effect cures. Sage was repugnant to the spirits of evil, and the buffalo skull warded off evil influences.

It was from the gods that men obtained strength and comfort. Power was received in visions wherein men actively sought communication with the gods. Young men, under the tutelage of a shaman, or "dreamer," might "go on the hill" to fast for four days and nights. There they would hope to receive instructions from an emissary of the gods: the Bear, the Elk, the Wolf, the Deer, or the Eagle. Men who dreamt of the Bear acquired the power to effect cures, while those who received visions of the Elk could make love flutes and potions. Wolf Dreamers could become powerful war leaders, while Deer Dreamers could make magical shields. Dreamers of the Eagle could find lost articles and, as *Heyokas*, became contrary men who did things backwards, wearing winter moccasins in the summer, for example, while going barefoot in the winter.

Self-torture provided another avenue for obtaining a vision. Young men might walk around the village dragging buffalo skulls on thongs attached to skewers stuck in their backs; or they might enter the Sun Dance, suspending themselves by thongs attached to skewers in their chest muscles from the sacred Sun Dance pole. The reward of priesthood came to those who endured all four phases of the Sun Dance and memorized the myths and ceremonies of the Sioux. Such men could paint their hands red, officiate at the sacred ceremonies, and interpret the cosmology and the supernatural for the benefit of the people.

White markers along the bluffs above the Little Big Horn River show where General George Armstrong Custer's troops died on June 25, 1876, in their eagerness to destroy the Sioux way of life. For years, the Sioux defied the white man's encroachment of their homelands. From the immigrants to the gold miners to the U.S. Cavalry, the Sioux resisted the aliens' inroads. So determined were the Indians that they closed the Bozeman Trail from the Platte River to Virginia City, Montana. Red Cloud, the Oglala chief, forced the government to rescind its treaty and close the forts — he was the only Indian statesman ever to force the U.S. government to surrender its terms.

The Custer battle was a culmination of the United States' policy of confining Indians to the despair of reservation life. Defiantly, the Indians won the battle; tragically, they lost the war. Over the next several years, anti-climactic skirmishes erupted between white man and Indian; military pressure and starvation led most of the Sioux remaining outside the reservations to surrender to the government agencies.

Sitting Bull, the great Hunkpapa chief, sought refuge in Canada, finally surrendering in July of 1881, when all possibilities of a free existence for his people had been exhausted. He was the last holdout. Sioux life was now destroyed. Only a hollow vestige remained of what was once a vibrant life style.

1. Unless otherwise noted, the source material for this essay is drawn from R. B. Hassrick, *The Sioux* (Norman, Okla.: 1964). The ensuing sections on hide preparation, quilling, and beading are borrowed directly from passages in this book.

2. Ibid., pp. 191–92.

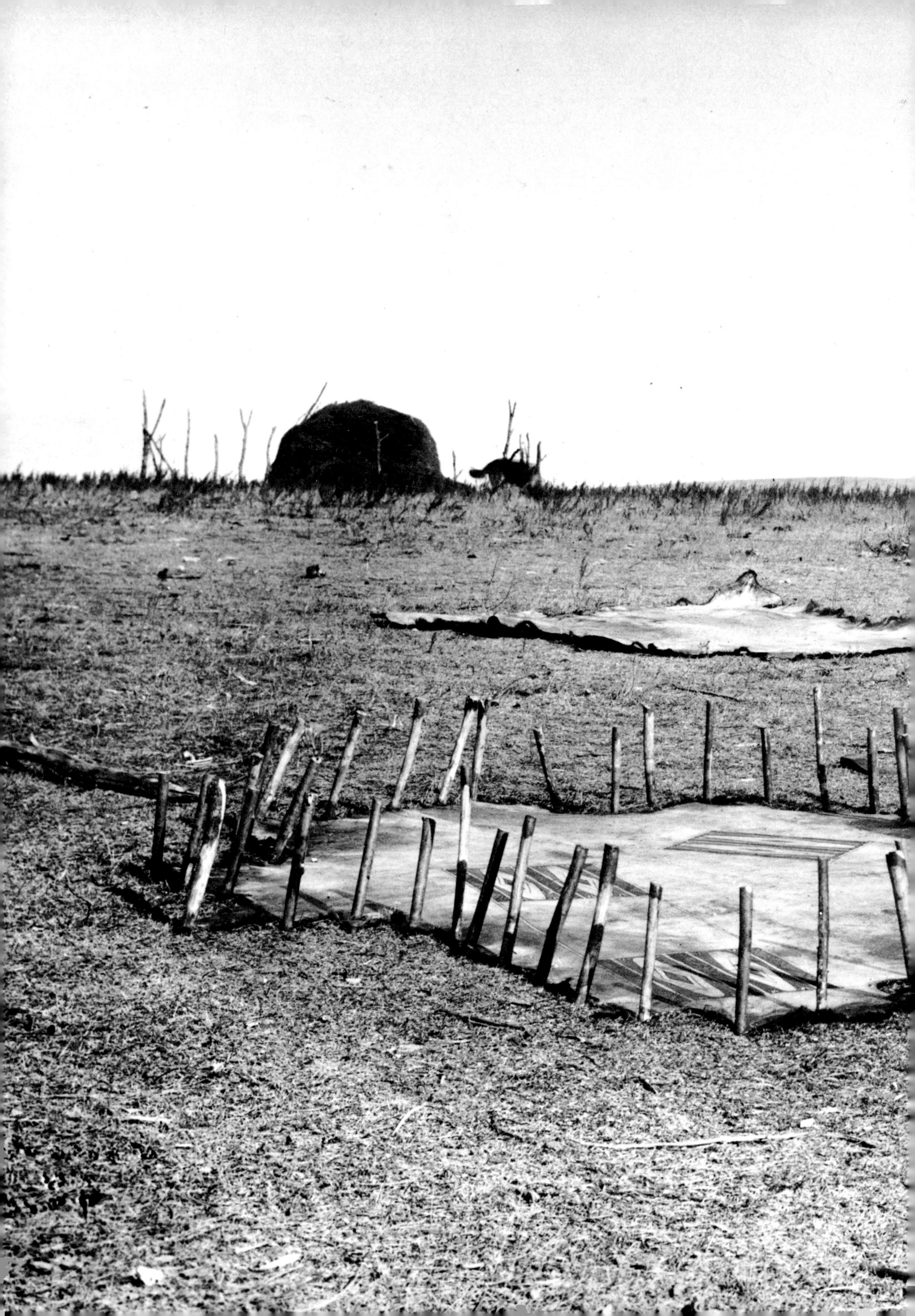

The Read Collection

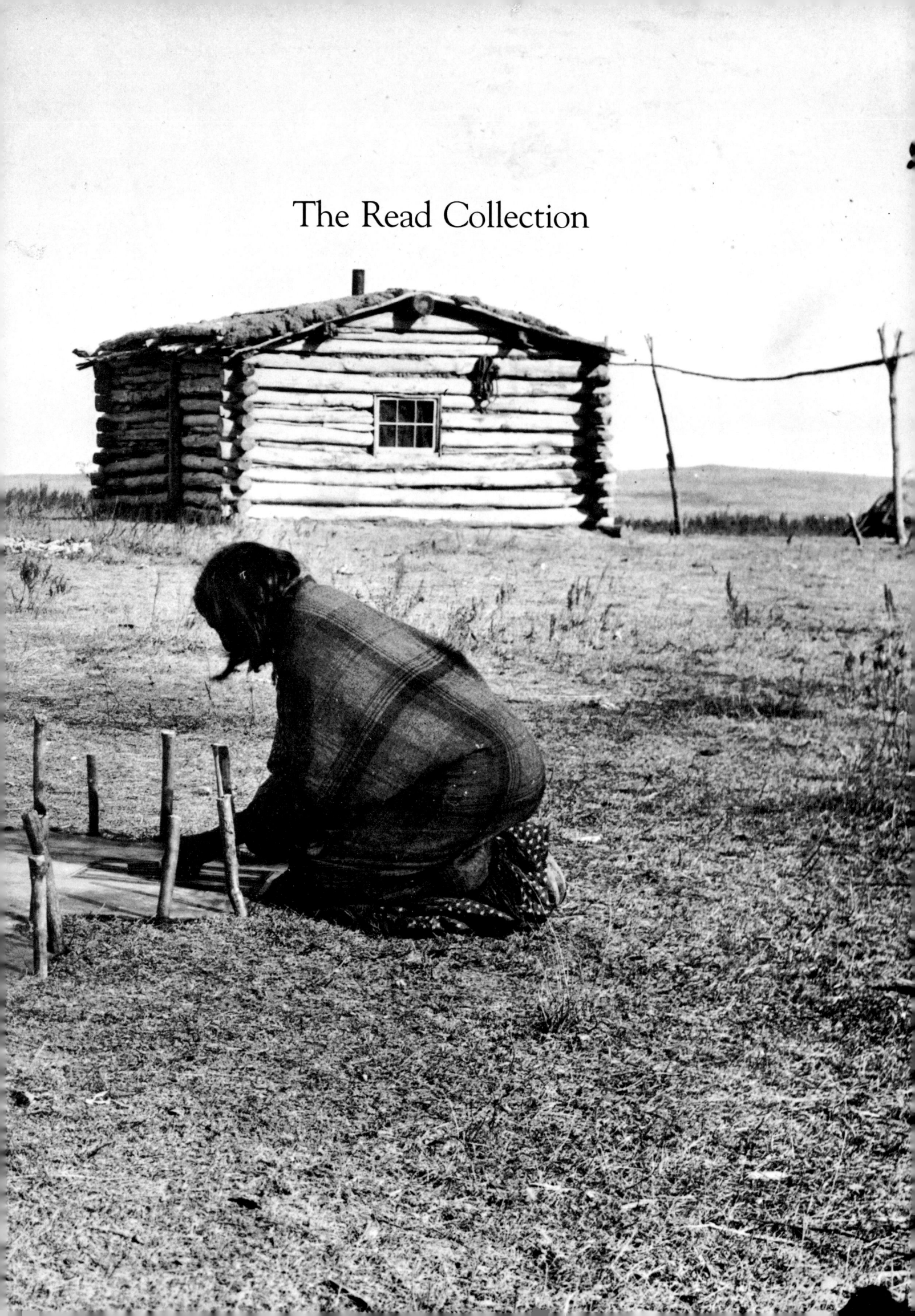

Men's Costume and Accessories

Cat. no. 5. Hair-Fringed Shirt (front)

Cat. no. 5. Hair-Fringed Shirt (back)

Cat. no. 9. Eagle Feather Bonnet

Cat. no. 10. Roach

Cat. no. 11. Horned Headdress

Cat. no. 12. Horned Headdress

Cat. no. 1. Grizzly Bear Claw Moccasins

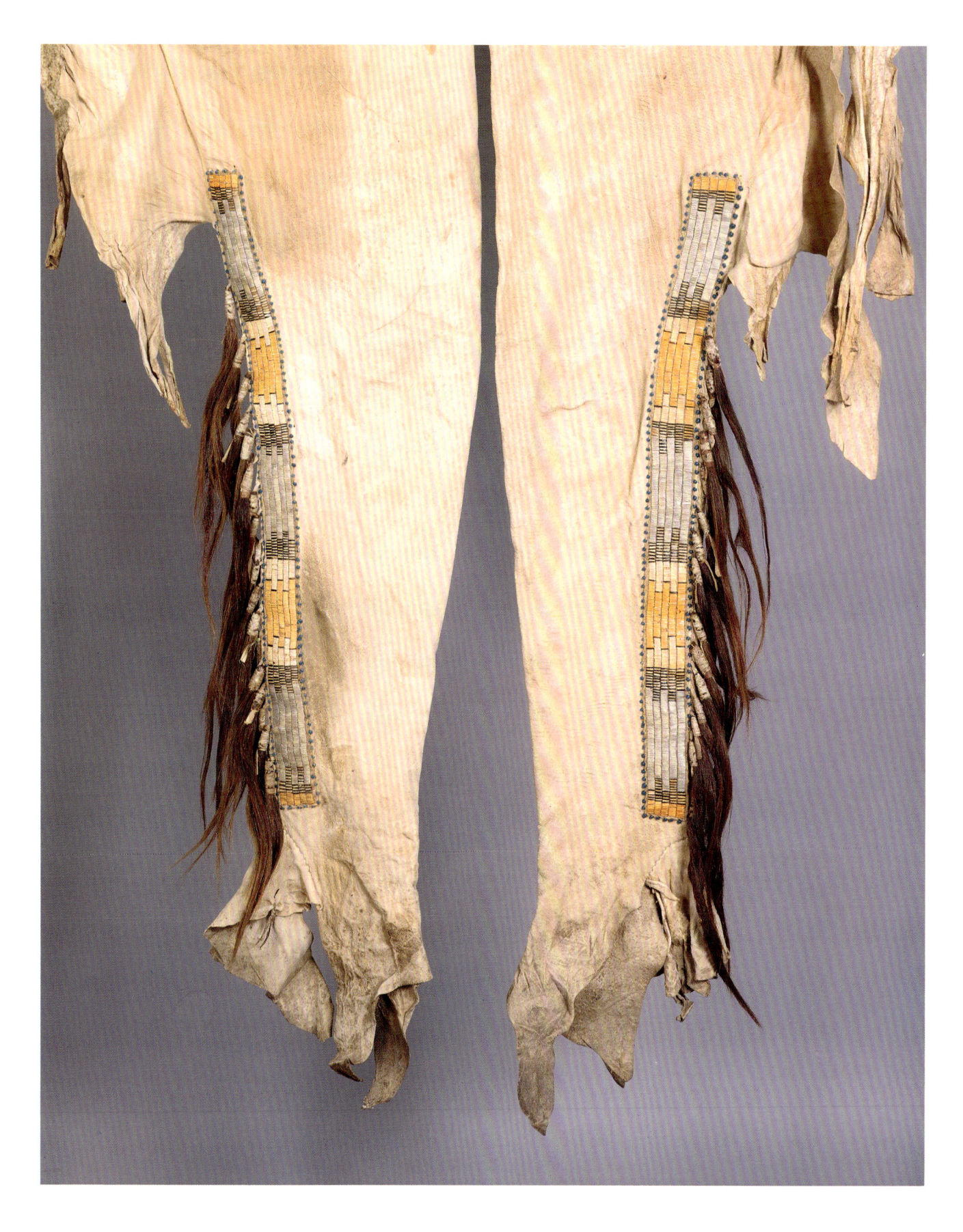

Cat. no. 8. Leggings (detail)

Cat. no. 7. Hair-Fringed Shirt (back)

Cat. no. 7. Hair-Fringed Shirt (front)

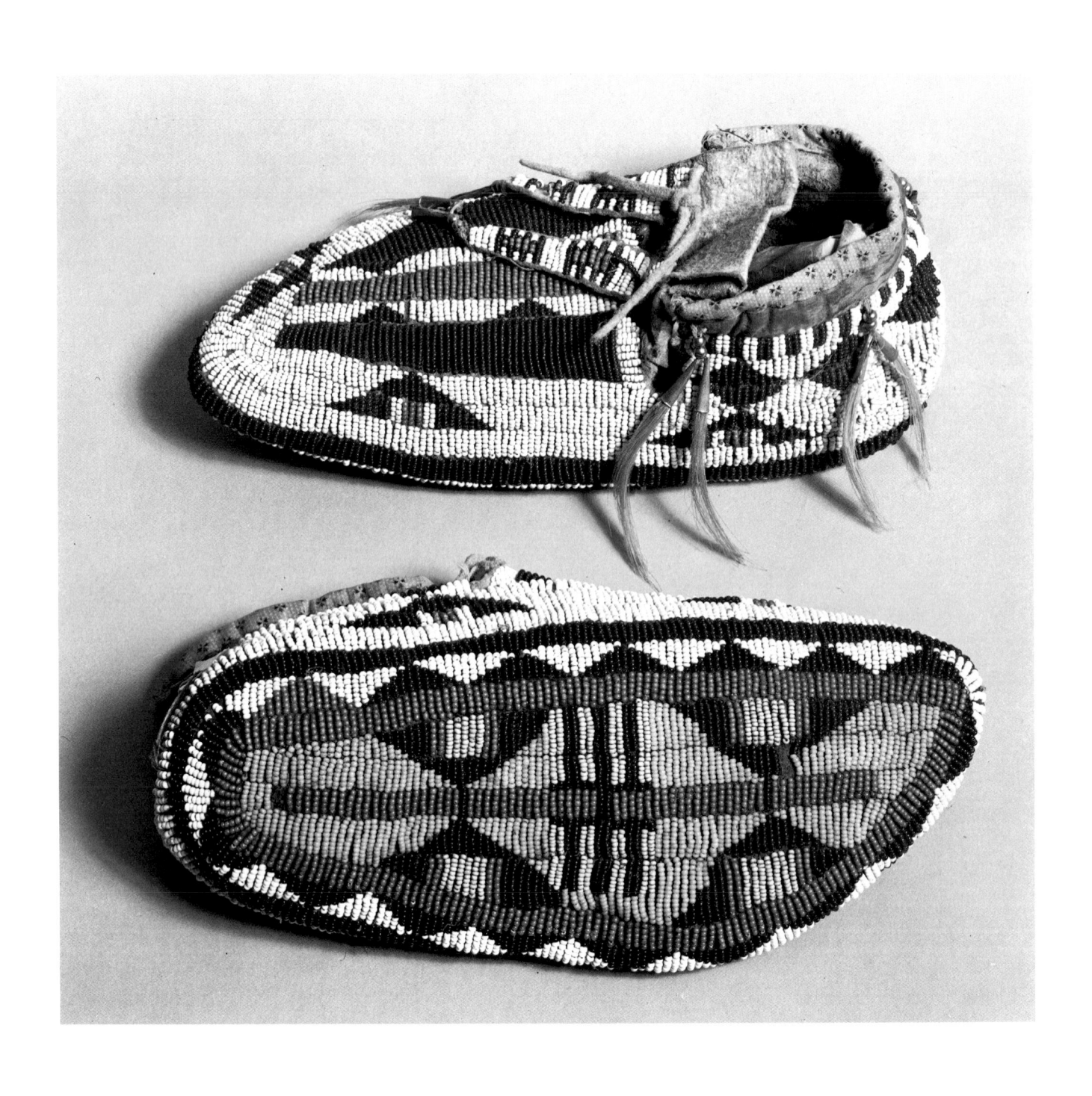

Cat. no. 3. Fully Beaded Moccasins

Cat. no. 2. Moccasins

Cat. no. 4. Moccasins

Men's Costume and Accessories

1. Grizzly Bear Claw Moccasins

Sioux, probably Yanktonai Dakota
L: 27 cm   W: 10 cm
Presented to Captain Read by Medicine Bear, principal chief of the Yanktonais.
1881.3.73   Read no. 73

Buffalo rawhide sole sinew-sewn to upper of deerskin; straight cut ankle bound with red stroud; separately added triangular tongue with beaded multiple triangles in pink and green on light blue ground, terminating in metal cone dangles with yellow horsehair tufts; upper beaded in white-core rose, yellow, and dark blue on a light blue ground; grizzly bear claw attachments with red stroud trim (with single beaded strand) sinew-sewn to cuff; claws and bear hide show traces of red pigment; thong lacing.

In his inventory, Read notes that these moccasins were awarded to the bravest warrior in the tribe and that Medicine Bear exhibited six wounds as proof of his right to wear them. The grizzly bear was regarded as the bravest and fiercest of all animals, and the display of its claws indicated the status of its owner. The killing of a grizzly was the equivalent of the killing of a man. Thus, bear claws became a badge of bravery. Grizzly bear claws were normally worn as necklaces by warriors who had killed a grizzly or performed a different, equally valorous act. Attachment to moccasins, however, is unusual.

2. Moccasins

Cheyenne
L: 27 cm   W: 9.5 cm
Purchased from Cheyenne Indian at Terry's Landing, M.T., Nov., 1878.
1881.3.76   Read no. 76

Buffalo rawhide sole sinew-sewn to upper of deer hide; straight cut ankle; separate, forked tongue trimmed with white seed beads; upper decorated with horse hooves (front) and paired dragonflies with eyes denoted by dark blue beads (back); originally painted blue; beaded borders around sole and ankle cuff and up back and across front of ankle; double vertical border ornamented with double row of metal cone dangles bisects front half of upper; heel fringe; thong lacing.

The Cheyenne favored the use of a central row of fringe or tin cones to delineate the front decorative panels on their moccasins. The horse hooves depicted on the front signify that the owner had captured many horses. The dragonflies symbolize speed and invincibility, thus offering the wearer protection in battle.

3. Fully Beaded Moccasins

Sioux
L: 26 cm   W: 8 cm
Presented by Joe Culbertson at Poplar River, M.T., 1881.
1881.3.74   Read no. 74

Separate pieces of deerskin form upper and sole; each fully beaded with geometric patterns in white-core rose, yellow, and light and dark blue on a white ground; separate beaded, forked tongue terminating in metal beads and cones with orange horsehair tufts; straight cut ankle with calico and purple ribbon sewn onto cuff; lower edge of cuff decorated with metal beads and cone dangles with orange horsehair tufts; thong lacing.

This pair of moccasins is distinguished by the fact that it is beaded on both the uppers and the soles. Fully beaded moccasins such as these were known as "love moccasins," since they were made by young women for their would-be husbands. Read notes in his inventory that they were buried with the warrior to whom they belonged, and it may well be that such moccasins served a funerary purpose as well. In this connection, it may be noted that fully beaded moccasins were observed by General Terry's troops after the Custer battle as they investigated the burial lodges containing the bodies of fallen warriors in the Indian villages (E.S. Connell, *Son of the Morning Star* [San Francisco, 1984] 3–4). It was customary to be buried in one's finest attire, and it could well be that these young men were wearing their "love moccasins." The upper design of long parallel triangles, or gores, visible on this example was referred to as "buffalo tracks" by the Sioux.

4. Moccasins

Yanktonai Dakota
L: 26 cm   W: 9.5 cm
Made by wife of Two Bears, Yanktonai.
1881.3.116   Read no. 116

Buffalo rawhide sole sinew-sewn to upper of deer hide; straight cut ankle bound with dark blue stroud and lined with calico; dark blue stroud instep; trapezoidal tongue separately attached with plaited quillwork and metal cone dangles; plaited porcupine-quill decoration on uppers: purple background with joined lozenge designs in turquoise; beaded border around edge of uppers consisting of triangles and box designs (yellow and medium blue) trimmed with translucent dark red on a light blue ground; heel fringe; thong lacing.

5. Hair-Fringed Shirt

Sioux
L: 75 cm (1.30 m including leg pendants)
W: 90 cm   Sleeve L: 65 cm
1881.3.156 LA   Not in Read inventory list

Antelope skin, sinew-sewn; poncho style; separately attached antelope leg pendants with attached dewclaws under arms; legs retained as pendants at bottom; open sides, half-sewn sleeves; self-fringed on edges and cuffs; rectangular neck flaps of red stroud beaded in four rows of white with light and dark blue bands; quilled hide strips sinew-sewn on shoulders and sleeves; quillwork plaited between four threads of sinew using multiple quills in alternating panels of yellow and white with dark blue feather designs; quillwork bands trimmed with light blue beads; dark brown human-hair pendants on quill-wrapped leather thongs attached to lower edges of arm bands, outer edges of shoulder bands, and bottom edges of neck flaps; upper half of shirt and sleeves decorated with light blue vertical stripes.

This hair-fringed shirt is in the style of the 1870s, particularly in the width and design motifs of the arm and shoulder bands. In a lecture presented to the Women's Indian Association at the University of Vermont in 1888, Read displayed a war shirt which he believed to be Sitting Bull's, reputedly worn by the leader in the Custer battle. He claimed that the shirt had been given to him by a trader who had acquired it from Sitting Bull himself on his way to Canada (abstract of lecture in Burlington *Daily Free Press*, May 16, 1888, p. 8). Stanley Vestal, Sitting Bull's biographer, states that the chief was, in fact, wearing a hair-fringed shirt with matching leggings during the Custer battle (S. Vestal, *Sitting Bull* [Boston, 1932] 164). That the shirt in Read's possession was worn by Sitting Bull during the battle may be apocryphal. As headman of the Hunkpapa, Sitting Bull was certainly entitled to wear such a shirt; however, the fact that he gave it to a trader rather than sold or traded it seems strange, although he may have given it in exchange for something else. That the trader would make a gift to Read of so historic an article rather than ask a high price for it is also unusual, but would seem to add some credence to the story insofar as it seems to indicate that Read himself was not sold a bill of goods.

6. Ermine Skin Pendants *(not illus.)*

Northern Plains
L: 20–33 cm
1881.3.157 LA   Possibly from Read no. 114

Eight strips of white weasel (ermine) skin wrapped with red stroud and strands of light and dark blue beads; originally attached to the sleeves or shoulders of a man's shirt or suspended from a headdress.

7. Hair-Fringed Shirt

Northern Plains, ca. 1850
L: 80 cm   W: 1.52 m (sleeves extended)
1986.2.1 LA   Not in Read Collection

Antelope skin, sinew-sewn; poncho style; antelope legs retained as pendants on bottom and on sleeves; self-fringed on edges and cuffs; triangular neck flaps with long fringe decorated with blue pony beads; hide shoulder bands consist of four columns of blue pony beads; shoulders and arms decorated with painted strips in black (right side) and fugitive red (left side); brown and blond human-hair pendants (on thong strips with white and blue quill wrapping) attached to outer edges of beaded shoulder bands and along sleeves; front and back of shirt decorated with central disk quill-plaited in five concentric bands and trimmed with single border of blue (front) and white (back) pony beads; medallions decorated with tripartite divisions in orange trimmed with brown.

Shirts were worn principally as badges of office, as symbols of prowess, or as protective devices, guarding the wearer against harm in battle. In its latter function, the shirt might be decorated with magical symbols. The *Wicasas* were invested with hair-fringed shirts and were known as "Shirt Wearers." The locks of hair that decorated the shoulders and sleeves of such shirts did not represent scalps but, rather, the people of the tribe for whom the leader was responsible. (Among some groups, the hair fringe is said to have denoted scalps, trophies of the wearer's valor.) The stripes on the shoulder and arm flaps probably represent a tally of some sort.

This garment is an example of an early hair-fringed and painted shirt with quilled rosette at the breast. A Yankton Sioux and an Assiniboine, both painted by Bodmer in 1833, wear shirts of this style (D. Thomas and K. Ronnefeldt, eds., *People of the First Man* [New York, 1982] 45 and 53). A shirt worn by One Horn, a Teton Sioux pictured by Catlin in 1832, is of the same type (R. B. Hassrick, *The George Catlin Book of American Indians* [New York, 1977] 154).

8. Leggings

Northern Plains, ca. 1850
L: 1.20 m   Bottom W: 14 cm
1986.2.2 LA   Not in Read Collection

Deerskin, folded and sinew-sewn along one side; separately added flap at bottom; decorated along outer edge with band of quillwork in two-thread, one-quill, straight technique; quilled band consists of five rows in blue, yellow, and black dyes; band trimmed with single row of blue pony beads; outer edge of legging decorated with hair pendants wrapped with hide thongs.

9. Eagle Feather Bonnet

Sioux
H: 50 cm   L: 26 cm
Acquired at Poplar River, M.T., 1881.
1881.3.56   Read no. 56

Skull cap of buffalo hide decorated with crow feathers attached by thongs; forty upright golden eagle tail and secondary wing feathers form outer circle, strung together on thong; yellow horsehair tufts attached with resin to tips of feathers; red-dyed down feathers sinew-sewn onto brow; red stroud triangular strips at sides, trailing to rear; hide fringe attached to sides, piercing the stroud; thong fastening straps.

Plains Indian men wore a variety of headdresses, the most popular of which was the eagle feather war bonnet. Among the Sioux, these bonnets were composed of eagle feathers mounted on a leather cap. The number of feathers employed usually totaled thirty-six, representing the tail feathers of three eagles. Such headdresses were commonly ornamented with a beaded brow band terminating with rosettes from which were suspended hawk feathers and ermine skins. Shamans made bonnets, endowing them with magical power which protected the wearer from harm in battle. The power of the eagle feather alone served to ward off harm. Like the ermine, the hawk was swift and elusive and conveyed these attributes to the wearer. This eagle feather bonnet is comprised of a buffalo-skin cap covered with crow feathers. Red-dyed down feathers are placed along the brow, and red flannel strips trail at the sides and rear. This example is most unusual in that it lacks a brow band. A similar bonnet is worn by the Pawnee chief Petalesharo in a portrait painted by Charles Bird King in 1821 (see P. H. Hassrick, *The Way West* [New York, 1977] 29).

10. Roach

Northern Plains
L (at base): 12.5 cm
1881.3.93   Read no. 93

Black and purple-dyed deer hair secured by base of wrapped porcupine quills; single golden eagle feather in center.

Headdresses of deer and porcupine hair, referred to as "roaches," were common throughout much of the Great Plains and Eastern Woodlands. Among the Sioux, for example, members of certain warrior societies, such as the Kit Foxes, were entitled to shave the sides of their heads. By cutting the central area short so the hairs stood erect, being careful to leave the scalp lock intact, they effectively "roached" their hair. It may be that these headdresses were originally signs of membership in particular clubs. However, in reservation days, when warrior societies had lost their meaning, roaches became part of the costume of men engaged in a form of social dancing known as the "Grass Dance."

11. Horned Headdress

Sioux, probably Hunkpapa, Teton Dakota
Cap H: 10 cm   Cap Diam: 17 cm
Captured in engagement of Jan. 2, 1881, from Yellow Horse, Hunkpapa Indian.
1881.3.54   Read no. 54

Buffalo-hide cap, sinew-sewn in three sections; covered with strips of matted ermine; split antelope horns attached to cap with hide thongs through three perforations in base of horns, and sewn onto rectangular rawhide backing on underside; brow band of red stroud sinew-sewn to front, with beaded decoration in white, yellow, lavender, medium blue, dark purple, and translucent green and dark blue; beaded design consists of central crescent between circles with rectangular border in five panels below; stroud fastening straps.

At one time horned headdresses were worn only by the outstanding warriors and, as such, were badges of their prowess. Split-horn headdresses with caps of matted ermine skins such as this one were especially popular among the Blackfeet and the Crow, but they also were found among the Mandan and the Sioux.

12. Horned Headdress

Sioux
Band H: 5 cm   Band L: 35 cm
1881.3.150 LA   Read no. 123 (?)

Buffalo-hide brow band; beaded design of three stepped triangles in light blue trimmed in dark blue on white ground; split antelope horns sinew-sewn to brow band through single perforation in base of each horn; yellow horsehair tufts attached to tips of horns with sinew and red-dyed porcupine-quill wrapping; quill-wrapped pendant hide thongs (in yellow, orange, blue, and white) hold horns in place; row of clipped crow feathers sinew-sewn to uppper edge of brow band between horns; bundles of split hawk feathers attached on either side of horns; thong fastening straps.

Split-horn headdresses with crowns of clipped crow feathers were unusual. Bodmer illustrates one worn by the Assiniboine Noapeh in 1833 (Joslyn Museum, *Karl Bodmer's America* [1984] pl. 199). A similar headdress, dating around 1830, with horns cut from rawhide is in the collection of the University Museum, Philadelphia; no tribal identification is made. A horned headdress with cropped feathers is in the Peabody Museum, Harvard; the specimen was collected in 1886 at Fort Berthold, North Dakota, and is identified either as Mandan or Hidatsa (J.C. Ewers, "Assiniboine Antelope-horn Headdresses," *American Indian Magazine* [Autumn 1982] 46, fig. 2); cf. also an example in the National Museum of Natural History, Smithsonian Institution (Inv. no. 153,983; acquired 1892).

Women's Costume and Accessories

Cat. no. 13. Dress

Cat. no. 13. Dress (detail)

Cat. no. 14. Dress

Cat. no. 15. Buffalo Robe

Cat. no. 17. Baby Carrier (detail)

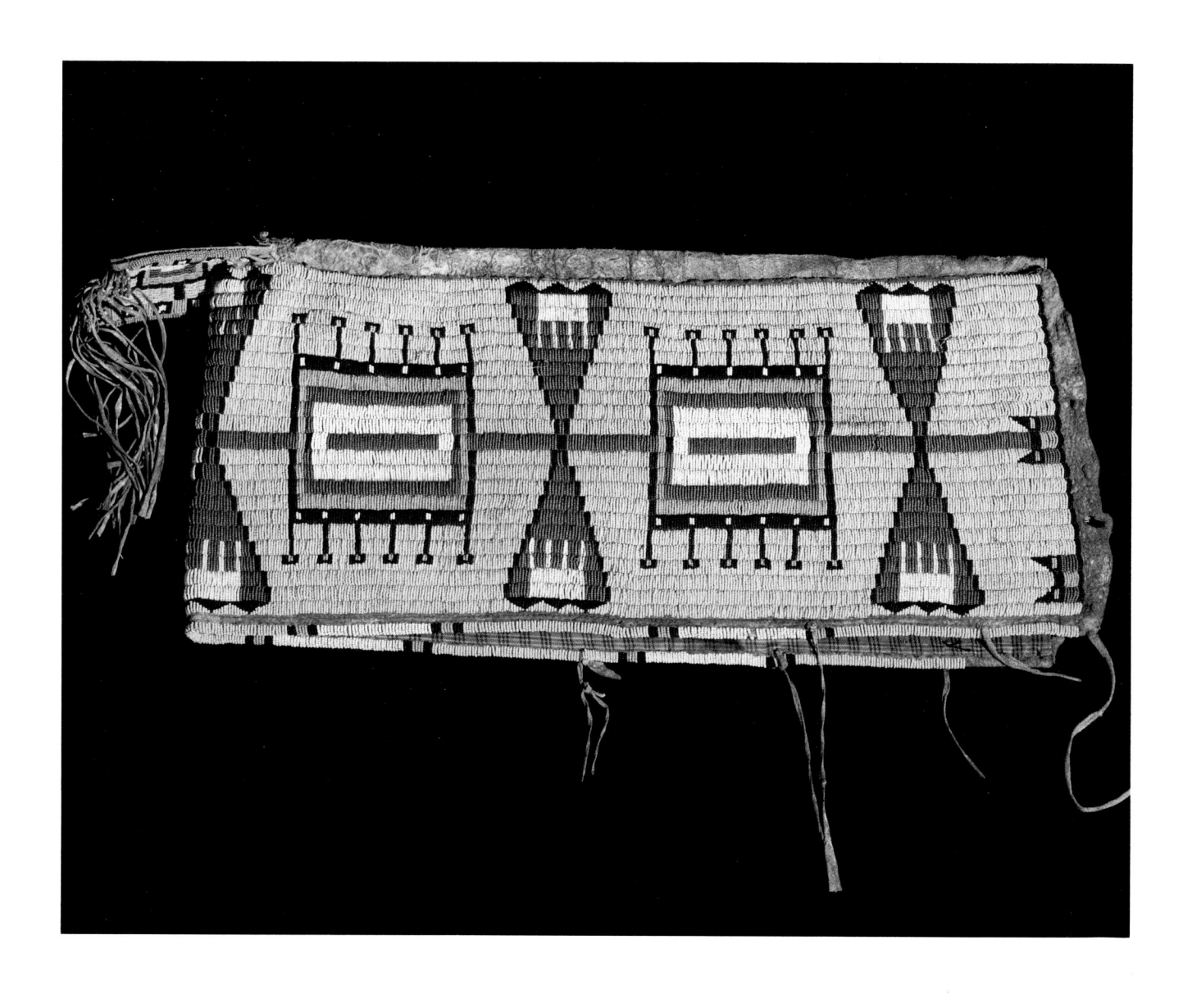

Cat. no. 17. Baby Carrier

Cat. no. 19. Legging

Cat. no. 18. Leggings

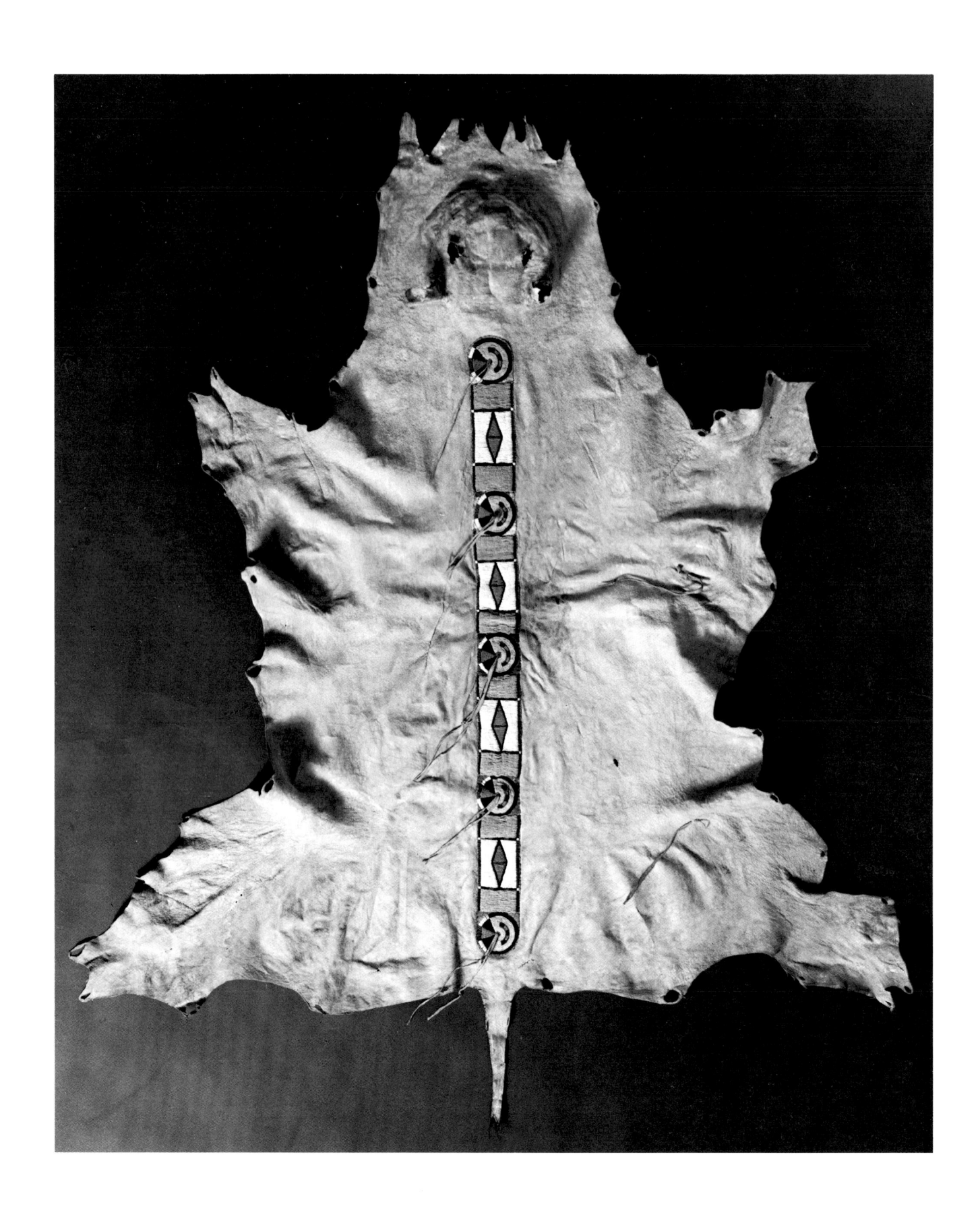

Cat. no. 16. Child's Buffalo Robe

Women's Costume and Accessories

13. Dress

Nez Percé
L: 1.50 m W: 52 cm (at waist)
Nez Percé manufacture. Captured by Crow Indian in action at Bear Paw Mountains, M.T., 1877.
1881.3.28 Read no. 28

Two elkskins, sinew-sewn, form front and back of dress; separately added cape with elkskin tail on front and back; added fringe along sides, hem, sleeves, and shoulders; long pendant skin strips attached to front and back of dress: beneath shoulder piece and in three rows on lower half of skirt; clusters of glass seed beads form rectangles and triangles in red, pink, green, yellow, and light and dark blue at base of pendant fringe on skirt; collar decorated with sinew-sewn red stroud trimmed below with three rows of blue pony beads.

Early Sioux dresses were fashioned of two elkskins sewn together at the hindquarters with an opening for the neck. The tails folded over at the neckline to form a narrow yoke. Narrow bands of beading covered the seams. With its red flannel collar and its skirt with beads and fringe, this double-elkskin dress is an interesting example of an early style of women's garment. It is interesting to note that the Nez Percé, a mountain people, were still wearing a fashion that was popular fifty years earlier on the plains.

14. Dress

Sioux
L: 1.40 m W (sleeves extended): 1.50 m
Purchased from sister of Scout Bear Soldier, Poplar River, M.T., March, 1882.
1881.3.113 Read no. 113

Two elkskins, sinew-sewn, form front and back of dress; separately added yoke, fully beaded front and back; decoration consists of concentric rectangles, lozenges, triangles, oblongs, and curvilinear bands in yellow, green, dark blue, and translucent red on a light blue ground; separately added fringe along sleeves and hem; separately added hem flaps embroidered with three registers of dark blue and white beads trimmed with metal cone dangles.

Cf. a dress in the National Museum of Natural History, Smithsonian Institution (Inv. no. 200,632); cf. also a dress in the Smithsonian Brotherton Collection (Inv. no. 384,130; collected at Fort Buford, 1880–81).

When solidly beaded yokes became fashionable among the Sioux during the last quarter of the nineteenth century, or early reservation period, the yoke itself became a single element to which a skirt was sewn. Design elements consisted of bold triangles, boxes, and diamonds. At the base of the yoke it was common to place a U-shaped figure called a turtle, which was a vestige of the elk tail found on earlier dresses. This dress is a handsome example of early Sioux reservation costume. The two rows of tin cones added music as the wearer walked.

15. Buffalo Robe

Crow
L: 2.40 m W: 1.60 m
Crow manufacture. Purchased at Terry's Landing, M.T., Dec., 1878.
1881.3.18 Read no. 18

Bison hide, in two halves, sinew-sewn down the middle; beaded blanket strip in red, green, light and dark blue, and pink on a white ground bordered by green; design consists of four medallions beaded in concentric circular rows in alternation with lozenge designs between horizontal bars; triangular device of red stroud embroidered with horizontal bars in light and dark blue and trimmed in dark blue and white with small beaded triangles at the points; hide thong pendants attached to centers of medallions; edges of robe perforated for thong lacing.

Buffalo robes were worn as outer clothing by both sexes and were decorated with paint or with bands of quillwork and, later, beads. Painted robes exhibited various geometric patterns, while the bands of beading, later referred to as "blanket strips," consisted of four or five bars interspersed by disks. Much of the decoration on Indian attire was used to cover or hide seams, and so it was with the blanket strip. When the buffalo was killed, it often fell to its knees and was skinned down the back in this position. In fashioning a robe, the two halves were sewn together, forming a seam, and it was this seam that the blanket strip covered.

This buffalo-skin robe is ornamented with a beaded blanket strip of typical Crow design and style. The triangular device, frequently found on Crow women's dresses and men's leggings, is said to represent either the head of a buffalo (symbolizing sustenance) or a uterus (symbolizing birth). In Read's inventory, it is identified as "the outer dress of a wealthy squaw."

16. Child's Buffalo Robe

Crow
L: 1.60 m W: 1.0 m
Presented to Agnes Read (age four years) by one of her Crow playmates.
1881.3.20 Read no. 20

Hide of bison calf, in two halves, sinew-sewn down the middle; beaded blanket strip in green, yellow, and light and dark blue on alternating panels of pink and white; decoration consists of five medallions beaded in concentric circular rows in alternation with tripartite vertical panels with lozenges in the center section; thong lacing attached to centers of medallions; edges of robe perforated for hide lacing.

As Read's notes indicate, this child's buffalo robe, fashioned from the hide of a bison calf, was given to his four-year-old daughter by one of her Crow playmates. Children's clothing, including robes, were small replicas of adult attire.

17. Baby Carrier

Sioux (?)
L: 66 cm   W: 31 cm
Purchased from Yanktonai squaw at Poplar River, M.T., 1880.
1881.3.30   Read no. 30

Buffalo hide, fully beaded in red, orange, white, and green on a pink ground; repeated design of alternating concentric rectangles with extending lines and opposed triangles outlined in dark blue; calico lining; rawhide back; rectangular commercial leather tab with beaded design (in aforementioned colors) of concentric rectangles with extending lines, surrounded by a paneled border, the whole trimmed with light blue beads; tab has quill-wrapped, red-dyed skin fringe joined at base by a single strand of light blue beads; hood fastened in front by three sets of thong ties.

Baby carriers were lavishly decorated and often given as gifts in honor of newborn. They were, in fact, elaborate bundles in which infants were wrapped and carried in their mothers' arms. Some were equipped with a frame and strap. This served as a tump line placed over the mother's forehead or chest, thus supporting the carrier on her back. Carriers with straps could be hung from the pommel of a saddle or from a post. With its elaborately beaded decoration, this piece is a particularly handsome example. The use of a pink beaded background is an unusual feature in Sioux work and suggests that the carrier may be Assiniboine in origin.

18. Leggings

Yanktonai Dakota
L: 52 cm   W: 14 cm
Made by wife of Two Bears, Yanktonai.
1881.3.57   Read no. 57

Deerskin, folded and sinew-sewn to vertical skin strip; strip embroidered with quillwork, two-thread, one-quill, crossed technique; decoration consists of paired turquoise and dark blue diagonal bands against a purple ground; quilled strips decorated with applied skin fringe stained with yellow ochre; top of leggings terminate in red ochre-stained self fringe; dark blue stroud hem sewn around lower edge.

19. Legging

Métis
L: 45 cm   W: 57 cm
Half-breed work. Presented by David Roberts, Terry's Landing, M.T., 1879.
1881.3.59   Read no. 59

Deerskin; pocket flap sewn along bottom of legging; trimmed with calico; chintz lining; elaborate beaded floral pattern decorates left side of legging; drop-stitch technique in white-core rose, yellow, pink, light blue, and faceted green, grey, pink, purple, and black, trimmed in white.

The Métis, a people of mixed Indian and white descent, had settlements in the northeastern plains. Here they carried on a semi-nomadic lifestyle, adopting many Northern Plains Indian customs, including decorative designs. Floral designs are common in the Great Lakes region and the Northern Plains. The English chintz used as lining displays an elaborate "chinoiserie" pattern.

20. Belt

Sioux, probably Yanktonai Dakota
L: 85 cm plus 77 cm dangle   W: 10.5 cm
(Acquired from) Yanktonai, 1882.
1881.3.130a   Read no. 130

Commercial leather; metal buckle; belt and dangle decorated along edges with brass upholstery tacks; suspended from the belt is a beaded "Strike-a-light" pouch (see cat. no. 77).

Women's belts were often equipped with a variety of accessories, such as knife sheaths and awl cases. The beaded "Strike-a-light" pouch suspended from this belt probably held flint and steel. The dangle — that part of the belt that was inserted through the buckle — often hung down in front of the wearer two or three feet.

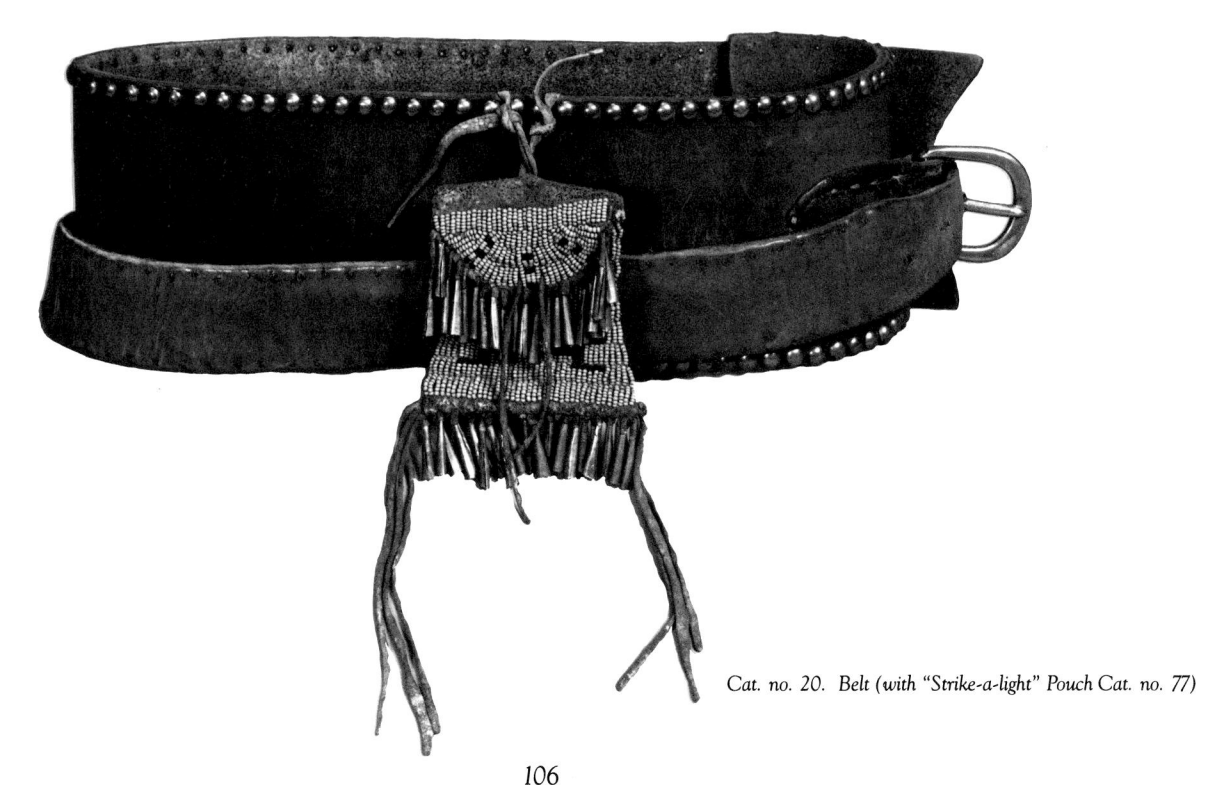

Cat. no. 20. Belt (with "Strike-a-light" Pouch Cat. no. 77)

Ornaments and Jewelry

Cat. no. 21. Man's Choker

21. Man's Choker

Northern Plains
L: 33 cm
Presented by Bad Soup, Yanktonai.
1881.3.94 Read no. 94

Four pairs of elk dewclaws, sinew-sewn together; choker fastened by hide thong.

22. Man's Earrings

Northern Plains
L: 16 cm
1881.3.105a,b Read no. 105

Dentalia shells in three sections, sinew-strung through both ends and through rawhide separating strips; attached pendants of four dentalia shells strung with dark blue bead spacers and terminating in trapezoidal sheetmetal plaques; earrings terminate in elongated round-bottomed abalone shell pendants sinew-strung through a pair of perforations at the top.

Cf. a pair of woman's earrings of identical construction in the National Museum of Natural History, Smithsonian Institution (Inv. no. 8504-A; Dakota Territory; acquired 1867).

23. Choker

Northern Plains
L: 33.5 cm
1881.3.96 Read no. 96

Dentalia shells, eleven sections of ten, sinew-strung through both ends and through rawhide separating strips; the middle six sections are decorated with brass upholstery tacks; ties of braided, orange-dyed cloth.

24. Woman's Choker

Northern Plains
L: 29 cm
Purchased from Yanktonai squaw at Poplar River, M.T., 1881.
1881.3.95c Read no. 95

Dentalia shells, nine sections of ten, sinew-strung through both ends and through rawhide separating strips ornamented with brass upholstery tacks; hide fastening thongs.

25. Woman's Earrings

Northern Plains
L: 36 cm
Purchased from Yanktonai squaw at Poplar River, M.T., 1881.
1881.3.95a,b Read no. 95

Dentalia shells, nine and ten sections of six, sinew-strung through both ends and through rawhide separating strips ornamented with brass upholstery tacks; earrings terminate in large trapezoidal sheetmetal pendants.

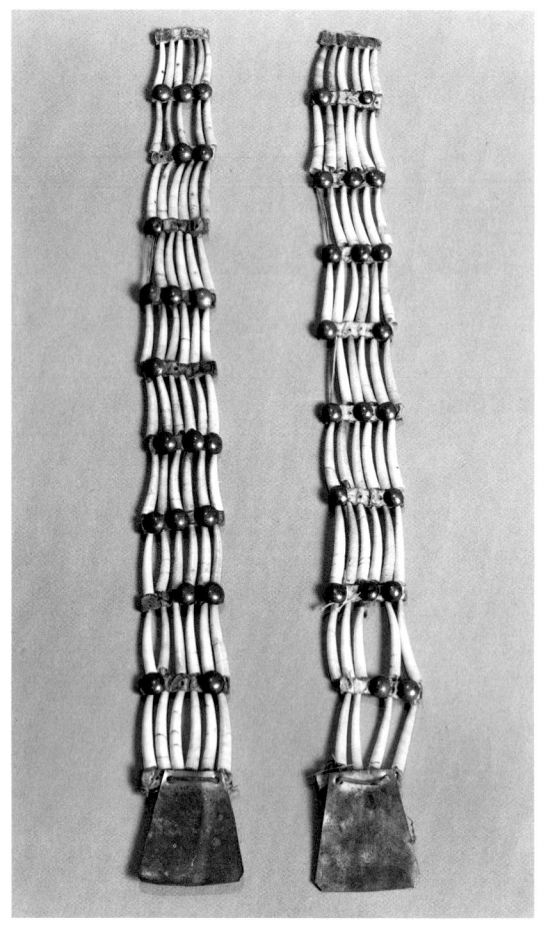

Cat. no. 25. Woman's Earrings

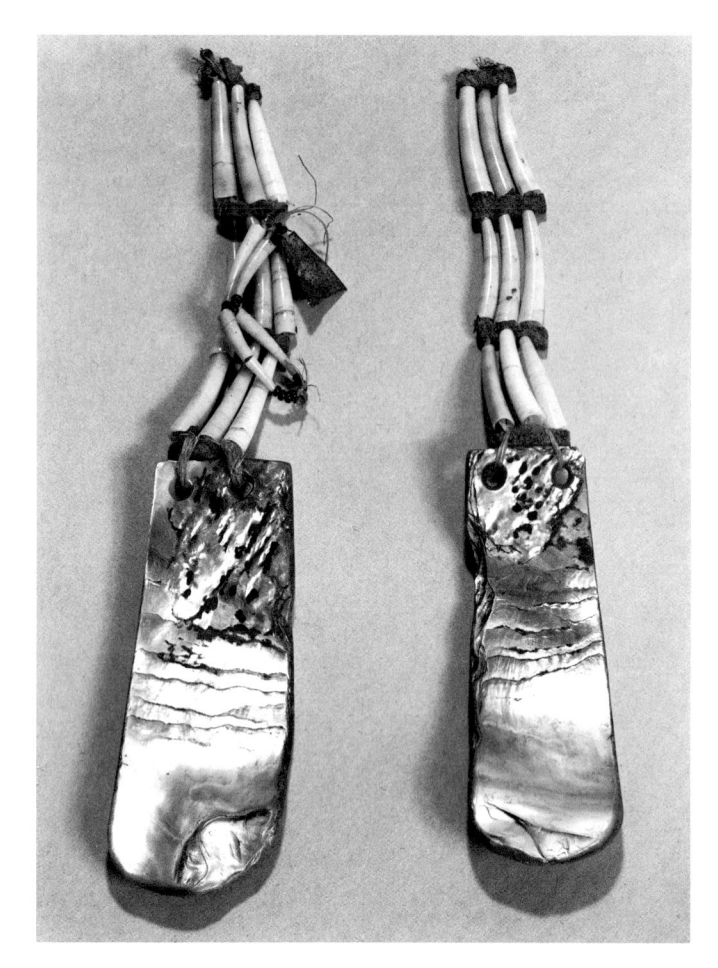

Cat. no. 22. Man's Earrings

Cat. no. 23. Choker (top)   Cat. no. 24. Woman's Choker (bottom)

Ritual and Ceremonial Objects

Cat. no. 29. Rattle

Cat. no. 27. Hand Drum (front)

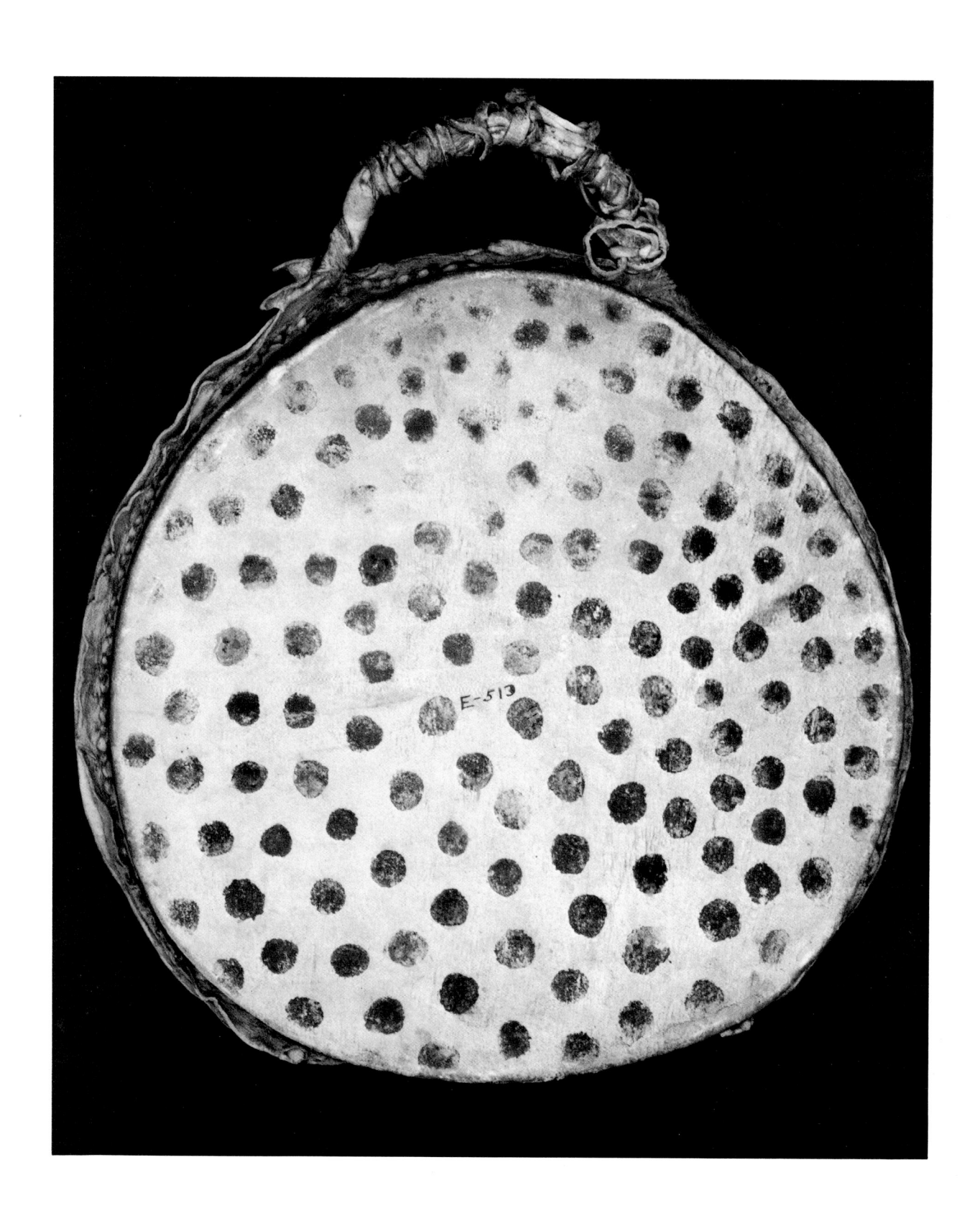

Cat. no. 27. Hand Drum (back)

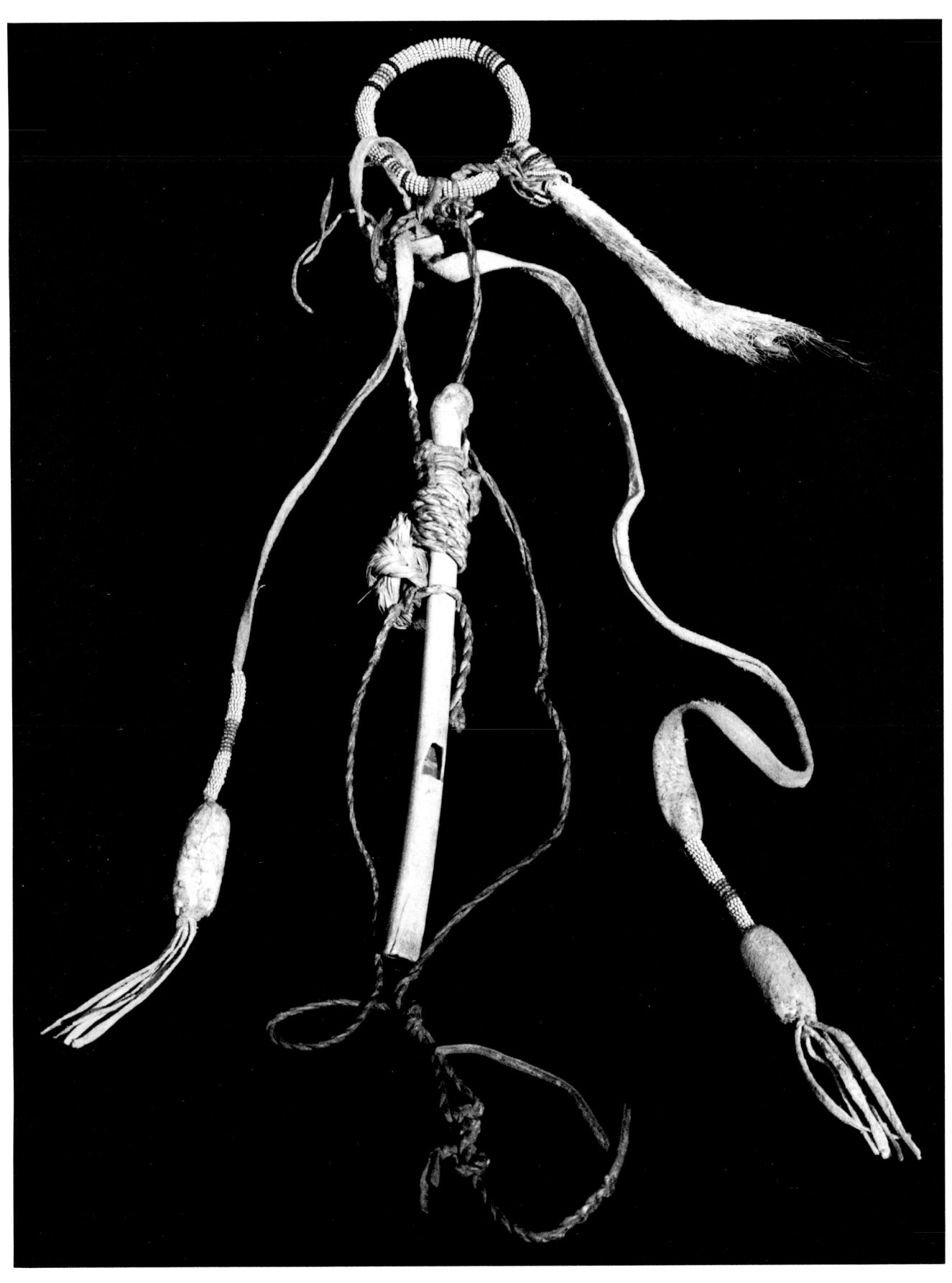

Cat. no. 26. Eagle Wing Bone Whistle

Cat. no. 35. Medicine Pouch (enlarged detail)

Cat. no. 39. Bowl

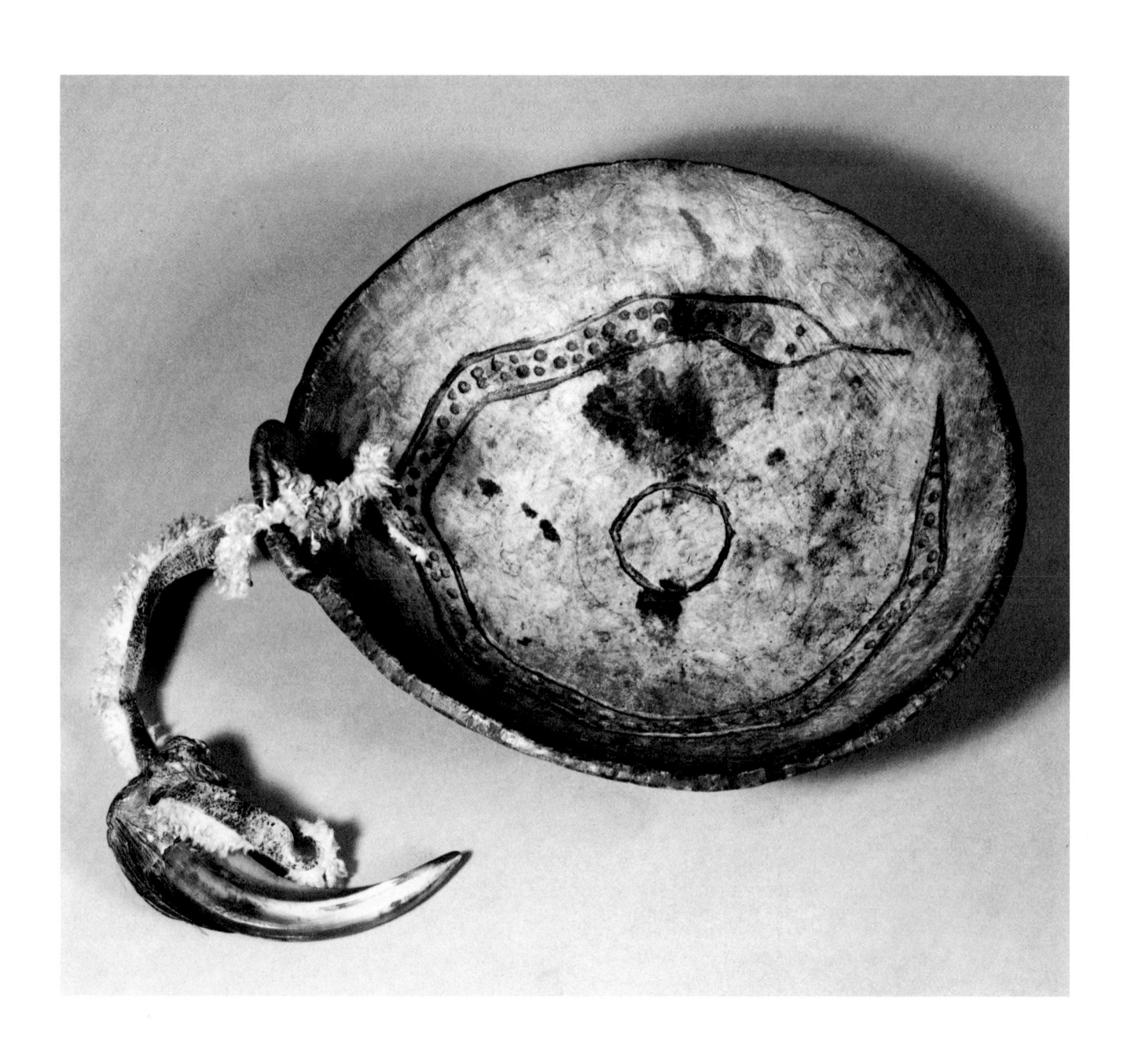

Cat. no. 41. Bowl

Cat. no. 38. Cup

Cat. no. 40. Cup

116

Cat. no. 32. Dance Sash

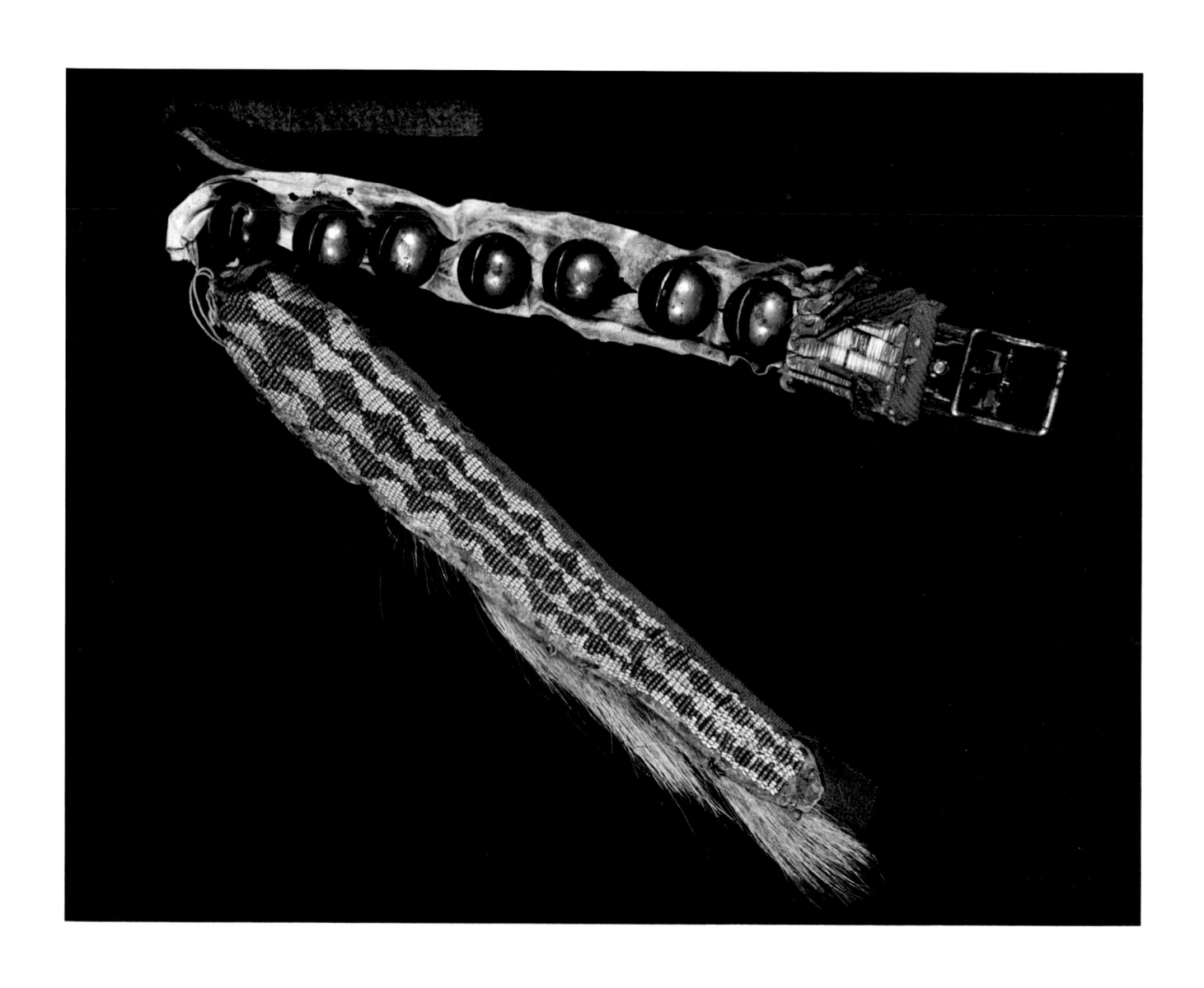

Cat. no. 30. Dance Garter or Anklet

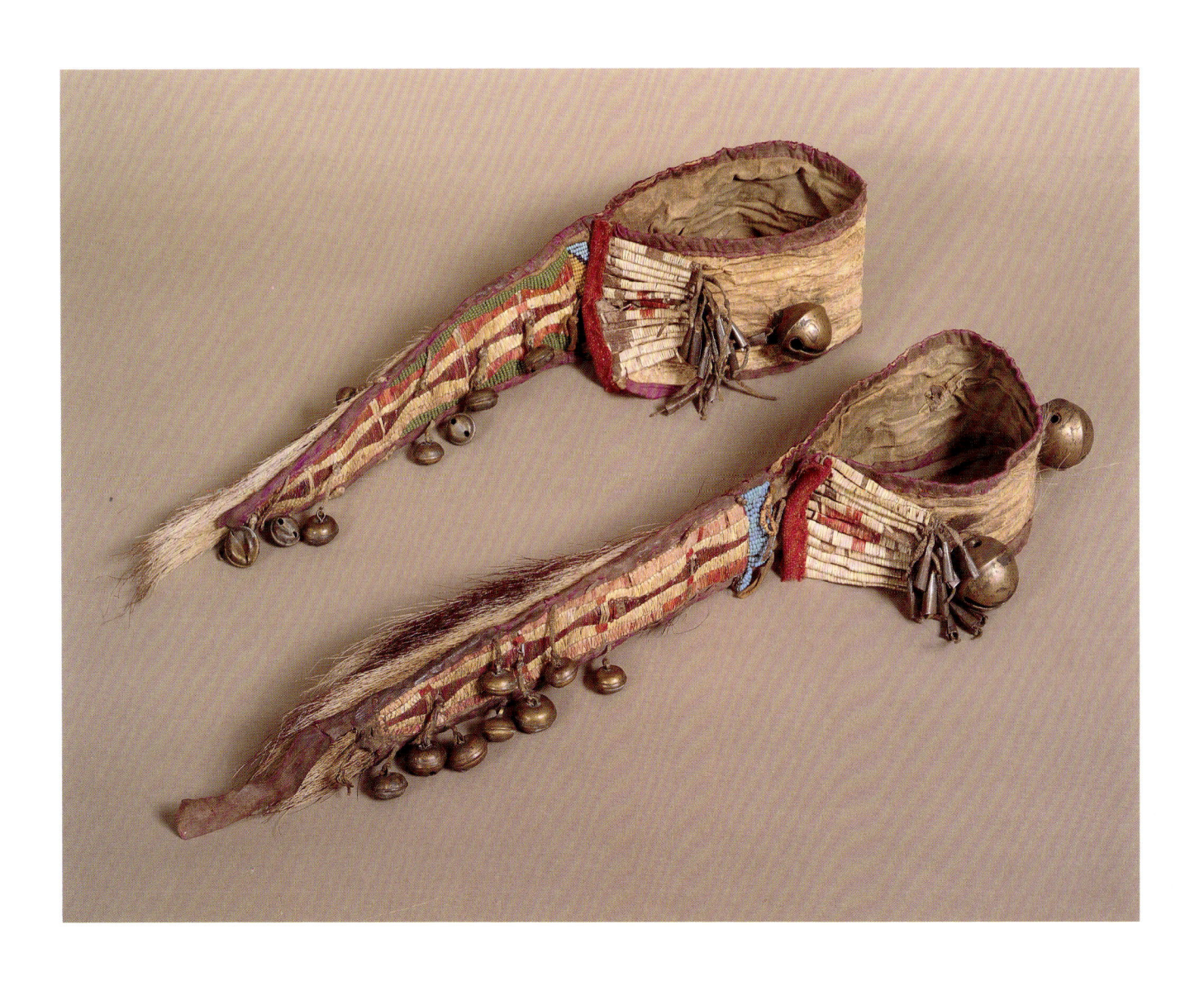

Cat. no. 31. Dance Garters or Anklets

Cat. no. 33. Dance Bustle

Cat. no. 34. Dance Shield

Cat. nos. 36, 37. Umbilical Cord Amulets

Ritual and Ceremonial Objects

26. Eagle Wing Bone Whistle

Sioux, probably Teton Dakota
Whistle L: 21 cm
Purchased from Little Assiniboine, chief-of-staff to Sitting Bull, while in irons at Camp Poplar River, M.T., Feb. 12, 1881.
1881.3.90   Read no. 90

Eagle wing bone whistle wrapped with hide rope to which a plaited bundle of sweet grass is secured; suspended from the rope is a beaded rawhide ring (embroidered with four bands each in white-core rose, yellow, and dark blue on a light blue beaded ground) to which is attached a stick wrapped in antelope skin and wound with a single beaded strand, and a long hide thong terminating at either end in red-dyed skin bundles with yellow buckskin fringe.

This eagle wing bone whistle is equipped with sweet grass and other medicines and provided with a thong for suspending it from the neck. Such whistles were blown by warriors in battle and by participants in the Sun Dance, who blew incessantly while gazing at the sun.

27. Hand Drum

Sioux, probably Yanktonai Dakota
H: 8 cm   Diam: 35.5 cm
Purchased from Black Chicken, Yanktonai, Poplar River, M.T., 1882.
1881.3.118a   Read no. 118

Two pieces of rawhide stretched over a bent wooden frame and stitched around the sides with a rawhide thong; drum painted on both faces: a) stylized frontal face with yellow eyes (and green pupils) and a red mouth on a red background with black dots; b) a white background with black dots; rawhide strap handle wrapped with hide strap.

The principal musical instruments of the Plains Indians were the rattle, drum, whistle, and flute. Rattling and drumming were nearly always accompanied by singing, all of which were employed in curing the sick and in ceremonial dancing. This hand drum was purchased from Yanktonai shaman Black Chicken, to whom a rattle (cat. no. 28 or 29) and several vessels (cat. nos. 38, 40) belonged. This drum is double-headed, a rather uncommon feature in the Plains area. The symbolism of the painting, both in its use of color and design, was known only to the owner. The dots which form the background of both faces are often referred to as hail spots and apparently served a protective function. Shamans usually sat beside their patients, holding the drum in one hand and beating it with a drum stick with the other.

28. Rattle *(not illus.)*

Sioux
L: 20 cm   Head W: 10 cm
1881.3.152 LA   Read no. 89 or 118

Sinew-sewn rawhide rattle formed from a buffalo's scrotum turned inside out; stick handle within buffalo-hide casing; head of rattle stained with red ochre; filled with pebbles.

29. Rattle

Sioux
L: 33 cm   W: 9 cm
1881.3.153 LA   Read no. 89 or 118

Sinew-sewn rawhide rattle formed from a buffalo's scrotum; stick handle wrapped at end with skin strap handle; filled with pebbles.

30. Dance Garter or Anklet

Sioux
Belt L: 54 cm   Pendant L: 29 cm
1881.3.155 LA   Read no. 70 or 71

Belt of commercial leather with skunk skin outer covering and blue felt backing, decorated with large brass bells; quill-wrapped, rawhide fringed ornament trimmed with red stroud and terminating in metal cone dangles with green yarn tufts sinew-sewn to belt; long triangular pendant of skunk skin edged with red stroud and beaded with triangular patterns in white-core rose on a light blue ground; belt inscribed "Bevin's Patent, April 8, 1862   Dec. 18, 1866."

31. Pair of Dance Garters or Anklets

Sioux
Garter L: 35 cm (58 cm with pendant)   W: 8 cm
1881.3.154 LA   Read no. 70 or 71

Elongated strips of skunk skin tapering gradually to a point; trimmed at top with red stroud and bordered on sides with purple ribbon; inner face of garter backed with cloth triangular pendant extension embroidered with quillwork, two-thread, one-quill, crossed technique, in red, green, and light and dark purple on white; one pendant has plain blue beaded upper border; the other, a border with triangles in yellow trimmed with dark blue on a light blue ground; on the latter, a green beaded border flanks the quillwork design; small brass bells attached to sides of pendant flap and along center; outside of garter decorated with four large brass bells; cut rawhide, quill-wrapped fringe (red and white) with metal cone dangles attached to top end beneath red stroud; triangular flap ends of pendant covered with skunk fur; hide thongs for fastening.

In the early 1830s and before, a number of Plains Indian tribes attached tabs or animal tails to their moccasins to commemorate specific accomplishments. The Mandans, for example, attached wolf tails to their moccasin heels to signify accomplishment in battle. The decorated skunk fur tabs employed here may have served a similar function.

32. Dance Sash

Sioux, probably Yanktonai Dakota
L: 56 cm
(Acquired from) Yanktonai, Poplar River, M.T., 1882.
1881.3.126   Read no. 126

Deer-hide strip, red-dyed, with cut deer hoof pendants; pendants include three bird claws and one large brass bell.

Cf. an example in the Haffenreffer Museum (B. Hail, Hau, Kóla! [Bristol, R.I., 1890] cat. no. 224 [labeled "Teton Dakota"]).

Sashes of deer hoofs were worn by men when dancing. Worn over the shoulder, they produced a pleasant rattling sound.

33. Dance Bustle

Sioux, probably Teton Dakota
L: 85 cm
Purchased from Rush After Thunder, Oglala Sioux, 1881.
1881.3.45   Read no. 45

Rawhide panel to which head and body plumage of eagle attached by hide thongs; bird mounted on backing of calico cloth; attached to this cloth is a rawhide plate (reused parfleche) in which five feathers were originally inserted; sweet grass bundle beneath bird's head; quill-wrapped rawhide strips (red, purple, and white) with brass bell attachments; pendant woolen strips pierced with eagle tail feathers attached to either side of rawhide panel with hide thongs; thong-wrapped bundles of hawk and eagle wing feathers attached to rawhide panel, one on either side of bird; a single, long quill-wrapped rawhide strip (blue, yellow, and white) with sinew-wrapped horsehair terminals in either bundle; finger-woven multicolored yarn sash.

Cf. a similar bustle with eagle carcass in the National Museum of Natural History, Smithsonian Institution (V. J. Evans Collection; Inv. no. 357,488); cf. also an eagle-feather bustle collected by Major James W. Bell at Poplar River, M.T. (Inv. no. L68) and an example in the Brotherton Collection (Inv. no. 384,123; collected at Fort Buford in 1880–1881); both pieces are in the Smithsonian.

Feather bustles, usually attached to a finger-woven sash, were often worn by men as part of a dance costume. They were sometimes referred to as crow bustles, probably because they often contained a stuffed crow's head as part of the decoration. A portrait by Catlin executed in 1833 shows the Sauk-Fox chief Bear Track wearing a similar bustle (R.B. Hassrick, *The George Catlin Book of American Indians* [New York, 1977] 86).

34. Dance Shield

Sioux
H: 48 cm
Taken from Sioux grave near Poplar River, M.T., 1881.
1881.3.72   Read no. 72

Deerskin, stretched around a willow hoop (lashed together with skin thong) and gathered to circle on underside; painted decoration on front consists of a stylized buffalo head in blue (with white eyes and rectangular mouth) on a yellow background with zigzag border framed in red; brass bells and cropped feathers suspended from each of the points of the zigzag border; rope attached through perforation in skin cover above buffalo head; two perforations in area of buffalo mouth; skin repaired in areas; skin strap handle on back to which a medicine bundle wrapped in calico is attached.

War shields were made from fire-hardened buffalo hide with a soft deerskin cover. On this were painted magical designs and figures originally in native pigments and later in trade colors. Shields were worn around the neck, supported by a skin strap. When attacking, the warrior wore the shield over his chest; when retreating, he swung it to the rear to protect his back. This example is a dance shield. It is probably a replica of the owner's true shield cover carried in battle, although it may, in fact, be the actual war-shield cover itself. The horned head of a buffalo(?) with the vestige of a down feather suspended from the forehead, the clipped feathers, the bells, and even the colors all had symbolic meaning to the owner.

35. Medicine Pouch

Sioux
L: 6 cm
1881.3.83   Read no. 83

Two pieces of hide, sinew-sewn together; both sides with beaded decoration in dark and light blue, orange, and red, forming a cross (top) and a vertical band (bottom); perimeter trimmed with light blue beads; long hide suspension strap.

While listed as an umbilical cord container, this piece is more likely a medicine pouch containing a round stone worn suspended from the neck by a warrior as a protection against harm. Such stones, through their association with the god Rock, were thought to have magical power.

36. Umbilical Cord Amulet

Sioux
L: 15 cm   W: 5 cm
1881.3.138b   Read no. 138

Effigy of lizard made of two pieces of buffalo skin sewn together; top beaded, with central lozenge in green and dark blue on light blue ground, the whole bordered in white-core rose (also tail and limbs) and trimmed with purplish blue beads; legs, tail, and head terminate in metal cone dangles with orange horsehair tufts; underside slit and sewn closed; originally contained umbilical cord.

Charms such as this and the following example contained the child's umbilical cord and were worn by little children, who were laughingly called "carry their navels." The charms were later thrown away. It was believed dangerous to one's life if someone gained possession of one's umbilical cord. In view of this, these little containers were often fashioned in the shape of a tortoise, which is hard to kill, or a lizard, which is difficult to catch. In Read's inventory, these navel amulets are identified as "ornaments taken from a Sun Dance pole." It was during the Sun Dance that small children had their ears pierced, and it may be that at this time these charms were discarded and hung on the sacred pole.

37. Umbilical Cord Amulet

Sioux
L: 14 cm   W: 6 cm
1881.3.138a   Read no. 138

Effigy of turtle made of two pieces of buffalo skin sewn together; top fully beaded with a concentric stepped lozenge pattern in checkerboard design of dark blue, yellow, white-core rose, and opaque and faceted green on a light blue ground; separately added legs and tail; tail beaded, legs quill-wrapped with metal cone dangles; thong for hanging attached to underside; underside slit and sewn closed; originally contained umbilical cord.

38. Cup

Sioux, probably Yanktonai Dakota
L: 28 cm   Diam: 8 cm
(Acquired from) Black Chicken, Poplar River, M.T., 1882.
1881.3.129   Read no. 129

Buffalo horn; deerskin band around rim with beaded geometric designs (concentric boxes, stepped triangles) in white-core rose, green, yellow, and dark blue on a background of translucent white beads; hide thong pendants wrapped with metal cones attached to lower edge of beaded band; suspension loop of colored cloth rope attached to perforation in rim.

39. Bowl

Sioux, probably Yanktonai Dakota
H: 6 cm   Diam: 19 cm
(Acquired from) Yanktonai, Poplar River, M.T., 1882.
1881.3.127   Read no. 127

Wood; perforated tab with cloth rope; pair of antelope hooves attached to back of bowl with brass upholstery tacks; tacks also decorate claw attachment and perimeter of base; inside of bowl decorated with red (perimeter) and black pigment (center).

The antelope hoof attachment and the ornamental use of brass upholstery tacks suggest a ceremonial use for this bowl, which probably belonged to the shaman Black Chicken, owner of vessels cat. nos. 38 and 40.

40. Cup

Sioux, probably Yanktonai Dakota
L: 29 cm   Diam: 9 cm
Purchased from Black Chicken, principal medicine man at the Yanktonai tribe.
1881.3.88   Read no. 88

Buffalo horn; buffalo-calf strip suspended from one of four holes around rim; cup ornamented on outside with designs composed of incision and red ochre-filled drilled depressions, including a zigzag serpent, an incised cross with drilled terminals, and a looped design with central white-filled drill hole and T-shaped terminal.

41. Bowl

Sioux, probably Yanktonai Dakota
H: 5 cm   Diam: 20 cm
(Acquired from) Yanktonai, Poplar River, M.T., 1882.
1881.3.128   Read no. 128

Wood; perforated tab handle with grizzly bear claw pendant on buffalo calfskin thong; interior of bowl decorated with incised figure of coiled snake around a circular medallion; drilled depressions along length of body and to denote eyes; bowl rubbed with red ochre underneath.

The snake motif on this bowl is similar to that found on cup cat. no. 40 and suggests that it was the property of the shaman Black Chicken. No doubt the snake represented the reptilian intermediary from which Black Chicken received supernatural powers to cure.

Weapons and War Paraphernalia

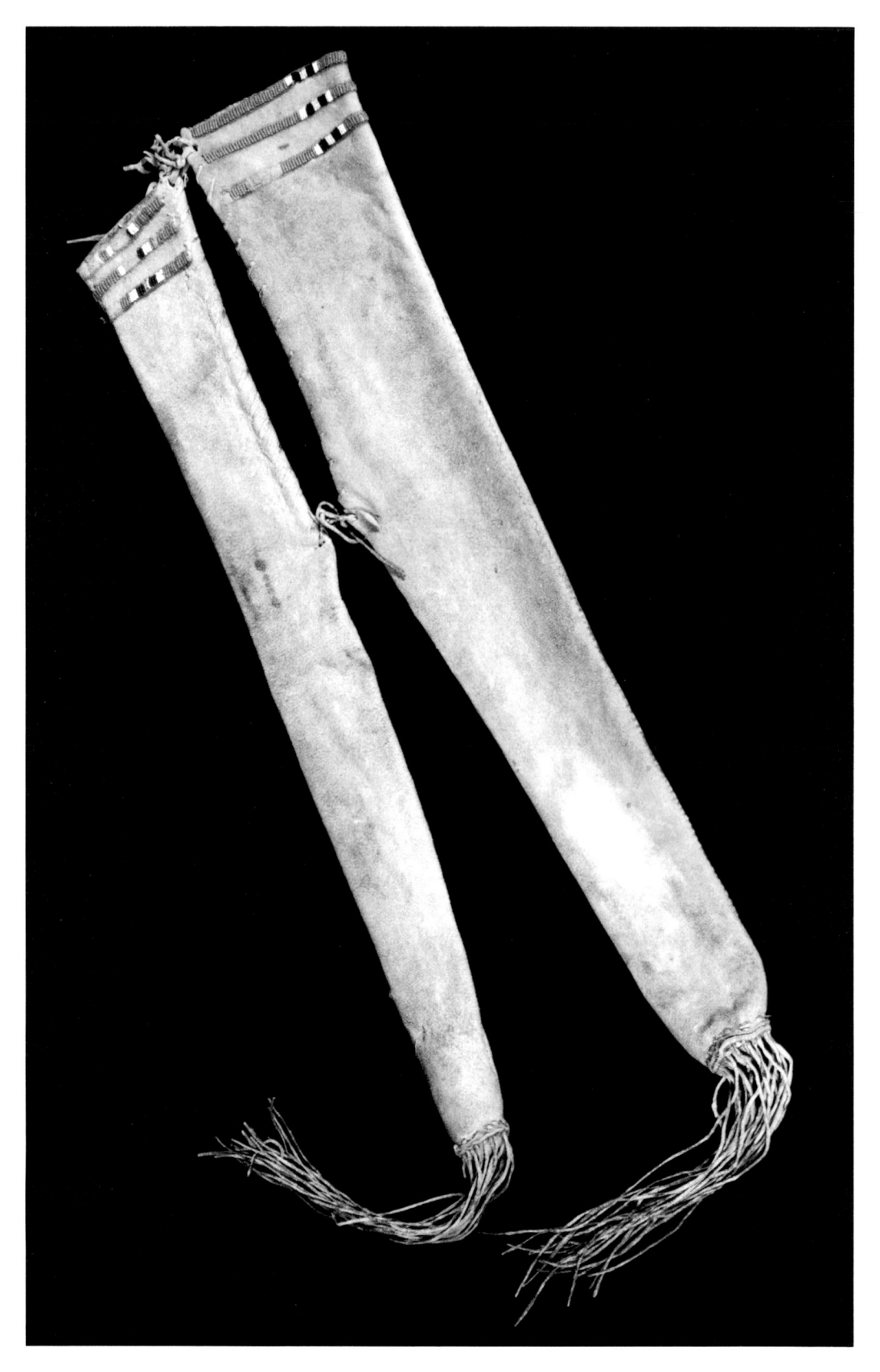

Cat. no. 43. Quiver and Bow Case

Cat. no. 44. Quiver

Cat. no. 56. Coup Stick

Cat. no. 56. Coup Stick (detail)

Cat. no. 51. War Club (top)   Cat. no. 52. Gunstock Club (bottom)

Cat. no. 53. Pipe Tomahawk

Cat. no. 48. Gun Case

Weapons and War Paraphernalia

42. Quiver and Bow Case (not illus.)

Hunkpapa, Teton Dakota
Quiver L: 60 cm (without fringe)   Bow Case L: 90 cm (without fringe)
Purchased from captive Hunkpapa at Camp Poplar River, M.T., Feb. 11, 1881 (along with bow and arrows, cat. no. 46).
1881.3.2   Read no. 2

Rawhide, folded and sinew-sewn on one side; bow case has separate bottom piece sinew-stitched to main section; cut fringe at top and bottom; top edge of quiver folded over and sinew-stitched to form hem; hide disk with cropped fringe forms base of quiver; bow case and quiver attached with rawhide thong in three places; hide carrying strap.

43. Quiver and Bow Case

Crow
Quiver L: 69 cm plus 25 cm fringe
Bow Case L: 68 cm plus 25 cm fringe
Crow manufacture.
1881.3.102   Read no. 102

Elk hide, folded and sinew-stitched on one side; stitched with rawhide laces along upper back; quiver and bow case embroidered at top with three beaded bands in light and dark blue, yellow, and dark purple; beaded bands stained above and below with orange ochre; hide disks, with rawhide fringe, form bottoms of case and quiver.

In his inventory, Read identifies this as a boy's quiver and bow case.

44. Quiver

Northern Plains, ca. 1850
L: 66 cm plus 16 cm fringe
1986.2.3 LA   Not in Read Collection

Deerskin, folded and sinew-stitched along one side; sinew-sewn skin disk forms base; disk base ornamented around its perimeter with quill-wrapped hide thongs in white and orange; long, triangular flap sinew-sewn to upper edge; flap stained with red ochre and embroidered with three rosette ornaments in blue and white pony beads; upper edge of quiver also decorated with border of blue and white pony beads; two pendant attachments (at the top and one third of the way down the back) consisting of braided rawhide thongs (top), a single strand of blue pony beads (top and back), red stroud square (top), and a green stroud ribbon and a light brown stroud ribbon with red-dyed borders (back).

In both its construction and its decoration, this quiver is very similar in style to a Mandan case depicted by Karl Bodmer in 1833 (Joslyn Art Museum, *Karl Bodmer's America* [1984] pl. 347). The beaded rosettes on the long triangular pendant hark back to an early origin.

45. Unfinished Bow and Arrows (not illus.)

Hunkpapa, Teton Dakota
Bow L: 1.25 m   Arrow L: 64 cm
Taken from lodge while burning Hunkpapa villages after engagement near Poplar River, M.T., on Jan. 2, 1881.
1881.3.4   Read no. 4

Ash bow; ends slightly worked. Bundle of eleven peeled willow shafts bound together with hide thong; only one shaft has notched end.

46. Sinew-Backed Bow and Arrows (not illus.)

Hunkpapa, Teton Dakota
Bow L: 1.03 m   Arrow L: 60–66 cm
Purchased from captive Hunkpapa at Camp Poplar River, M.T., Feb. 11, 1881 (along with quiver and bow case, cat. no. 42).
1881.3.2   Read no. 2

Ash; recurved; backed with thick strips of sinew the full length of bow; bow center tapered; ends reinforced by sinew wrappings encased in buffalo hide; twisted sinew bowstring. Nine willow shafts, peeled, smoothed, decorated with paint and incised lines along length; triple-fletched with long quills; tied with sinew top and bottom; sheetmetal points hafted by inserting into split shaft and wrapping with sinew.

It was reported that Indian men could release their arrows faster than an average man could fire a six-shooter. The effective range of the arrows was fifty yards, although they could be dangerous at one hundred. At close range, an arrow could be driven through a buffalo (see M. I. Carrington, *Absaraka, Home of the Crows* [Philadelphia, 1868]).

47. Sinew-Backed Bow (not illus.)

Yanktonai Dakota
L: 1.14 m
Purchased from Yanktonai Indian at Camp Poplar River, M.T., 1881.
1881.3.3   Read no. 3

Ash; recurved; backed with thick strips of sinew the full length of bow; ends reinforced by sinew wrappings; twisted sinew bowstring.

48. Gun Case

Sioux
L: 1.03 m
1881.3.137   Read no. 137

Elk hide, folded and sinew-sewn along one side; embroidered at top and bottom with beaded panels; geometric designs consist of opposed multiple triangles in medium and dark blue, orange, white-core rose, and green on a light blue ground; panels trimmed with red stroud border (also along side seam); skin fringe attached to top and bottom edges and along side seam; shoulder strap handle.

Although no tribal identification is mentioned in Read's inventory, the design motifs and the beading techniques suggest this gun case to be of either Yanktonai Dakota or Hunkpapa manufacture.

49. Cartridge Pouch (illus. in Bags and Containers)

Crow(?)
L: 13 cm plus 8 cm fringe   W: 14 cm
1881.3.79   Read no. 79

Deerskin; round-bottomed pouch and flap; front fully beaded with curvilinear tear-shaped designs in yellow trimmed with blue on blue-trimmed white-core rose ground; hide fringe at bottom.

50. Holster (not illus.)

L: 45 cm   Flap W: 18 cm
Picked up on the Custer battlefield, Little Big Horn, M.T.
1881.3.108   Read no. 108

Commercial leather, sinew-sewn; separate end piece with self fringe.

51. War Club

Northern Plains
L: 87 cm
1881.3.149 LA Read Collection(?)

Wooden shaft (white pine) decorated with brass upholstery tacks; cluster of brass bells and a pair of cord-wrapped horsehair bundles attached to upper end; medicine bundle wrapped in calico cloth hangs from handle end by braided cloth wrist strap; leather cut-out star ornament nailed to upper edge of shaft below blade; various sides of shaft decorated with commercial paint in different colors: light and dark green, dark blue, and red; commercially manufactured steel blade with manufacturer's mark: J. Russell & Co., Green River Works.

Established in 1836, the J. Russell & Co. firm played a very prominent role in supplying cutlery to various fur trading companies and dealers on the frontier. In the late 1860s the company operated the Green River Works near Deerfield, Massachusetts. For a detailed discussion of its operations, see R. L. Merriam et al., *The History of the John Russell Cutlery Company, 1833–1936* (Greenfield, Mass., 1976).

52. Gunstock Club

Northern Plains
L: 98 cm
1881.3.148 LA Read Collection(?)

Wooden shaft (cottonwood), gunstock-shaped, studded on either side with brass upholstery tacks; perforated, disk-shaped butt end (wrist strap missing); thong with remains of feather at upper end; hammered steel blade secured to shaft with nails; traces of diagonal blue bands that originally decorated either side of shaft.

53. Pipe Tomahawk

Crow
Shaft L: 57 cm Blade L: 20 cm
Pendant L: 83 cm
Purchased from Crow Indian at Terry's Landing, M.T., 1879.
1881.3.8 Read no. 8

Steel head cast in one piece; oval eye; figure of standing bird (hawk or eagle) enclosed within zigzag border incised on one side of face; maple(?) wood handle the upper half of which is decorated with rows of brass upholstery tacks and tightly coiled brass wire; lower portion of shaft has beaded hide wrapping with red stroud border; end of handle wrapped with buffalo-hide thong; long red stroud pendant upper half of which is beaded on buffalo-hide backing; beaded design consists of three stepped triangles in dark blue trimmed with white-core rose (top and bottom) and yellow trimmed with dark blue (middle) on a light blue ground, the whole surrounded by a white border; willow stick brace at base of stroud pendant.

Pipe tomahawks of brass or steel were more ornamental than functional. Of European manufacture, they were popular items of trade. Since the stem of this specimen is solid, it could not have been smoked; the nicks on the blade suggest that it may have been used as a weapon. The beaded pendant is typically Crow in its use of color and design.

54. Fixed-Stone-Head Club

Sioux, probably Hunkpapa, Teton Dakota
L: 76 cm Head L: 10 cm
Presented to Mrs. Captain Read at Camp Poplar River, M.T., Feb. 1, 1881, by a Hunkpapa Indian.
1881.3.11 Read no. 11

Oval head; rawhide-encased wooden shaft with pendant rawhide thong; single golden eagle feather attached with cotton cloth strip to end of rawhide casing enclosing head; yellow ochre rubbed into rawhide casing around head.

Stone-headed war clubs were used in battle until the end of the Indian wars. The nature of Indian warfare was such that only by striking the enemy could a warrior earn points, or coups. Thus, the club, the lance, or coup stick, and the quirt remained essential weapons after firearms were introduced. According to Read's inventory, this club was presented to his wife by a Hunkpapa warrior who claimed to have killed three soldiers with it.

55. Fixed-Stone-Head Club

Sioux, probably Yanktonai Dakota
L: 92 cm Head L: 14 cm
Purchased from Yanktonai Indian at Camp Poplar River, M.T., 1881.
1881.3.12 Read no. 12

Oval head with pointed ends; red ochre decorates one end of head; rawhide-encased wooden shaft; facsimile scalp lock of horsehair sinew-sewn to pendant leather disk with stroud covering (red and blue) attached with rawhide thong.

The facsimile scalp of horsehair that decorates the end of this club serves as a sign of victory. According to the owner, the red paint on one end of the club indicates the point to which he had driven it through the skull of a Crow Indian.

56. Coup Stick

Sioux, probably Hunkpapa, Teton Dakota
L: 1.77 m
Captured from Hunkpapa Indian near Poplar River, M.T., Feb. 11, 1881, by Scout Bear Soldier and presented by him to Captain Read.
1881.3.1 Read no. 1

Willow shaft wrapped with quill plaiting and weasel skins; elongated steel blade; four groups of pendant weasel strips bound at intervals around lance with rawhide thongs; bundle of hawk feathers and horsehair fastened at base of blade with hide thong; red ribbon fastened at base.

Coup sticks were, in fact, lances used by warriors to strike the enemy. In many instances, these lances were carried by officers of the police societies as symbols of authority, thus serving both a ceremonial and a practical function.

Cat. no. 54. Fixed-Stone-Head Club

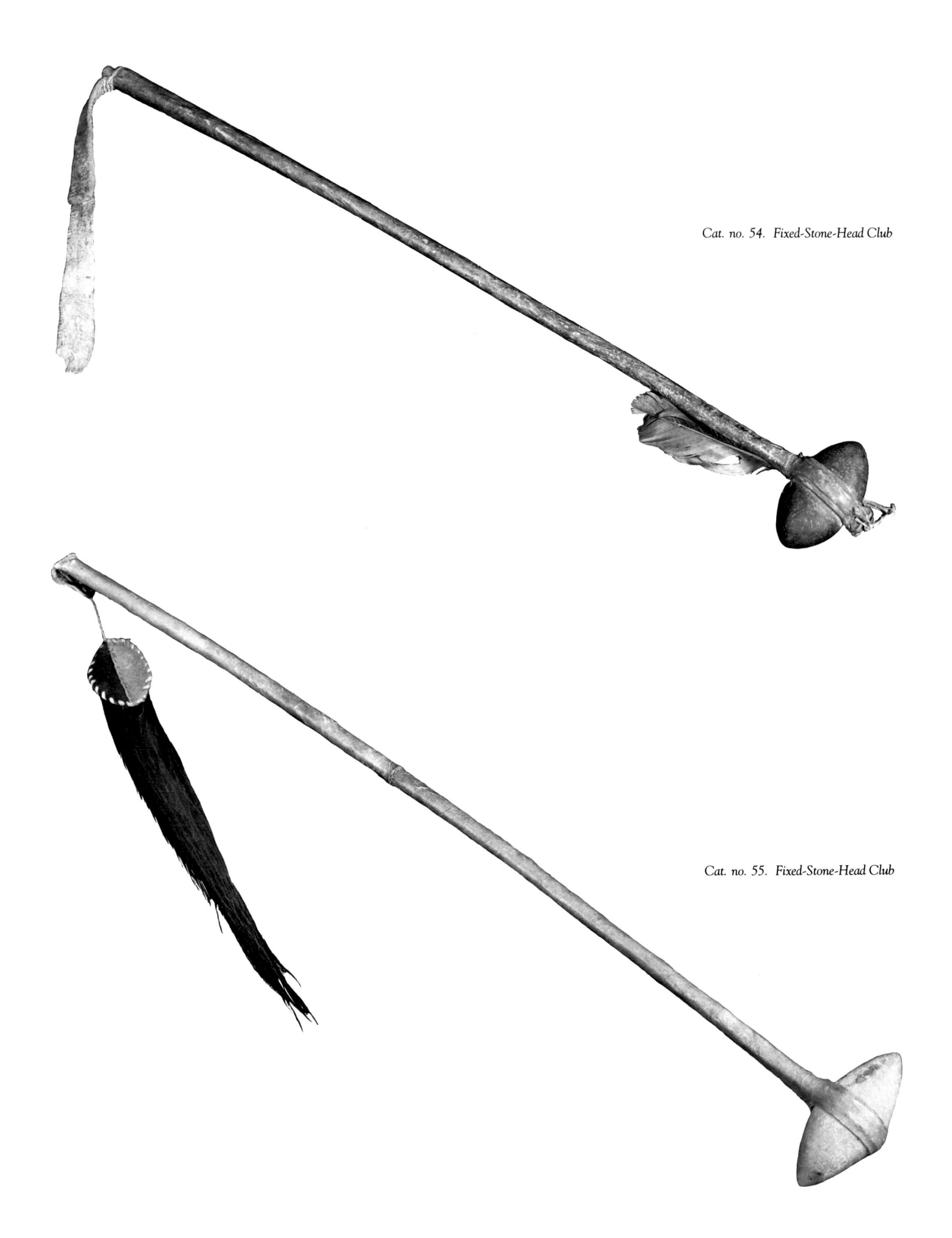

Cat. no. 55. Fixed-Stone-Head Club

135

57. Scalp Lock *(not illus.)*

Taken from Yanktonai Indian named Little Big Toad killed in engagement with Crow scouts under Lt. Kislingbury, Eleventh Infantry, near mouth of Musselshell River, M.T., Nov., 1880.
1881.3.47   Read no. 47

Scalp with red stroud covering sinew-stitched on bent twig frame.

58. Scalp Lock *(not illus.)*

Purchased from Black Chicken, Yanktonai, 1881.
1881.3.49   Read no. 49

Scalp decorated with green-dyed brass upholstery tacks and painted concentric circles in green and red; braided yarn pendant in blue and red.

Read's inventory states that this scalp was believed to be that of a white woman. In restoring the body of a casualty by presenting a scalp to a female relative, the scalp of a woman or child was as effective as that of a man.

59. Scalp Lock *(not illus.)*

From Crow Indian.
1881.3.50   Read no. 50

Piece of scalp with long blond hair.

60. Scalp Lock *(not illus.)*

1881.3.146 LA   Read no. 48 or 131

Scalp to which cloth strips and three feathers (one eagle, two crow[?]) are affixed with hide thong.

The addition of feathers indicates that this scalp lock had been worn as a headdress.

61. Scalp Lock *(not illus.)*

1881.3.145 LA   Read no. 48 or 131

Scalp with orange yarn and braided thong of red and yellow hide affixed to hair.

62. Scout Feather

1881.3.132   Read no. 132

Eagle feather stripped down to 12 cm; stem wrapped with orange-dyed quills; horsehair tuft fixed with resin to feather tip; orange and blue yarn affixed through perforation at base of stem; long, braided, red-dyed, horsehair pendant suspended.

The scout feather, a hair ornament consisting of a golden eagle feather stripped down, its stem quill-wrapped, was awarded to a scout who either spotted the enemy or discovered the location of the enemy camp.

Cat. no. 62. Scout Feather

Horse Gear and Riding Accessories

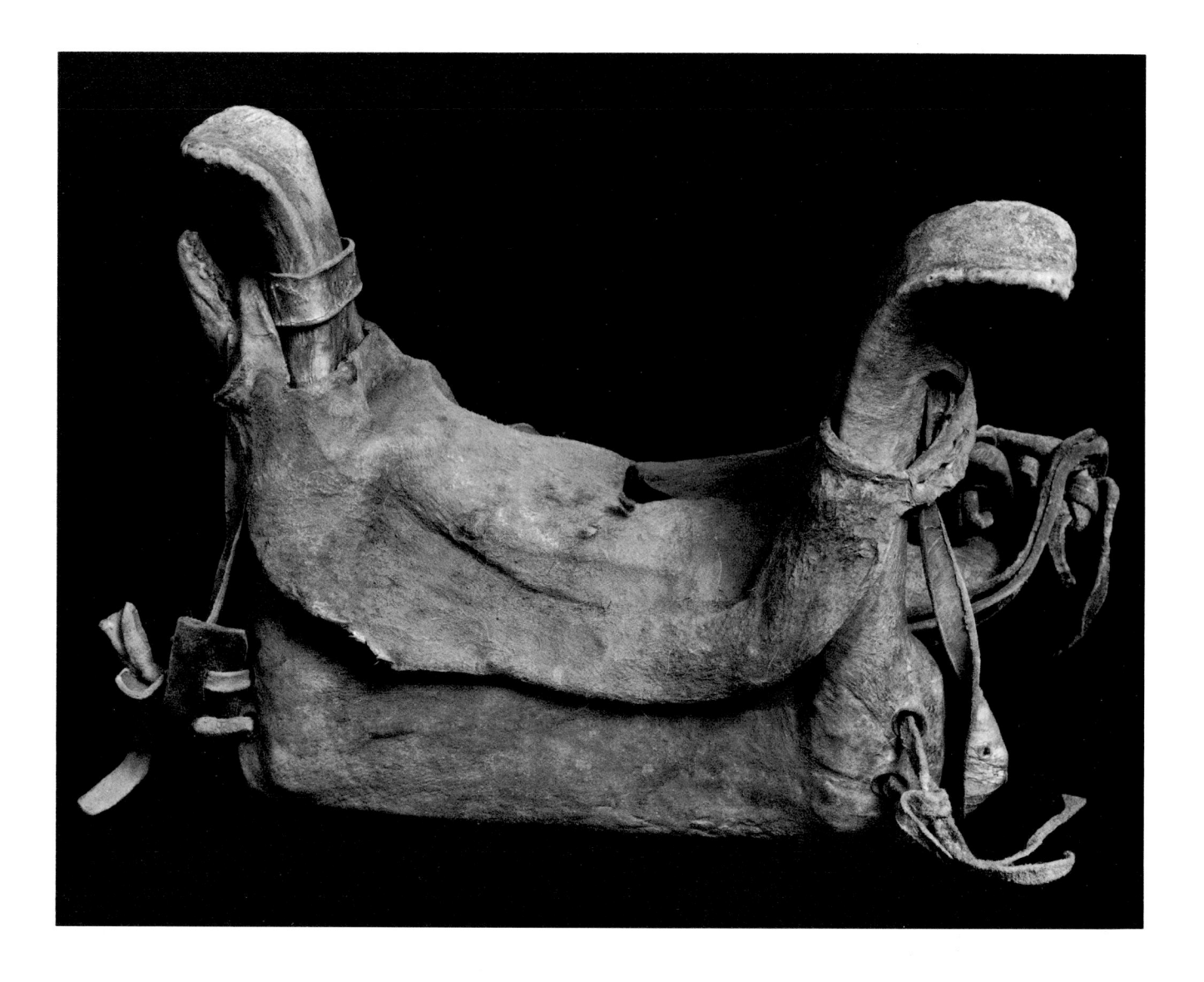

Cat. no. 63. Girl's Saddle

Cat. no. 64. Man's Pad Saddle

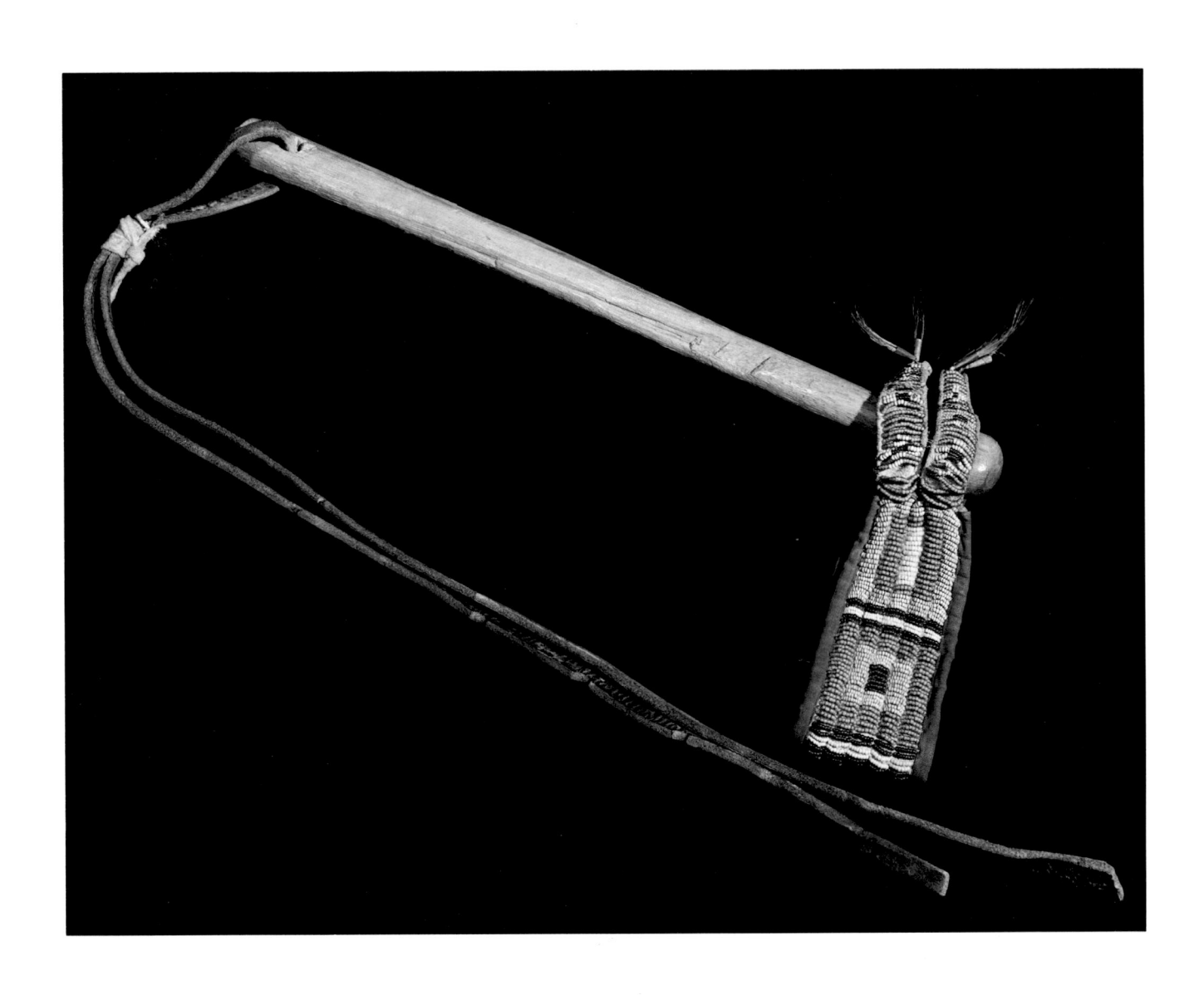

Cat. no. 67. Quirt

Horse Gear and Riding Accessories

63. Girl's Saddle

Hunkpapa, Teton Dakota
Base L: 30 cm   W: 20 cm   H: 27 cm
Picked up from Hunkpapa Camp near Poplar River, M.T., after engagement of Jan. 2, 1881.
1881.3.41   Read no. 41

Sinew-sewn wood frame (consisting of pommel, cantle, and slat side pieces) covered with bison rawhide; rawhide saddle seat fits over frame; rawhide girth and rigging straps.

Women's saddles with high pommels and cantles were adapted from early Spanish saddles. Wet rawhide stretched over a wooden frame made for a rigid structure when dried. The small dimensions of this example suggest that it was a young girl's saddle.

64. Man's Pad Saddle

Sioux, probably Teton Dakota
L: 47 cm   Max W: 33 cm
1881.3.158 LA   Probably Read no. 43

Two pieces of deerskin, sinew-sewn together and stuffed to form four oblong pads; red stroud trim around edges; rawhide strap laced across center and covered by self-fringed deerskin saddle seat; separately attached skin side flaps perforated for attachment of girth straps (missing); beaded rectangular flaps with colored yarn fringe and cloth backing attached to corners; four loop pendants with black cloth interiors trimmed with skin decorated with pink and white beads and yarn tassles; corners of saddle embroidered with beaded decoration of concentric diamonds and circles; beaded decoration of saddle and flaps in light, medium, and dark blue, white, yellow, orange, white-core rose, and translucent red and green.

65. Man's Pad Saddle

Northern Plains, ca. 1860
L: 43 cm   Max W: 31 cm
1986.2.5 LA   Not in Read Collection

Two pieces of deerskin, sinew-sewn together and stuffed with buffalo fur(?) to form two oblong pads; deerskin saddle cover with denticulated side borders and fringed ends sinew-sewn to pad saddle; four circular skin medallions attached one to each of four corners; rim of fringe attached to underside of each disk; fringe quill-wrapped at base in red, white, green, and red; front of medallion is plaited with an elaborate quillwork design consisting of a medallion surrounded by six concentric registers decorated with alternating chevrons and small triangles in red and brown on white; pads trimmed with quill-wrapped decoration in red, white, blue, and green.

Cf. a very similar pad saddle of Blackfoot manufacture with quilled corner disks in the National Museum of Natural History, Smithsonian Institution (Inv. no. 2,656; collected by Capt. H. Stansbury; acquired 1867).

66. Double Saddlebag

Hunkpapa, Teton Dakota
L: 1.10 m (1.90 m with fringe)   W: 32 cm
Hunkpapa manufacture. Presented by Joe Culbertson at Camp Poplar River, 1881.
1881.3.27   Read no. 27

Deerskin(?), folded and sinew-sewn on one side and at either end; skin fringe sewn into stitched side (single layer) and ends (double layer); lower edge of bags decorated with brass bells; skin has 18-cm opening cut into area of top fold to accommodate cantle; fully beaded square panels on either side are connected by a narrow band along the stitched side; each panel decorated with geometric designs in light and dark blue, yellow, and translucent red on a white beaded ground: a central stepped diamond with multiple side prongs and a repeated rectangular design with gabled top and triangular finial in each corner; connecting strip decorated with three double-ended, three-pronged bands in light and dark blue and translucent red; skin stained with orange ochre, especially on underside and end borders.

Double saddlebags were popular among the Sioux, Cheyenne, and Arapaho. For a Sioux example with related decorative scheme, cf. a saddlebag in the Louis Warren Hill Collection (A. Walton, ed., After the Buffalo Were Gone [St. Paul, 1984] cat. no. 293).

67. Quirt

Sioux
Handle L: 40 cm   Lash L: 64 cm
1881.3.64   Read no. 64

Carved hickory stem; beaded deerskin wrist band attached by thong through hole in knobbed base of wood stem; wristlet is covered on its underside and top borders with green cotton cloth and has two flaps, each ending in metal cone dangles with yellow horsehair tufts; front of handle and flaps beaded with concentric boxed design in light and dark blue, yellow, and white-core rose; lash of commercial leather.

Cat. no. 66. *Double Saddlebag*

Cat. no. 65. Man's Pad Saddle

Pipes and Smoking Equipment

Cat. no. 73. Tobacco Bag

Cat. no. 74. Tobacco Bag (detail)

Cat. no. 74. Tobacco Bag

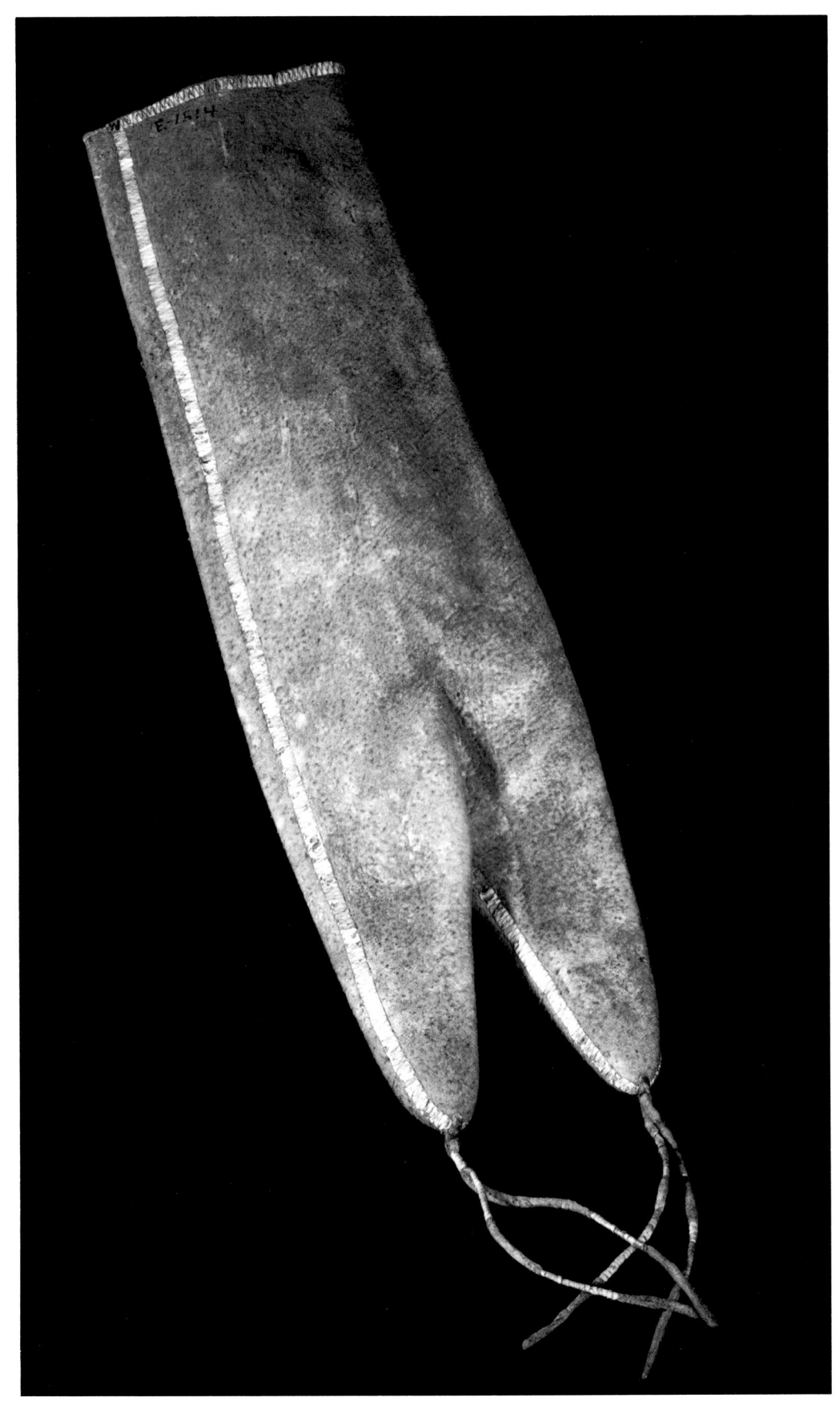

Cat. no. 75. Tobacco Bag

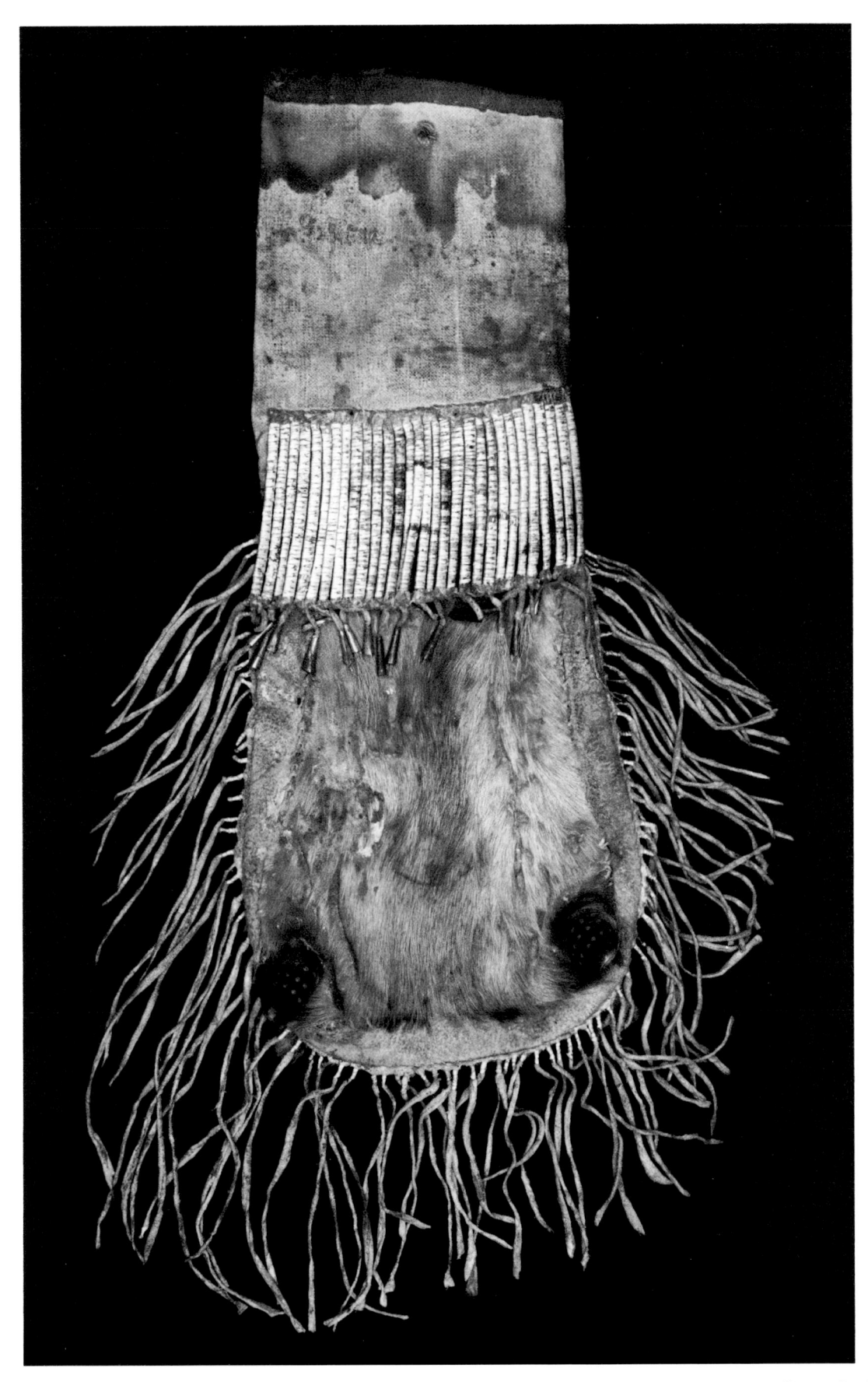

Cat. no. 72. Tobacco Bag

Pipes and Smoking Equipment

68. Pipe Stem and Bowl

Stem probably Yanktonai Dakota
Stem L: 46.5 cm
Bowl L: 20.7 cm   H: 10.2 cm   Diam: 1.4 cm
Purchased from Black Tiger, Yanktonai chief at Poplar River, M.T., 1881.
1881.3.67a,b   Read no. 67

Hardwood stem (white ash), upper half with carved spiral twists, lower half flattened in cross-section; cylindrical center piece decorated with brass upholstery tacks; catlinite T-shaped bowl, round in cross-section, with anterior projection of stem base; tall straight bowl portion; tapered, fire-blackened borings.

Ceremonial pipes were differentiated from ordinary smoking pipes by their flat stems ornamented with quill embroidery, horsehair, and ribbon streamers, and the green-feathered neck of a mallard duck at the extremity. Ordinary pipes might have a simple tubular stem or might be carved with animal figures or spirals (as here). Commonly L-shaped or in the shape of an inverted T, pipe bowls were usually carved from catlinite, a soft, red clay stone which hardened when exposed to air. This pipe bowl may have been manufactured by white men as a trade item; the carved twisted stem, however, is characteristic of Fort Peck reservation work.

69. Pipe Bowl

Northern Plains
L: 11 cm   H: 7.5 cm   Diam: 1.5 cm
1881.3.139 LA   Read no. 66, 68, or 69

Catlinite; rectangular with small pointed anterior projection and low serrated crest (broken); round in cross-section; bowl expands toward rim; inlaid with lead bands; tapered borings.

70. Pipe Bowl

Northern or Eastern Plains
L: 13.5 cm   H: 7.4 cm   Diam: 2.2 cm
1881.3.141 LA   Read no. 66, 68, or 69

Black pipestone; rectangular with sloping anterior projection; hexagonal base with high serrated crest and one aperture; two incised bands below rim and nine relief bands at base; tapered borings.

This style with vertical fin with serrated edge was favored by the Indian inhabitants of the Eastern Plains.

71. Pipe Stem *(not illus.)*

Northern Plains
L: 52 cm
1881.3.140 LA   Read no. 66, 68, or 69

Hardwood stem (box elder), round in cross-section; branch butts decorated with brass tacks; bone mouthpiece. May belong with pipe bowl cat. no. 69.

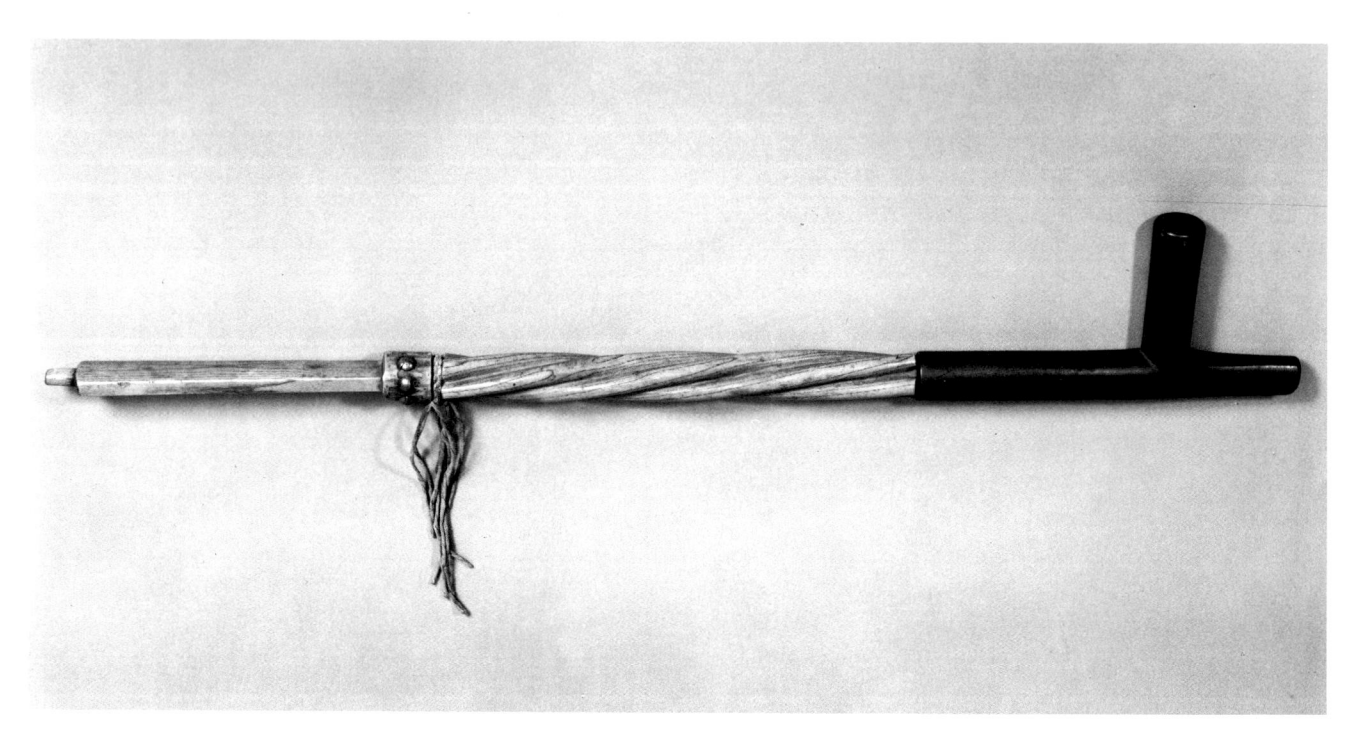

Cat. no. 68. Pipe Stem and Bowl

Cat. nos. 69, 70. Pipe Bowls

72. Tobacco Bag

Sioux
L: 46 cm plus 12 cm fringe   W: 19 cm
1881.3.125   Read no. 125

Fashioned from the lower portion of an elk's leg, sinew-stitched to a rawhide border; woven cloth neck extension with red stroud upper border; attached to front of neck is a flap of cut, quill-wrapped, rawhide fringe terminating in rawhide thongs with metal cone dangles and lavender horsehair tufts; rawhide fringe along entire lower border, wrapped at base with red and purple-dyed quillwork; the four dewclaws are ornamented with various drilled abstract designs.

Cf. a bag in the Louis Warren Hill Collection (A. Walton, ed., After the Buffalo Were Gone [St. Paul, 1984], cat. no. 273).

In this tobacco bag fashioned from an elk's leg, the animal's dewclaws are retained as a decorative element.

73. Tobacco Bag

Sioux
L: 38 cm plus 44 cm fringe   W: 12.5 cm
1881.3.142 LA   Read no. 62, 63, or 66

Deerskin, folded into narrow tube and sinew-sewn on one side; beaded border along upper edge in alternating bands of light and dark blue; central portion has beaded geometric designs of concentric boxes and triangular borders in light and dark blue, yellow, green, pink, and translucent red; bottom section of quill-wrapped rawhide thongs (from reused painted parfleche) with red background and white box designs; double row of hide fringe attached to bottom of thongs.

Typical tobacco bags consist of three design elements: a beaded or quill-embroidered central panel, a section of quill-wrapped rawhide strips, and long, pendant deerskin fringe. The beaded panels on the obverse and reverse sides always bore different designs; the reason for this differentiation is now unknown. While each tobacco bag displayed similar designs, no two were precisely the same. This bag is typical of the stylized ceremonial equipment once carried by the Wakincuzas, or "Pipe Bearers." When the Indians were confined to reservations and tribal governments had broken down, anyone could carry a ceremonial tobacco bag.

74. Tobacco Bag

Sioux
L: 47 cm plus 65 cm fringe   Max W: 14.5 cm
1881.3.143 LA   Read no. 62, 63, or 66

Two pieces of deerskin stitched together and folded into a narrow tube sewn on one side; border of glass seed beads along each side and along top edge of bag; two triangular beaded feather elements at base of skin bag on either side; central section embroidered on one face with two triangular stepped patterns and, on the other, with an overall checkerboard pattern in orange, lavender, and translucent red and green on a light blue beaded ground; bottom section of quill-wrapped rawhide strips with red background and white, yellow, and red inset box designs; double row of long hide fringe attached to bottom of strips.

75. Tobacco Bag

Sioux
L: 42 cm   W: 11 cm
1881.3.144 LA   Read no. 62, 63, or 66

Deerskin, folded and sinew-sewn on one side and bottom; bag bifurcates at bottom into two tapering sacks; single band of plaited purple quillwork along upper edge and side and bottom seams; quill-wrapped hide thong pendants hang from bottom.

For a tobacco bag of similar construction, cf. an example in the collection of the National Museum of Natural History, Smithsonian Institution (Mooney Collection; Inv. no. 152006).

This small, swallow-tail tobacco bag may have been used by a woman.

76. "Strike-a-light" Pouch (illus. in Bags and Containers)

Crow
L: 12 cm   W: 9 cm
Presented by or purchased from Yanktonai Indian at Camp Poplar River, M.T., 1881.
1881.3.80a   Read no. 80

Commercial leather; flap fastened with hide thongs; flap, front, and edges of back beaded in geometric motifs in dark blue, white-core rose, and white; brass carpet tacks originally decorated lower front edge; metal cones hang from edge of flap and bottom on short thongs; long braided double thongs decorated with brass beads and (at the bottom) with tubular white beads hung from lower corners.

77. "Strike-a-light" Pouch (illus. in Women's Costume)

Crow
L: 8.5 cm   W: 8 cm
Attached to woman's belt acquired from a Yanktonai in 1882.
1881.3.130c   Read no. 130

Deerskin, folded and sinew-sewn on one side; front and flap beaded in dark blue and yellow on light blue ground; central design of rectangle flanked above and below by horizontal pronged lines; metal cone fringe decorates flap and lower edge.

78. Match Pocket (not illus.)

Sioux
L: 11.8 cm plus 7 cm fringe   W: 7.7 cm
Presented by or purchased from Yanktonai Indian at Camp Poplar River, M.T., 1881.
1881.3.80b   Read no. 80

Deerskin, folded and sinew-sewn on one side; two long quill-wrapped rawhide thongs ending in loops attached to upper right corner; quill-wrapped, purple-dyed rawhide fringe below, the ends of which are sinew-stitched together; stroud loop attachment at back; beaded front features a rectangle between two opposed step triangles in orange trimmed with translucent red over a light blue ground; front of flap decorated with light blue beads trimmed with a single row of translucent red beads.

79. Match Pocket (not illus.)

Sioux
L: 24 cm plus 10 cm fringe   W: 5 cm
Presented by or purchased from Yanktonai Indian at Camp Poplar River, M.T., 1881.
1881.3.80c   Read no. 80

Deerskin, folded and sinew-sewn on one side; long strap handle; front and borders of back beaded in opaque white and translucent yellow, green, rose, red, and burgundy; front is decorated with four "feather" motifs within a border of triangles and concentric boxes; hide fringe at bottom.

80. Match Pocket (not illus.)

Sioux
L: 9.3 cm   W: 6.5 cm
1881.3.82   Read no. 82

Commercial leather, folded and stitched together on both sides with rawhide lacing; front of flap decorated with brass upholstery tacks and pendant metal cones; two rawhide metal-wrapped thongs attached to corners.

Bags and Containers

Cat. no. 83. Bandolier

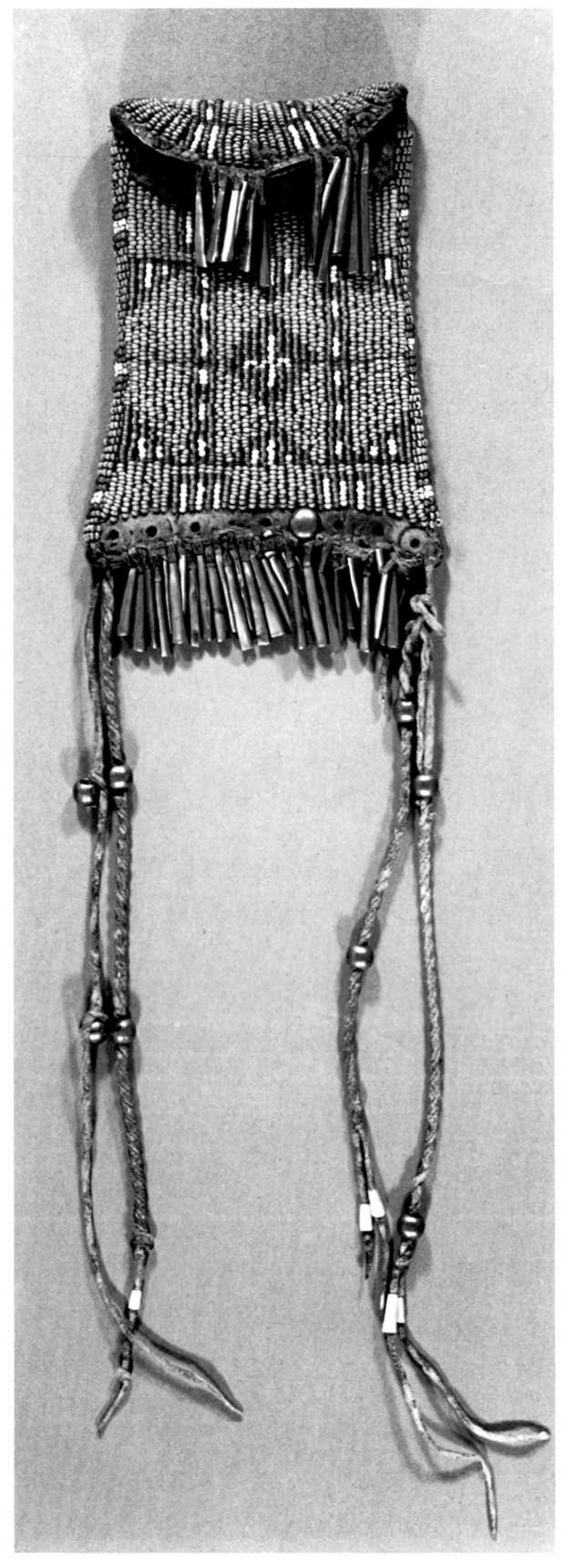

Cat. no. 76. *"Strike-a-light" Pouch (entry in Pipes and Smoking Equipment)*

Cat. no. 49. *Cartridge Pouch (entry in Weapons and War Paraphernalia)*

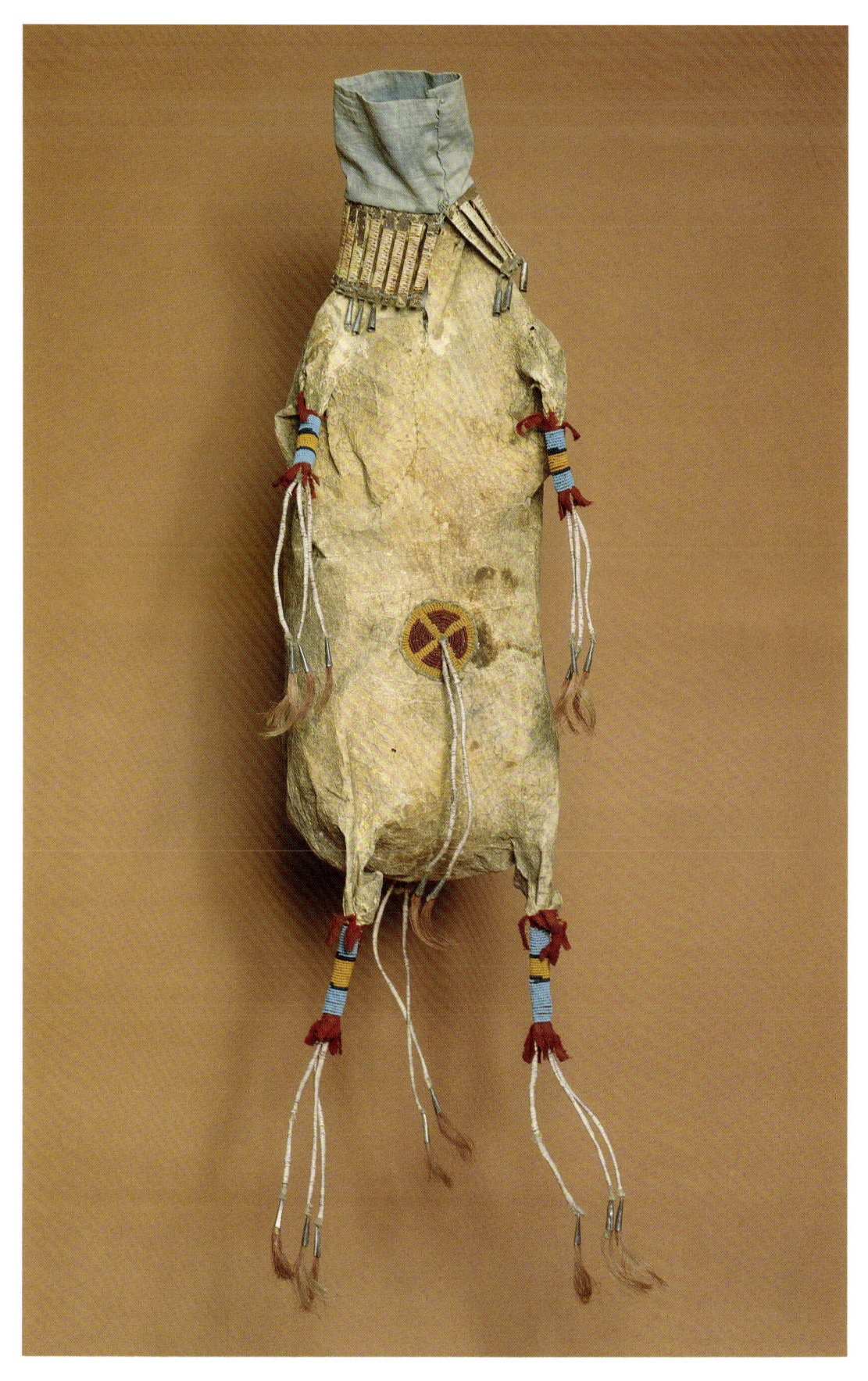

Cat. no. 82. Bag

Cat. no. 85. Bonnet Case

Cat. no. 84. Bandolier (with Paint Pouch Cat. no. 90)

Cat. no. 86. Pair of Parfleches

Cat. no. 87. *Painted Rawhide Container*

Cat. no. 89. *Painted Rawhide Container*

Cat. no. 88. *Painted Rawhide Container*

Cat. no. 81. Quilled Bag

Bags and Containers

81. Quilled Bag

Sioux, probably Teton Dakota
L: 13 cm plus 5 cm fringe   W: 17 cm
Captured from Hunkpapa camp near Poplar River, M.T., in engagement of Jan. 2, 1881.
1881.3.92   Read no. 92

Deerskin, folded and sinew-sewn along one side and bottom; decorated on both sides with quillwork, two-thread, one-quill, crossed technique, fourteen rows; lozenge and elongated chevrons in red and dark purple; pendant metal cones with red wool tufts; top edge of bag trimmed with single strand of white beads; thong carrying strap.

This piece is identified as a "medicine bag" in Read's inventory. It is referred to as such not because of its form or decoration, but rather because the owner probably kept his medicine in it. The bag appears to have been cut down from an older quilled container.

82. Bag

Sioux
L: 59 cm   W: 21 cm
1881.3.124   Read no. 124

Fashioned from skin of unborn buffalo calf; blue-dyed cloth extension sewn to neck; limb extensions gathered together and wrapped with sinew-strung beads in light and dark blue and yellow in banded design over red stroud; each extension terminates in three pink quill-wrapped rawhide slats equipped with metal cone dangles with lavender horsehair tufts; center of front and underside decorated with leather disks beaded in a square-cross design (translucent red and yellow on front, red and light blue on underside); from the center of each medallion extends a pair of quill-wrapped hide thongs; red quill-wrapped rawhide fringe around neck, sewn in pairs at the end with rawhide lacing terminating in metal cone dangles, the whole threaded at the lower end with a single strand of light blue beads.

Cf. a calfskin bag with central beaded medallion in the National Museum of Natural History, Smithsonian Institution (Inv. no. 154037; acquired 1892).

Containers fashioned from the skin of an unborn buffalo calf were considered to be quite stylish. In his inventory, Read refers to this item as a woman's "work bag." In such a bag, handiwork and supplies would have been kept.

83. Bandolier

Sioux
Pouch W: 25 cm   Pouch L: 25.5 cm
Strap L: 50 cm   Strap W: 7 cm
1881.3.147 LA   Possibly Read no. 44 or 91

Deerskin pouch with flap; composed of two pieces sinew-sewn on three sides; trimmed with orange cloth; perimeter of front and flap beaded with continuous geometric design in green and white-core rose on a light blue beaded ground with "feather" designs in corners (half dark blue and half white-core rose with single yellow median strand); outside of pouch stained with yellow ochre; loom-beaded shoulder strap with running geometric designs in green, burgundy, white-core rose, medium blue, and white on a light blue beaded background.

84. Bandolier

Crow
L: 90 cm   W: 38 cm
Purchased from White Dog, Assiniboine, Nov., 1881.
1881.3.87a   Read no. 87

Buffalo-hide strip forms shoulder strap attached to a central pocket composed of two buffalo-hide panels sinew-sewn on three sides; red stroud flap (trimmed in dark blue) sewn to bottom; front of bandolier fully beaded in white-core rose, green, yellow, white, dark blue, and translucent red on a light blue beaded ground; design consists of decorative panels with rectangles, concentric squares, triangles, diagonals, hourglass designs, and paneled borders; a pair of deerskin paint pouches were originally attached to lower corners of bandolier (the lefthand pouch now detached); see cat. nos. 90 and 91 for description of pouches.

Formerly used for carrying shot and firearm equipment, bandoliers became decorative items of apparel. Read identifies this example as a "dressing case." This function is confirmed by the two ochre-stained paint pouches, originally attached at its lower corners, which contained the owner's facial paints. Although Read's inventory states this bandolier to have been purchased from the Assiniboine White Dog, it is stylistically of Crow origin. Quite possibly, White Dog captured this piece from a Crow enemy.

85. Bonnet Case

Sioux
L: 39 cm   Diam: 15 cm
1881.3.151 LA   Read no. 91 (?)

Deerskin cover rolled around cylindrical rawhide form; cover sinew-sewn together on one side and stitched to rawhide form along its top and bottom edges; rawhide base sewn to lower edge of skin covering along bottom; removable skin top attached to outer skin covering with hide lacing; cover and front half of case beaded in white-core rose, yellow, green, and light and dark blue; cover is divided into four quadrants decorated alternately with three horse hooves and single-square crosses; front decorated with central lozenge chain and triangle-ornamented border in green, yellow, dark blue, and translucent red on light blue beaded ground; central lozenge flanked by horn motif; upper and lower edge of case decorated with metal pendants (bells, upper; crimped brass ornaments, lower); hide fringe along upper and lower edges and along vertical seam; hide shoulder strap attached to back.

Cylindrical cases for storing feathered war bonnets were generally made of rawhide decorated with painted geometric designs. This example is unusual in that it is beaded on soft skin over a cylinder of rawhide, yet it bears design elements applied to painted rawhide containers. Cylindrical rawhide cases were sometimes used as medicine bags (cf. an example filled with medicine bundles in the National Museum of Natural History, Smithsonian Institution, collected by Major James W. Bell at Fort Buford, N.D. [Inv. no. L55; acquired 1894]).

86. Pair of Parfleches

Sioux
L: 63 cm   W: 36 cm
Purchased at Poplar River, M.T.
1881.3.23a,b   Read no. 23

Rawhide, folded; painted on rectangular upper flaps; design on front consists of geometric and curvilinear shapes in red, green, yellow, blue, and black, outlined in black; fastened at center with rawhide thongs through one pair of holes.

As Read notes in his inventory, painted rawhide envelope-like cases, or parfleches, were used primarily to store dried meat. They were always made in pairs and no two pair ever displayed the same geometric design. A combination of curved and straight lines characterized the Sioux style. Blue, red, and green were the predominating colors, with much of the background in yellow; as here, the design was outlined in black.

87. Painted Rawhide Container

Yanktonai Dakota
L: 73 cm plus 16 cm fringe   W: 29.5 cm
Yanktonai manufacture.
1881.3.25   Read no. 25

Rawhide, folded and sewn together on one side with deerskin lacing; deerskin bottom and upper extension with rawhide fringe on three sides and skin drawstring at top; painted design on front consists of geometric and curvilinear patterns in red, yellow, green, and blue, outlined in black, with use of yellow crosshatching in central lozenge and triangles; the back is undecorated except for a central lozenge in green, yellow, and blue and four small triangles (in yellow with blue borders) in corners.

88. Painted Rawhide Container

Sioux
L: 28 cm plus 58 cm fringe   W: 26 cm
1881.3.159 LA   Read no. 44 or 91

Rawhide, folded and sewn together on either side with deerskin lacing over red stroud trim; long skin fringe sewn to each side seam; overhanging flap fastened at center with thongs through one pair of holes; short hide carrying strap at back; painted design on front composed of geometric forms in red, yellow, and green, outlined in black, framed above and below by a brown striped band trimmed with green.

Often referred to as medicine bags, rawhide cases such as this might contain a warrior's paint or medicine. Sometimes known as wall pockets, they were often hung from a lodge pole or suspended from a tripod outside the tipi (see illustration in M. Morrow, *Indian Rawhide: A Folk Art* [Norman, Oklahoma, 1975] 5).

89. Painted Rawhide Container

Yanktonai Dakota
L: 63 cm   W: 34 cm
Yanktonai manufacture.
1881.3.24   Read no. 24

Rawhide, folded, sewn together on one side with sinew stitches; deerskin bottom and upper extension stitched with sinew lacing to rawhide body; the skin sections are decorated with vertical and horizontal rows of purple quillwork; below the upper edge, a horizontal beaded band in blue, white-core rose, yellow, and orange; rawhide panels with painted design of vertical stripes (red on one side, blue on the other) framed by a blue border of alternating semicircles and triangles (above) and broad triangles (below) in red and yellow.

90. Paint Pouch *(illus. with Cat. no. 84)*

Crow (?)
L: 15 cm plus 18 cm fringe   W: 6.5 cm
Attached to bandolier no. 87 purchased from the Assiniboine White Dog, Nov., 1881.
1881.3.87b   Read no. 87

Deerskin, folded and sinew-stitched on one side; opening decorated with four lobed flaps; lower portion fully beaded with concentric boxes and triangles in yellow, pink, light and dark blue, and translucent red and green; skin stained inside and out with orange ochre; skin fringe at bottom.

91. Paint Pouch *(not illus.)*

Crow (?)
L: 18 cm plus 18 cm fringe   W: 6.5 cm
Originally belonged to bandolier cat. no. 84 purchased from the Assiniboine White Dog, Nov., 1881.
1881.3.87c   Read no. 87

Deerskin, folded and sinew-stitched on one side; opening decorated with four lobed flaps edged with light blue and orange glass seed beads; lower portion fully beaded with geometric patterns in light and dark blue, orange, and burgundy; skin stained inside and out with orange ochre; skin fringe at bottom.

92. Paint Pouch *(not illus.)*

Crow
L: 12.5 cm   W: 4 cm
Purchased at Terry's Landing, M.T., 1879.
1881.3.84   Read no. 84

Animal hide, sinew-sewn; body in two pieces with separately added flap and triangular bottom piece; beaded on both sides with geometric designs in light and dark blue, white, yellow, and white-core rose; hide laces attached at back, upper front, and bottom; inside stained with orange ochre.

See also under *Pipes and Smoking Equipment; Weapons and War Paraphernalia; Utensils, Implements, and Vessels;* and *Ritual and Ceremonial Objects.*

Utensils, Implements, and Vessels

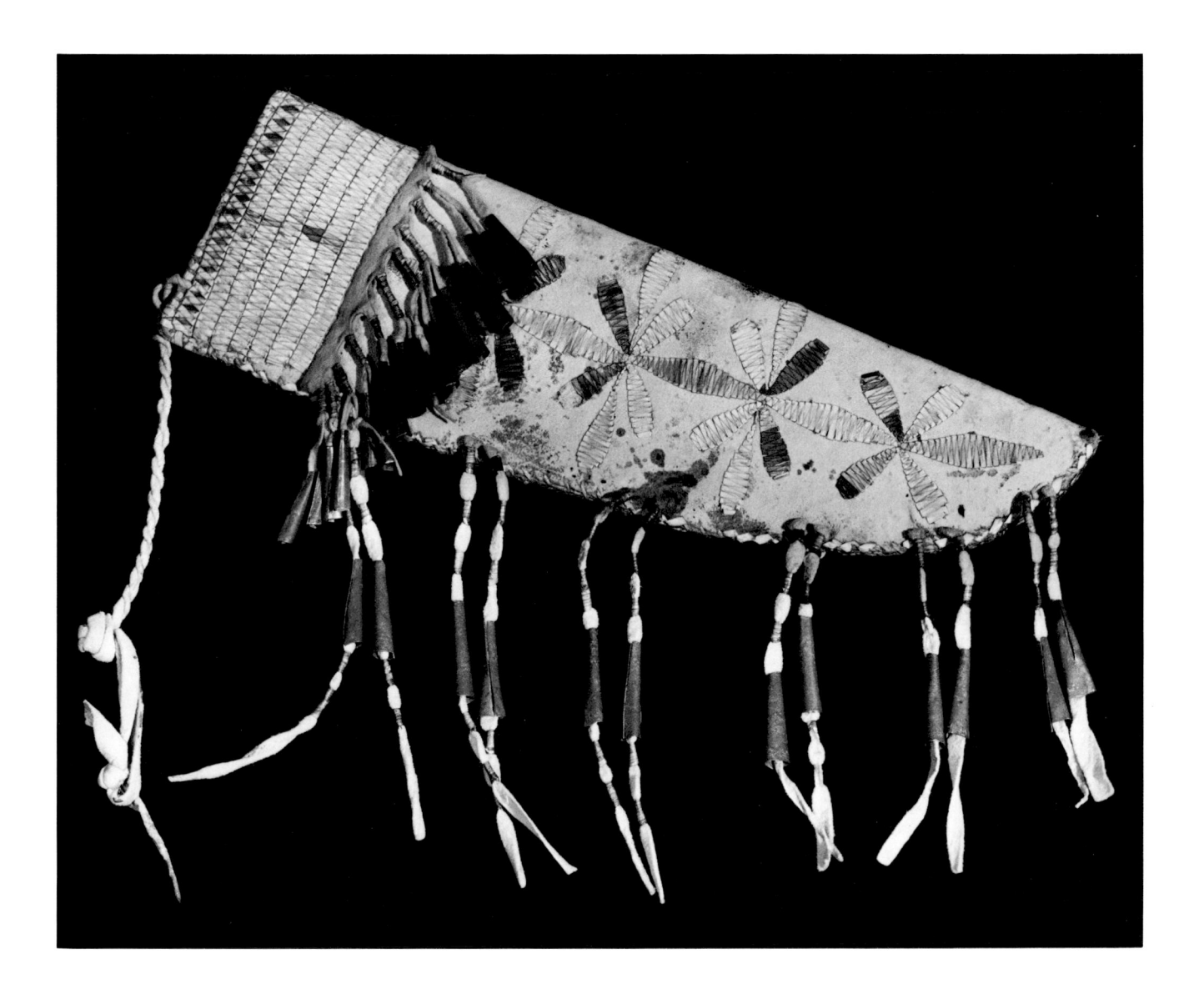

Cat. no. 107. *Woman's Knife Case*

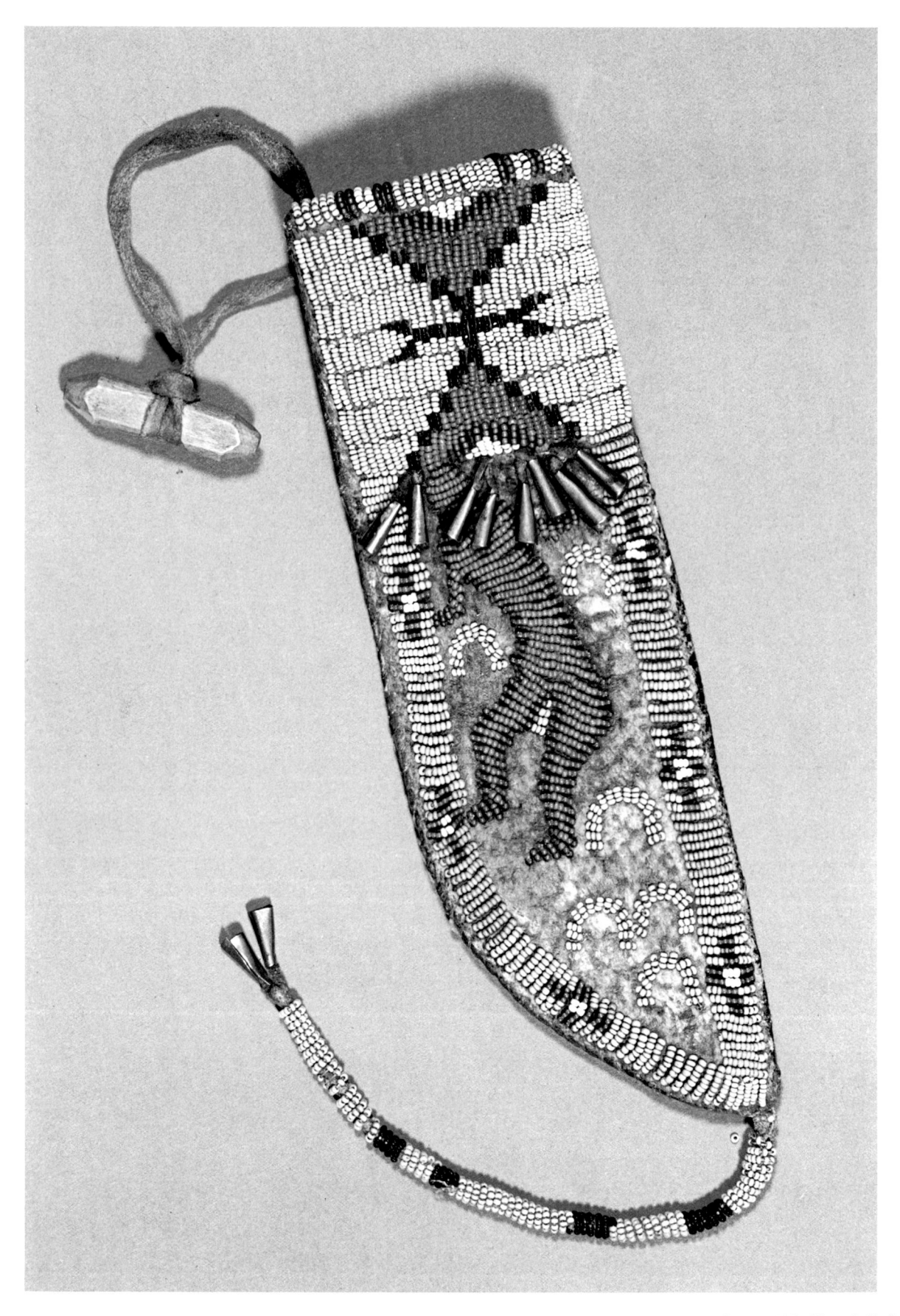

Cat. no. 106. Woman's Knife Case

Cat. nos. 95 (middle), 97 (top), 98 (bottom). Ladles

Cat. no. 99. Bowl

Cat. no. 93. Maul

Utensils, Implements, and Vessels

93. Maul

Hunkpapa, Teton Dakota
L: 46 cm   Head L: 16 cm
Picked up in Hunkpapa Camp near Poplar River, M.T., after engagement of Jan. 2, 1881.
1881.3.32   Read no. 32

Stone head, rounded at one end, flat pounding face, central groove; split wood haft bent around groove and covered with bison rawhide (stitched together from two pieces); rawhide covers entire stone head to within 3 cm of pounding surface.

Rawhide-covered stone mauls were used to pulverize dried meats and berries which were mixed with fat to make a small pressed cake, or pemican.

94. Maul Head *(not illus.)*

Northern Plains
Head L: 8 cm
1881.3.160 LA   Not in Read inventory list

Stone head, rounded at one end, flat pounding face, central groove; without wooden handle or rawhide wrapping.

95. Ladle

Hunkpapa, Teton Dakota
L: 30 cm   W: 10 cm
Picked up in Hunkpapa Camp near Poplar River, M.T., after engagement of Jan. 2, 1881.
1881.3.35a   Read no. 35

Buffalo horn.

96. Ladle *(not illus.)*

Hunkpapa, Teton Dakota
L: 23.5 cm   W: 6.5 cm
Picked up in Hunkpapa Camp near Poplar River, M.T., after engagement of Jan. 2, 1881.
1881.3.35b   Read no. 35

Buffalo horn.

97. Ladle

Hunkpapa, Teton Dakota
L: 23.5 cm   W: 7.5 cm
Picked up in Hunkpapa Camp near Poplar River, M.T., after engagement of Jan. 2, 1881.
1881.3.35c   Read no. 35

Cow horn.

98. Ladle

Hunkpapa, Teton Dakota
L: 37 cm   W: 9 cm
Picked up in Hunkpapa Camp near Poplar River, M.T., while burning lodges, Jan. 2, 1881.
1881.3.34   Read no. 34

Box elder wood.

99. Bowl

Sioux
H: 4 cm   Diam: 13 cm
Purchased from Indian at Poplar River, M.T., 1881.
1881.3.37   Read no. 37

Buffalo horn; perforated tab handle with cloth rope.

100. Bowl *(not illus.)*

Sioux, probably Hunkpapa, Teton Dakota
H: 5 cm   Diam: 13 cm
Purchased from Little Shield, a messenger from Sitting Bull captured at Poplar River, M.T., Feb., 1881.
1881.3.36   Read no. 36

Box elder wood; perforated tab handle with hide thong rope.

Bowls were commonly carved of wood, frequently from the burl of a maple or box elder.

101. Cup *(not illus.)*

Sioux, probably Hunkpapa, Teton Dakota
L: 28 cm
Purchased from Man Who Hides Under the Snow, a stepson of Sitting Bull, at Camp Poplar River, M.T., 1881.
1881.3.40   Read no. 40

Buffalo horn; decorated around upper portion with drilled designs; row of seven horse hooves encircles horn ca. 5 cm below rim; decorative band immediately beneath rim consists of ten small horse hooves on one side and a chain of drilled dots on the other; hide rope loop through perforation in rim.

102. Knife *(not illus.)*

L: 29 cm
Taken from hostile Indians captured near Poplar River, M.T., Feb. 9, 1881.
1881.3.16a   Read no. 16

Commercial knife with wood handle and steel blade (worn, tip broken); manufacturer's mark: Lamson & Goodnow S. Falls.

The Lamson & Goodnow Manufacturing Company, headquartered at Shelburne Falls, Massachusetts, was probably the largest cutlery firm in the United States in the 1860s. The firm made a number of sales to the Office of Indian Affairs. An order from that office to Lamson & Goodnow on May 24, 1877, consisted of 1,116 dozen butcher knives, 351 dozen hunting knives, and 104 dozen skinning knives (Indian Office — Finance Division, Contracts and Bonds — Supplies, Vol. 1: National Archives, Washington, D.C.). A number of Lamson Goodnow & Co. butcher knives were found in the remains of the steamboat *Bertrand*, which sank in the Missouri River in present-day Iowa while on a trip from St. Louis to Fort Benton, Montana Territory, in 1865 (see R. R. Switzer, *Museum of the Fur Trade Quarterly* 8:1 [1972] 5–7).

103. Knife *(not illus.)*

L: 23 cm
Taken from hostile Indians captured near Poplar River, M.T., Feb. 9, 1881.
1881.3.16b   Read no. 16

Commercial knife with wood handle and steel blade; manufacturer's mark: Lamson & Goodnow Mfg. Co.

104. Knife *(not illus.)*

L: 25.5 cm
Taken from hostile Indians captured near Poplar River, M.T., Feb. 9, 1881.
1881.3.16c   Read no. 16

Commercial knife with wood handle and steel blade.

105. Knife *(not illus.)*

L: 28.5 cm
Taken from hostile Indians captured near Poplar River, M.T., Feb. 9, 1881.
1881.3.16d   Read no. 16

Commercial knife with wood handle and steel blade; manufacturer's mark: Lamson & Goodnow Mfg. Co.

106. Woman's Knife Case

Yanktonai Dakota
L: 23 cm   W: 7 cm
Yanktonai manufacture.
1881.3.17   Read no. 17

Rawhide, folded and sinew-sewn on one side; front face with beaded decoration in two sections divided by a row of metal cone dangles; the upper zone contains two opposed stepped triangles in green trimmed with faceted dark blue beads on a light blue beaded ground; the lower zone has a stylized upright human figure in green trimmed with white-core rose and six horse hooves in light blue against a painted blue hide ground, the whole surrounded by a light blue border with square crosses in red with white centers; beaded rawhide pendant (light and dark blue, yellow) with metal cone dangles attached to tip; rawhide loop with wood toggle attached to upper edge.

This woman's knife sheath is elaborately decorated with beadwork and tin cones. It is unusual to find horse hooves and the human figure as decorative elements on a woman's sheath; undoubtedly they represented exploits of a brother or husband, which she wished to display.

107. Woman's Knife Case

Northern Plains, ca. 1850
L: 23 cm   W: 7 cm
1986.2.4 LA   Not in Read Collection

Deerskin, folded and sinew-sewn on one side; panel of plaited quillwork below rim with traces of red and orange dye; remainder of front face decorated with rosettes of plaited quillwork with petals in white, red, and orange; quill-wrapped skin thongs with metal cone dangles hang from skin strips below quilled rim panel and also from side seam (which is plaited with red and white quillwork); skin cord strap attached to rim.

108. Knife Case *(not illus.)*

Northern Plains
L: 25.5 cm
Taken from hostile Indians captured near Poplar River, M.T., Feb. 9, 1881.
1881.3.16f   Read no. 16

Rawhide (reused parfleche), folded and sewn with rawhide lacing on one side; reinforcing hide tabs sewn in upper corner.

109. Knife Case *(not illus.)*

Northern Plains
L: 24 cm
Taken from hostile Indians captured near Poplar River, M.T., Feb. 9, 1881.
1881.3.16g   Read no. 16

Rawhide, folded and sinew-sewn on one side; hide strap.

110. Knife Case *(not illus.)*

Northern Plains
L: 23.5 cm
Taken from hostile Indians captured near Poplar River, M.T., Feb. 9, 1881.
1881.3.16h   Read no. 16

Rawhide, folded and sinew-sewn on one side; sinew-sewn hide case with slate (?) whetstone attached to knife case by hide thong.

111. Awl Case

Sioux, probably Yanktonai Dakota
L: 21 cm plus 39 cm fringe
Purchased from Yanktonai, Poplar River, M.T., 1881.
1881.3.86a   Read no. 86

Rawhide tube with two pendant thongs wrapped with sinew-strung beads, yellow background with green and dark blue banded design; skin flap decorated with two panels of square-cross design (yellow and blue on green ground) and ending in a single beaded thong.

Cf. a pair of beaded awl cases in the Brotherton Collection in the National Museum of Natural History, Smithsonian Institution (collected in 1880–1881 at Fort Buford, N.D.; cat. nos. 384,137 and 384,138; the latter has precisely the same banded color scheme as the Read case).

Like knives, awl cases were worn by women on their belts as tokens of their occupation.

112. Backrest *(not illus.)*

Hunkpapa, Teton Dakota
L: 117 cm   W: 80 cm (bottom), 40 cm (top)
Picked up in Hunkpapa Camp near Poplar River, M.T., after engagement of Jan. 2, 1881.
1881.3.39   Read no. 39

Mat of peeled willow rods strung on and held parallel by three strips of sinew; mat tapers gradually toward the top.

113. Mat *(not illus.)*

Yanktonai Dakota
L: 46 cm   W: 16 cm
Acquired from Sweet Grass Hills. Braided by Magpie, a Yanktonai.
1881.3.106   Read no. 106

Mat of braided sweet grass; six plaited bundles with five horizontal wooden slats interwoven; bound at either end with hide thongs; each bundle bound at base with stroud strips.

114. Lariat *(not illus.)*

Northern Plains
Preserved L: 6.25 m
Presented by Thomas Henderson.
1881.3.100   Read no. 100

Rope of braided buffalo hair; looped rope handle wrapped with sinew-sewn rawhide covering and with red stroud at the base.

115. Sinew Strip *(not illus.)*

L: 68 cm
1881.3.133   Read no. 133

Strip of prepared sinew.

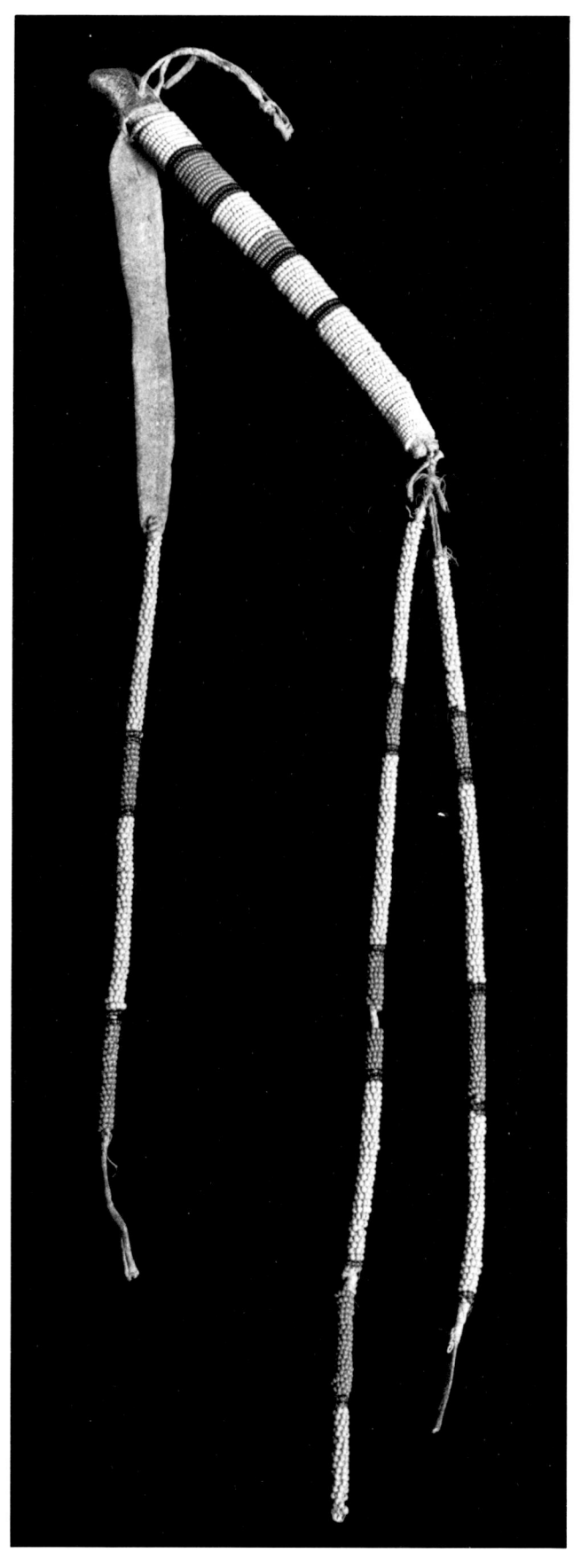

Cat. no. 111. Awl Case

List and Description of Articles in Indian Collection Belonging to Capt. O. B. Read, Eleventh Infantry, U.S.A.

* No. 1 Lance

Captured from Uncapapa Indian near Poplar River, M.T., Feb'y 11th, 1881, by Scout Bear Soldier and presented by him to Capt. Read.

* No. 2 Bow, Quiver and 15 Arrows

Purchased from captive Uncapapa at Camp Poplar, M.T., Feb'y 11, 1881.

* No. 3 Sinew Back Bow

Purchased from Yanktonais Indian at Camp Poplar River, M.T., 1881.

* No. 4 Unfinished Bow and Arrows

Taken from lodge while burning Uncapapa villages after engagement of Jan'y 2nd, 1881, near Poplar River, M.T.

+ No. 5 Medicine Sticks

Captured in action of Jan'y 2nd, 1881, by Lt. Avis, 5th Inf'ty.

+ No. 6 Springfield Carbine

Captured in action near Poplar River, M.T., Jan'y 2nd, 1881. Believed to be one of the carbines lost in the Custer Massacre.

+ No. 7 Gun Cover

Presented to Capt. Read by Bear Soldier, Yanktonais, at Camp Poplar River, Jan'y, 1881.

* No. 8 Tomahawk[1]

Purchased from Crow Indian at Terry's Landing, M.T., 1879.

+ No. 9 Tomahawk

Purchased from Yanktonais Indian at Poplar River, M.T., Dec., 1880.

+ No. 10 War Club

Purchased from Black Eagle, 2nd Chief under Crow King, who surrendered 325 hostile Indians at Ft. Buford, D.T., Feb'y 6th, 1881.

* No. 11 War Club

Presented to Mrs. Capt. Read at Camp Poplar, M.T., Feb'y 1st, 1881, by an Uncapapa Indian who claimed he had killed three soldiers with this club.

* No. 12 War Club

Purchased from Yanktonais Indian at Camp Poplar River, M.T., 1881. Red paint on one point indicates the point to which he had driven it through the skull of a Crow Indian.

+ No. 13 War Club

Manufactured by a Yanktonais Indian named "War Club," or "Break Sticks," the only one in the tribe skilled in work of this kind — presented by Joe Culbertson, who was a white scout employed by the Government.

+ No. 14 War Club

Nails in head. Yanktonais manufacture. Presented by Joe Culbertson.

+ No. 15 Belt, Knife and Scabbard, and reloaded cartridges

Taken from "Umpato Wakan," a messenger from Sitting Bull's Camp — arrested by Capt. Read at Poplar Creek Agency, May 3rd, 1881, and afterwards shot while attempting to escape.

* No. 16 Five Knives and Scabbards[2]

Taken from hostile Indians captured near Poplar River, Feb'y 9th, 1881.

* No. 17 Knife Scabbard — beaded

Yanktonais manufacture.

* No. 18 Buffalo Robe — beaded

Crow manufacture — purchased at Terry's Landing, M.T., Dec., 1878. The outer dress of a wealthy squaw.

+ No. 19 White Buffalo Robe

Purchased at Camp Poplar River, M.T., 1881.

* No. 20 Buffalo Calf Robe — beaded

Presented to Agnes Read (age 4 yrs) by one of her Crow playmates.

+ No. 21 Skin of a Mountain Lion

Presented by Thos. Henderson.

+ No. 22 Pony Skin

Presented by Thos. Henderson.

* No. 23 Pair of Parfleches

Purchased at Poplar River, M.T. Used chiefly for packing dried meat, and taking the place of trunks when travelling.

* No. 24 Rawhide Sack

Yanktonais manufacture — used by Indians as valises.

* No. 25 Same as 24

+ No. 26 Saddle Bags

Purchased from Crow King, Uncapapa Chief, Feb. 3, 1881, at Big Muddy, M.T.

* No. 27 Saddle Bags

Uncapapa manufacture — presented by J. Culbertson at Camp Poplar River, 1881.

* No. 28 Squaw Dress

Nez Percie manufacture — captured by Crow Indian in action at Bear Paw Mountains, M.T., 1877.

+ No. 29 Yoke for squaw dress

Purchased from "Rush After Thunder," an Ogalala Sioux, at Camp Poplar River, 1881.

* No. 30 Wau-Pu-sta, or Baby Hood — beaded

Purchased from Yanktonais squaw at Poplar River, 1880.

× No. 31 Baby Hood — Porcupine Quill

Purchased from Yanktonais squaw at Poplar River, 1881.

* No. 32 Stone Mallet

Used for pounding up dried meat, fruit, etc., for making pemican. Picked up in Uncapapa camp after engagement of Jan'y 2nd, 1881.

+ No. 33 Scraper for dressing buffalo hides

Picked up in Uncapapa camp while burning lodges, Jan'y 2nd, 1881.

* No. 34 Wooden Spoon

Picked up in Uncapapa camp while burning lodges, Jan'y 2nd, 1881.

* No. 35 Three (3) spoons — Buffalo Horn

Picked up in Uncapapa camp after engagement of Jan'y 2nd, 1881.

☆ No. 36 Wooden Bowl

Purchased from Little Shield, a messenger from Sitting Bull captured at Poplar River, Feb'y, 1881.

* No. 37 Bowl, made from Buffalo Horn

Purchased from Indian at Poplar River, 1881.

* No. 38 Snow Shoes

Presented by Fd'k Cadd, Wody[3] Mountain, N.W.T.

* No. 39 Willow Mat

Used to separate sleeping apartments in Indian Lodges.[4] Picked up in Uncapapa camp after engagement of Jan'y 2nd, 1881.

* No. 40 Buffalo Horn Drinking Cup

Purchased from "The man who hides under the Snow," a stepson of Sitting Bull, at Camp Poplar River, M.T., 1881.

* No. 41 Boy's Saddle[5]

Picked up after engagement of Jan'y 2nd, 1881.

× No. 42 Indian Stirrups

Picked up after engagement of Jan'y 2nd, 1881.

☆ No. 43 Riding Pad or Saddle

Picked up after engagement of Jan'y 2nd, 1881.

☆ No. 44 Medicine Pouch

Presented to Mrs. Capt. Read by White Eagle, Yanktonais.

* No. 45 Ornament of Eagle Feathers

Worn as a bustle in dances — purchased from "Rush after Thunder," 1881.

+ No. 46 Head-dress of hair and ornaments[6]

Taken from Crow Indian killed by "Bad Temper," a Yanktonais, now enlisted scout at Camp Poplar River, M.T.

* No. 47 Scalp

Taken from Yanktonais Indian named "Little Big Toad," killed in engagement with Crow Scouts under Lt. Kislingbury, 11th Inf'ty, near mouth of Mussellshell River, M.T., Nov., 1880.

* No. 48 Scalp and Hair Ornaments

Blackfoot Indian killed by Yanktonais near Poplar River, Aug., 1881.

* No. 49 Scalp and Bead Hair Ornament

Scalp believed to be that of a white woman. Purchased from "Black Chicken," Yanktonais, 1881.

* No. 50 Piece of Crow Scalp

* No. 51 Braid of Hair

Cut from her own head by the wife of Scout John Brughier, while mourning because her husband was being tried for murder.

+ No. 52 Cap — Coyote Skin

Purchased from "Fast Dog," Yanktonais, at Poplar River, 1881.

+ No. 53 Cap — Badger's Head

* No. 54 Medicine Cap

Captured in engagement of Jan'y 2nd, 1881, from "Yellow Horse," Uncapapa Indian.

+ No. 55 Boy's Cap — Crow

Presented by H. L. Williams, Terry's Landing, M.T., 1879.

* No. 56 Dance Head-dress

Poplar River, 1881.

* No. 57 Leggings ornamented with porcupine quills

Made by wife of "Two Bears," Yanktonais.

+ No. 58 Leggings — beaded

Made by wife of "White Eagle," Yanktonais.

* No. 59 One Legging

Half-Breed work — presented by David Roberts, Terry's Landing, 1879.

× No. 60 Breech Cloth

Made by wife of "Two Bears." Usually made of plain flannel. This ornamented to be worn at dances.

+ No. 61 Doll

Purchased from captive Uncapapa squaw at Poplar River, M.T., Jan'y 10th, 1881. This doll is a perfect specimen of the usual dress and ornaments of a Sioux squaw.

☆ No. 62 Tobacco Pouch

Presented to Capt. Read by Uncapapa Indian, at Poplar River, March, 1881.

☆ No. 63 Tobacco Pouch

Purchased from Sioux Indian at Standing Rock, D.T., 1876.

* No. 64 Riding Whip

+ No. 65 Guard for Riding Whip

Made by Uncapapa squaw, wife of Scout Joe Culbertson, Poplar River, 1881.

☆ No. 66 Tobacco Pouch and Pipe

Purchased from Ho-ha-Sa-pa ("Black Cat Fish"), Yanktonais Chief at Poplar River, M.T., 1881.

* No. 67 Pipe and Stem

Purchased from Ink-a-mo-Sa-pa ("Black Tiger"), Yanktonais Chief at Poplar River, 1881. Known throughout the tribe and its vicinity as the white man's friend.

☆ No. 68 Pipe and Stem

Presented to Capt. Read by captive Uncapapa, Feb'y 11th, 1881, Poplar River.

☆ No. 69 Pipe and Stem

Taken from Blackfoot Indian killed near Poplar River, Aug., 1881 (Scalp No. 48).

☆ No. 70 Dance Garters — Skunk Skin

Purchased from "Rush After Thunder," Poplar River, 1881.

☆ No. 71 Dance Garters — Skunk Skin

Presented by Thos. Henderson.

* No. 72 Medicine Shield

Taken from Sioux grave near Poplar River, 1881.

* No. 73 Moccasins — Bear Claws

Presented to Capt. Read by "Medicine Bear" (Mah-to-a-ka), principal Chief of Yanktonais. These moccasins were awarded to the bravest warrior in the tribe and Medicine Bear in his presentation speech claimed to have been wounded six times in gaining the right to wear them, and exhibited his wounds as proof of the assertion.

* No. 74 Moccasins — beaded

Used only at dances, and buried with the warrior to whom they belong. Presented to Joe Culbertson at Poplar River, 1881.

+ No. 75 Moccasins — Porcupine work

Made by wife of "Two Bears" (Mah-to-no-pa).

* No. 76 Moccasins — beaded

Purchased from Cheyenne Indian at Terry's Landing, M.T., Nov., 1878.

× No. 77 Moccasins — beaded

Purchased from messenger sent to Poplar River to negotiate surrender of the remnant of hostile camp, July, 1881.

× No. 78 Moccasins — beaded

Presented to Capt. Read by a daughter of Black Eagle, Uncapapa chief, Feb'y 5th, 1881.

* No. 79 Beaded Cartridge Pouch

* No. 80 Five Beaded Match Pockets[7]

Presented by or purchased from different Yanktonais Indians at Camp Poplar River, M.T., 1881. Worn on belt.

+ No. 81 Match Pocket, ornamented with elk teeth

Purchased from squaw in Iron Dog's band of Uncapapas after their surrender at Poplar River, Jan'y, 1881. These teeth, of which each elk has but two, trade among Indians for one dollar each and are used chiefly to ornament dresses of favorite children of rich Indians.

* No. 82 Match Pocket, leather

* No. 83 Charm[8]

Worn by children, and said to contain a portion of the umbilical cord of the person wearing it.

* No. 84 Needle Case — beaded[9]

Crow manufacture. Purchased at Terry's Landing, M.T., 1879.

+ No. 85 Knife Case

Crow manufacture.

* No. 86 Two Awl Cases[10]

Purchased from Yanktonais, Poplar River, 1881.

* No. 87 Dressing Case

Purchased from Shunka Ska (White Dog), Nov., 1881. Reputed to be the worst Indian in the Assinniboine Tribe. Since killed while on a horse-stealing expedition against the Crees.

* No. 88 Buffalo Horn Drinking Cup

Purchased from "Black Chicken," principal Medicine man at the Yanktonais tribe.

☆ No. 89 Medicine Rattle

Purchased from a squaw in Iron Dog's band, Jan'y, 1881.

* No. 90 Sun Dance Whistle, Ornaments and Medicine

Purchased from Little Assinniboine, chief-of-staff to Sitting Bull, while in irons at Camp Poplar River, Feb'y

12th, 1881, having been arrested as a spy. When this Indian was a child, the camp to which he belonged was attacked by Sitting Bull and all killed but himself. He came out of the brush where he had hidden, addressed Sitting Bull as "Father," was adopted by him, and afterwards became his chief adviser.

☆ No. 91 Medicine Bag

Captured in engagement of Jan'y 2, 1881, from "Fool Heart," who was a son of Chief Lame Deer, killed in Gen'l Miles' engagement at Wolf Mountain, M.T., May, 1877.

☆ No. 92 Medicine Bag — Porcupine Quill

Captured in engagement of Jan'y 2nd, 1881.

* No. 93 Hair Ornaments — Miscellaneous

* No. 94 Necklace — Antelope hoofs

Presented by "Bad Soup," Yanktonais.

* No. 95 Squaw Necklace and Earrings, Iroquois[11]

Purchased from Yanktonais Squaw at Poplar River, 1881.

* No. 96 Necklace, Iroquois

+ No. 97 Child's Bracelet, Beads and Elk Teeth

Presented to Agnes Read by one of her Crow playmates at Terry's Landing, 1879.

+ No. 98 Beaver Skin and Beads

Captured in engagement of Jan'y 2nd, 1881.

+ No. 99 Indian Bridle

* No. 100 Buffalo Hair Lariat

Presented by Thos. Henderson.

+ No. 101 Hoop netted with raw-hide

Used as a toy for children and also in gambling games, the hoop being rolled on the ground and arrows shot or spears thrown at it while rolling.

* No. 102 Boy's Quiver and Bow Cover

Crow manufacture.

× No. 103 Flint Lock Gun

Surrendered by hostile Indian at Poplar River, 1880. Presented by Frank Porter.

+ No. 104 Colt Revolver

Taken from "Iron Jaw," Ogalala Sioux, by Capt. Read at Camp Poplar River, March, 1881.

* No. 105 Earrings

* No. 106 Mat of Sweet Grass

From the Sweet Grass Hills, procured and braided by Magpie, Yanktonais.

+ No. 107 Horse Shoe

From the Custer Battlefield. Picked up by Mrs. Read on the point where Gen'l Custer was killed.

* No. 108 Pistol Holster

From the Custer Battlefield.

+ No. 109 Cartridge Shells and Horse Tooth

Picked up on Custer Battlefield by Capt. Read.

× No. 110 Buffalo Hoof

Deformed — supposed to be the result of a wound preventing use of the limb. Presented by Chas. Aubrey, Wolf Point, M.T., 1881.

+ No. 111 Indian Drawings or Paintings

The large sheet represents the Custer massacre, and was painted for Capt. Read by an Indian who took part in it. Others mostly painted by Wit-cho (The Fool), son of Crow, a prominent Uncapapa chief.

+ No. 112 Agency Ration Returns

Sent merely to show peculiar names of Indians.

* No. 113 Squaw Dress — beaded

Purchased from sister of Scout "Bear Soldier," Poplar River, M.T., March, 1882.

+ No. 114 War Shirt — Ermine and Beaver

Yanktonais — Poplar River, M.T., 1882.

+ No. 115 Boy's Coat — Buffalo Calf Skin
Poplar River, M.T., Feb'y, 1882.

* No. 116 Moccasins — Porcupine Quill and Beads
Made by wife of "Two Bears," Yanktonais.

+ No. 117 Buffalo Calf Skin ornamented with feathers, etc.
This is the "medicine" against lightning and from the superstitious fears connected with it. Was more valued by the Indians than any other article in this collection. It was purchased from "Black Chicken," a medicine man of the Yanktonais, and is believed to have been stolen by him from a medicine woman in the same camp.

* No. 118 Medicine Drum and Rattle
Purchased from "Black Chicken," Yanktonais — Poplar River, M.T., 1882.

+ No. 119 Buzzard Head, etc.
Medicine, "Black Chicken."

+ No. 120 Medicine Man's Cap — skin of White Pelican
"Black Chicken," 1882.

+ No. 121 Hat of "Medicine Bear," Principal Chief of Yanktonais — ornamented with wing of Pelican
Poplar River, M.T., 1882.

☆ No. 122 Beaded Pouch
Yanktonais — Poplar River, M.T., March, 1882.

☆ No. 123 Head Dress[12]
Crow skin — Yanktonais.

* No. 124 Squaw's Work Bag
Antelope skin.[13]

* No. 125 Tobacco Pouch — Skin of Elk Legs with its claws attached

* No. 126 Necklace — Antelope hoofs and Bird Claws[14]
Yanktonais — Poplar River, 1882.

* Nos. 127, 128 Wooden Bowls
Yanktonais — Poplar River, 1882.

* No. 129 Buffalo Horn Cup — ornamented with beads, etc.
Black Chicken — Poplar River, 1882.

* No. 130 Squaw Belt
Yanktonais — 1882.

☆ No. 131 Crow Scalp and Knife with which it was taken
Poplar River, 1882.

☆ No. 132 Hair Ornament

* No. 133 Sinew
Prepared for use as thread, the place of which it takes in nearly all Indian work.

* No. 134 Buffalo Head — 4-year-old Bull
Killed near Poplar River, M.T., 1881.

+ No. 135 Buffalo Hoof

* No. 136 Collection of Indian Photographs, viz.

  * 1. Sitting Bull   (Sioux)
  * 2. Rain-in-the-face   "
  * 3. Gall   "
  * 4. Gall   "
  * 5. Crow King   "
  * 6. Low Dog   "
  * 7. The man who hides under the Snow — stepson of Sitting Bull
  * 8. Yellow Eagle and two wives (Sioux)
  * 9. Tit-anta   (Kiowa)
   10. Kicking Bird   (Kiowa)
  *11. Little Raven   (Arapaho)
   12. Powder Face
  *13. Anapapo Camp
   14. Charlie   (Ton-ka-way Chief)
   15. Sam Houston   "
   16. Francis   (Ton-ka-way Squaw)
   17. Two Strike   (Sioux)
   18. Yankton Chiefs
  *19. Camp in Wickyups (Crook's expedition, 1875)
   20. Travois with wounded man "
   21. Stretchers "   " "
   22. Soldiers carrying off horse meat "

* No. 137 Gun Case — beaded

* No. 138 Ornaments — taken from a "Sun Dance pole"[15]

Annotations to Read Inventory

In an attempt to reproduce the original inventory as faithfully as possible, all abbreviations and spellings of proper names have been retained as they appear on the typed transcription.

Key to Status of Artifact in Read Collection

* * Object clearly identified with entry on list
* ☆ One or more objects attributable to entry
* × Object exchanged or discarded by Museum
* + Object missing or unaccounted for

Abbreviations

D.T.	Dakota Territory
M.T.	Montana Territory
N.W.T.	North West Territory
Gen'l	General
Inf'ty	Infantry
Lt.	Lieutenant
Capt.	Captain
Ft.	Fort

Modern Spellings and Transliterations of Indian Names (in singular)

Assiniboine	(Read sp. Assinniboine)
Hunkpapa	(Read sp. Uncapapa)
Nez Percé	(Read sp. Nez Percie)
Oglala	(Read sp. Ogalala)
Yanktonai	(Read sp. Yanktonais)

War club or "break stick." The Sioux word is c'annáksa, "war club"; it is etymologized as c'an, "wood," + naksa, "break with the foot." (no. 13)

Umpato Wakan. The name is almost certainly Anpétu wak'án, "Holy Day." (no. 15)

Wau-pu-sta. The correct form is wap'óštan. (no. 30)

Ho-ha-Sa-pa. The correct form is Hogán sápa, "black fish," the Sioux name for "catfish." In the historical literature this man is always called Black Catfish. (no. 66)

Ink-a-mo-Sa-pa. The correct form is Inkmú sápa, "Black Wildcat." (no. 67)

Mah-to-a-ka. The correct form is Mat'ó wak'án, "Holy Bear." In the historical literature he is always called Medicine Bear. (no. 73)

Mah-to-no-pa. The correct form is Mat'ó núnpa, "Two Bears." (no. 75)

Shunka Ska. The correct form is Šúnka ská, "White Dog." (no. 87)

Wit-cho. The correct form is Witkó, "Foolish." (no. 111)

Used here is the standard orthography of Eugene Beuchel, S.J., *A Dictionary of the Teton Dakota Sioux Language*, ed. Paul Manhart, S.J. (Pine Ridge: Red Cloud Indian School, 1970).

Identifications of Individuals Named in Inventory

Joseph Culbertson (nos. 13, 14, 27, 74)

Son of renowned Indian trader Alexander Culbertson, who served as general manager of the American Fur Company. Born in Peoria, Illinois, in 1858; moved to Fort Benton, Montana, with family in 1868. Joseph Culbertson served as an Indian scout and guide for the U.S. military under General Miles' command from 1876 to 1895. For two years, 1881–1883, he acted as Captain Read's chief scout and interpreter at Camp Poplar River. During this time, he was involved in reconnaissance operations against Sitting Bull. For an autobiography of Culbertson, see F. Delger, *Joseph Culbertson: Famous Indian Scout Who Served Under General Miles in 1876–1895* (Wolf Point, Montana, 1958). Culbertson's wife, mentioned in entry no. 65, was Spotted Harp, a Hunkpapa who was captured by General Miles' command in the 1870s (see ibid., p. 37).

John Brughier (no. 51)

White scout who served under General Miles. In 1878 Brughier was tried and acquitted in Fargo, North Dakota, for the killing of a man at Fort Yates, North Dakota, in 1875. For an account, see ibid., p. 90.

Frederick Cadd (no. 38)

White trader active at Wood Mountain trading post, N.W.T., in the 1870s and 1880s.

Thomas Henderson (nos. 21, 22, 71, 100)

Post trader at Camp Poplar River, M.T., in the early 1880s.

Notes

1. This is, in actuality, a pipe tomahawk.

2. Four knives and three cases are extant.

3. This is a misspelling for Woody Mountain or, more properly, Wood Mountain.

4. In reality, this is a backrest that was designed to be suspended from a tripod at the head of the bed.

5. The high pommel indicates that this was originally a girl's saddle, not a boy's.

6. An old Museum catalogue entry records that this headdress, now missing, was decorated with shell ornaments.

7. Three examples are extant.

8. This was probably a medicine pouch containing a round stone.

9. This identification is probably not correct, as the Indian inhabitants of the Northern Plains did not use needles. The presence of orange ochre stain on the inside of the container suggests that it was used as a paint pouch.

10. One example is extant.

11. The tribal identification of Iroquois for this and necklace no. 96 is incorrect.

12. A split horn headdress with clipped crow feathers has been tentatively assigned to this entry. The description "crow skin" may perhaps represent a misinterpretation of crow feathers.

13. This is actually a buffalo calf skin.

14. In reality, this is a sash. Misidentification as a necklace is completely understandable since the sash was worn over one shoulder.

15. These are actually umbilical cord amulets such as described (incorrectly) for no. 83.

Appendix: Other Documented Nineteenth-Century Plains Indian Collections

Although many small collections of Plains Indian material were assembled by private individuals, particularly military officers, stationed in the West during the nineteenth century, surprisingly few well-documented collections of such material survive in museum holdings today. The following is a list of collections from the region of the Upper Missouri assembled over the period ca. 1850–1885. For a more general listing of documented Plains Indian collections, see p. 249 in B. A. Hail, *Hau, Kóla!* (Haffenreffer Museum; Bristol, R.I., 1980).

All of the collections listed below are in the Department of Anthropology, National Museum of Natural History, Smithsonian Institution, Washington, D.C.

Lt. G. K. Warren Collection: assembled in the Upper Missouri region in the 1850s. Acquired by the Smithsonian in 1866.

Lt. Emmet Crawford Collection: collected from Dakota Territory. Crawford worked for the War Department, U.S. Ordnance Bureau. Acquired by the Smithsonian in 1877.

Lt. Col. D. H. Brotherton Collection: assembled by Brotherton while in command of Fort Buford, D.T., July 20, 1880, to August 30, 1881, and at Fort Stevenson, D.T., September 7, 1881, to October 20, 1881. Brotherton was commanding officer at Fort Buford on the occasion of Sitting Bull's surrender on July 19, 1881. Acquired by the Smithsonian in 1946.

Major James M. Bell Collection: assembled primarily at Fort Buford, D.T., and Camp Poplar River, M.T., presumably in 1880–81. Bell was sent by Brotherton from Fort Buford to Camp Poplar River on December 15, 1880, at the head of a company of the Seventh Cavalry, where he was subsequently involved in negotiations with Chief Gall prior to Ilges' attack on his Hunkpapa camp on January 2, 1881. The collection was acquired by the Smithsonian in 1894.